About the Author

Kavaljit Singh is the Coordinator of the Public Interest Research Centre in New Delhi. He has been writing on global finance and developmental issues in journals and newspapers in India and abroad. He is the author of *The Globalization of Finance: A Citizen's Guide* (DAGA, IPSR Books, Madhyam Books and Zed Books, 1999). Apart from several English language editions, the book has been translated and published in nine Asian languages. His previous books on foreign capital include *TNCs and India* (with Jed Greer, PIRG, 1995) and *The Reality of Foreign Investments* (Madhyam Books, 1997).

What the Critics said of Kavaljit Singh's previous book

THE GLOBALIZATION OF FINANCE: A CITIZEN'S GUIDE

"A very useful critical introduction to the workings, threats and possibilities of control of the global financial system. Highly recommended."
Edward S Herman

"This book is exactly what was needed... A real citizen's guide."
Samir Amin

"Don't be passively globalized: this book explains where you fit in the globalizers' plans and points towards new forms of resistance."
Susan George

"Strongly recommended for all who are not familiar with economic jargon."
Economic and Political Weekly

"Lucid... With minimal use of jargon... Singh achieves his objective: producing a useful layman's guide to the complex world of global finance."
Intelligent Investor

" This accessible survey of a widely debated topic is recommended for general readers [and] students."
Choice

"Although written for outsiders, this book should prove useful to the many... denizens of financial institutions."
Investment Adviser

"A sorely needed antidote to the hype about the benefits of globalization... Does a superb job of explaining the nature of the problem and showing how obvious the solution could be."
Labour Left Briefing

"It must be read by everyone who has to do with government policy on liberalization and globalization of financial sector policies and activities."
The Hindu

"The book justifies the author's claim that it can be a tool to understand the complex issues and his hope that it will help in wider citizen participation in popular campaigns to reform and regulate the global finance capital."
Mainstream

TAMING GLOBAL FINANCIAL FLOWS

Challenges and Alternatives in the Era of Financial Globalization:
A Citizen's Guide

KAVALJIT SINGH

HONG KONG UNIVERSITY PRESS
Hong Kong

MADHYAM BOOKS
Delhi

UNIVERSITY PRESS LTD
Dhaka

WHITE LOTUS
Bangkok

ZED BOOKS
London & New York

Taming Global Financial Flows: Challenges and Alternatives in the Era of Financial Globalization was first published in India by Madhyam Books, 142, Maitri Apartments, Plot No. 28, Patparganj, Delhi - 110 092, in 2000.
ISBN   81 86816 13 5 (hb)
         81 86816 12 7 (pb)

Published in Bangladesh by The University Press Limited, Red Crescent Building, 114 Motijheel C/A, PO Box 2611, Dhaka 1000
ISBN   984 05 1533 0 (pb)

Published in Burma, Cambodia, Laos and Thailand by White Lotus Company Ltd, GPO Boc 1141, Bangkok, 100501, Thailand

Published in Hong Kong by Hong Kong University Press, 14/F Hing Wai Centre, 7 Tin Wan Praya Road, Aberdeen, Hong Kong
ISBN   962 209 517 8 (pb)

Published in the rest of the world by Zed Books Ltd, 7 Cynthia Street, London, N1 9JF and Room 400, 175, Fifth Avenue, New York, NY 10010, USA
ISBN   1 85649 783 6 (hb)
        1 85649 784 4 (pb)

Distributed in the United States exclusively by St Martin's Press, Inc., 175 Fifth Avenue, New York, NY 10010, USA.

Printed and bound in India by Gopsons Papers Ltd., Noida
Cover design by Brij Raj Goel

A catalog record for this book is available from the British Library

Library of Congress Cataloging-in-Publication Data
Singh, Kavaljit
    Taming global financial flows: challenges and alternatives in the era of globalization / Kavaljit Singh.
      p.   cm.
    Includes bibliographical references and index.
    ISBN 1-85649-783-6 (hc.) – ISBN 1-85649-784-4 (pbk.)
    1. International finance. 2. Monetary policy. 3. Capital movements
    – Law and legislation. 4. Investments, Foreign – Law and legislation.
    5. Financial crises. I. Title.
HG3881.S5372   2000
330.4'6-dc21   00-025711
                                        CIP

Contents

List of Boxes

List of Tables

Acronyms

ACU	Asian Currency Unit
ADR	American Depository Receipt
AMF	Asian Monetary Fund
APEC	Asia-Pacific Economic Cooperation
ATTAC	Association for the Taxation of Financial Transactions
BCCI	Bank of Credit and Commerce International
BIBF	Bangkok International Banking Facility
BIS	Bank for International Settlements
BNP	Banque National de Paris
CAL	capital account liberalization
CHIPS	Clearing House Interbank Payments System
DESA	Department of Economic and Social Affairs of the UN
EC	European Community
ECLAC	United Nations Economic Commission for Latin America and the Caribbean
EMH	efficient market hypothesis
EMU	Economic and Monetary Union
EPU	European Payments Union
ERM	Exchange Rate Mechanism
EU	European Union
EUB	European Union Bank (Antigua)
FATF	Financial Action Task Force
FDI	foreign direct investment
FII	foreign institutional investor
FSA	Financial Services Agreement
FTAA	Free Trade Area of the Americas
FTWE	fundamental theorem of welfare economics
FX / Forex	foreign exchange
GATT	General Agreement on Tariffs and Trade
GATS	General Agreement on Trade in Services
GDP	gross domestic product
GE	General Electric
G-7	group of seven highly industrialized countries
HKMA	Hong Kong Monetary Authority
IAS	International Accounting Standards
IBF	international banking facilities
IIF	Institute for International Finance
IMF	International Monetary Fund

IOSCO	International Organisation of Securities Commissions
ISI	import substitution industrialization
JOM	Japanese Offshore Market
LIBOR	London Interbank Offered Rate
LIFFE	London International Financial Futures Exchange
LTCM	Long-Term Capital Management (US based Hedge Fund)
MAI	Multilateral Agreement on Investment
MFI	Multilateral Framework for Investment
MFN	most favored nation
NAFTA	North American Free Trade Agreement
NGO	non-governmental organization
NRI	non-resident Indians
NT	national treatment
OECD	Organization of Economic Cooperation and Development
OFC	offshore financial center
OTC	over the counter
PI	portfolio investment
RBI	Reserve Bank of India
RM	Malaysian Ringgit
RMB	Chinese Renminbi
RR	reserve requirement
SAFE	Synthetic Agreement for Foreign Exchange
SDDS	Special Data Dissemination Standard
SEC	Securities and Exchange Commission (US)
SWIFT	Society for Worldwide Interbank Financial Telecommunications
TRIMs	trade related investment measures
TNC	transnational corporation
UN	United Nations
UNCTAD	United Nations Conference on Trade and Development
UNDCP	United Nations International Drug Control Programme
UNDP	United Nations Development Programme
WTO	World Trade Organization

Data Notes

Million is 1000000.
Billion is 1000 million.
Trillion is 1000 billion.
Dollars are US dollars unless otherwise specified.

Acknowledgements

I would like to express my thanks to all those people who provided moral and intellectual support in bringing out this book. Since a very large number of people have helped in the preparation of this book in one way or the other, it is impossible to acknowledge their names. In particular, I would like to thank those who shared with me various documents, books and journals: Angela Woods, Carol Welch, Jan Joost Teunissen, K S Jomo, Marcia Caroll, Mathew Siegel, Max von Bonsdorff, Michelle Chan-Fisher, Navroz K Dubash, Nicola Bullard, Robert A Blecker, Robert Mills, Robert Weissman, Robin Round, Samir Amin, Sandy Buffett, Ward Morehouse and my colleagues at the Asia-Europe Dialogue Project. The library staff of the ADB, IDRC, IMF, Indian Social Institute, NCAER, United Nations Information Centre and World Bank offices in New Delhi provided excellent support in terms of research papers, publications, journals and press clippings. Thanks are also due to Jessica Gordon Nembhard, Sebastian Edwards and Yu Yongding whose writings and materials I have drawn upon in the preparation of the book. I am grateful to Arun Ghosh and Jo Marie Griesgraber for going through the manuscript and making valuable comments. However, the author remains solely responsible for any errors or flaws. Heinrich Boll Foundation, Germany, provided financial support. The book would not have been completed in a short time without the meticulous editorial support of Dilip Upadhyaya. In the initial stages, Anirudh Deshpande and Smita Gupta also helped in editing some of the chapters. Ranjeet Thakur provided efficient computer support. Finally, special thanks are due to Robert Molteno of Zed Books for encouraging this endeavor.

Preface

The success of my earlier book, *The Globalization of Finance: A Citizen's Guide*, was beyond expectation. Published in the wake of the Southeast Asian financial crisis, the response was overwhelming. Not only several English language editions of the book appeared, but more importantly, the book was translated and published in nine Asian languages. The book also gave me an opportunity to travel in India and abroad and speak to a diverse audience on the enigmatic world of global finance capital. Quite surprisingly, in almost every seminar, the participants raised identical questions. Are there any alternatives to financial globalization? Is financial globalization an irreversible process? What can ordinary citizens do to deal with global financial issues? To a large extent, these pointed questions prompted me to write another volume that specifically addresses these questions.

This book does not deal with all kinds of global financial flows such as FDI or official capital flows. It essentially focuses on one aspect of the global financial flows — the global finance capital — which is also popularly referred to as 'hot money.' In recent years, the role of 'hot money' flows has become quite controversial due to its destabilizing effects on both the financial system and the real economy. These financial flows are liquid and are attracted by short-term speculative gains, and can leave the country as quickly as they come. To a considerable extent, such financial flows have drastically altered one of the main objectives of the global financial system as a vehicle for overall economic development. Nowadays, financial flows are less associated with the flow of real resources and long-term productive investments, than was the case a couple of decades ago.

Of course, such speculative flows are not new. However, what is new presently is the speed with which the destabilizing effects of these financial flows are transmitted on a global scale. Particularly after the collapse of Bretton Woods system of fixed exchange rates and capital controls, the present system (rather 'non-system') of financial liberalization and floating exchange rates has induced greater volatility and fragility in the global financial system, which in turn, has given rise to recurring financial crises. Almost every episode of financial liberalization has been followed by a period of financial crisis. It is well recognized that a stable financial system is critical for the overall development, as various sectors of economy are integrally related to it.

Boom and bust have important repercussions on the level of economic activity and real investment. A failure in a large bank or financial institution can not only lead to the collapse of the financial system but also can quickly spread to other sectors of the economy thereby creating a prolonged recession, and in some instances, even a depression cannot be ruled out. Because of the potential large social costs associated with financial crises, a stable financial system is considered as a public good. Therefore, governments as well as people have a stake in maintaining a stable financial system.

Thanks to financial liberalization and technological advances, financial markets have become immensely complex. Nowadays, debt, equity, derivative and foreign exchange markets play a much greater role than they did two decades ago. Financial institutions other than banks now play an important role in the global financial markets. The transactions carried out by the financial institutions have become much more complex (e.g., derivatives) which makes the task of regulatory bodies all the more difficult to assess the systemic risks associated with such transactions. The present era of financial globalization poses new challenges to the regulatory authorities to keep pace with technological sophistication of global finance in both the developed and the developing countries. Regulatory authorities, therefore, have to remain alert and proactive even during periods of relative calm.

In the wake of recent financial crises, there is a renewed interest on issues related to new financial architecture. It appears that the pendulum is swinging away from the neo-liberal 'Washington Consensus' towards state intervention in the financial markets to curb volatility. Many 'experts' are still debating these issues within the framework of 'Washington Consensus,' while some others are calling for a new international financial architecture that can provide stability, growth and equity. Arguably, the emphasis has shifted from unbridled financial liberalization to proper 'sequencing,' but it remains problematic as countries often carry out financial liberalization haphazardly due to the pressure exerted by strong lobbies and vested interests.

Regulation of financial markets is no longer considered an anathema. In fact, all markets, particularly financial markets, are regulated to a lesser or greater degree. In the real world, there are no 'free markets.' For instance, the World Trade Organization (WTO) and the North American Free Trade Agreement (NAFTA), which are projected as free trade agreements, in reality, incorporate a plethora of rules running into several thousand pages. The debate should not be confined to regulation versus deregulation, but move beyond these parameters. Rather, it should focus on what kinds of regulations are required, and who would benefit from them. The notion that there are no alternatives is without substance as there is not just one but several alternatives. Take the case of portfolio investment. There is a Chilean model and a Malaysian model, besides, there is a Chinese model and an Indian model as well. Therefore, the moot question is — what kinds of alternatives are desirable and feasible in the present context? As the problems associated with regulation and supervision of financial markets are more political rather than technical, what is needed is a strong political will coupled with a radical transformation of the international economic order.

As global financial instability adversely affects the lives and livelihoods of ordinary citizens, these issues need to be discussed and debated by them as they have the greatest stake in a stable global financial system. It is high time that the debates on international financial architecture move beyond the charmed circles of 'experts' and academicians. There is an urgent need for democratization of debates on these issues to encourage public action on global financial issues. It is with this intention that I have written this book.

Chapter 1 charts out the recent trends in global financial flows, particularly in the 1990s, and identifies some of the factors responsible for the unprecedented surge in the financial flows. The chapter traces the growing dominance of the finance capital over the real economy. It is argued that the global financial system resembles a casino in which assets are traded primarily for speculative profits rather than for the benefit of the real economy.

Chapter 2 discusses, at length, some of the critical issues emanating from unfettered financial liberalization and its role in inducing financial fragility in the global financial system. It comes to the conclusion that unbridled financial liberalization, in almost all cases, was the contributory factor that precipitated the financial crises in various regions of the world, and therefore, advocates the need for regulatory and supervisory institutions, at the national as well as international levels.

Chapter 3 examines in detail the process of capital account liberalization and the devastating impact of such a measure on the domestic economies. International agreements that advocate capital account liberalization have also been analyzed. It debunks certain myths associated with the presumed benefits of capital account liberalization.

The role, strategies, investment style of hedge funds, with a mind boggling amount of capital at their command, constitute the contents of chapter 4. It is argued that unless prudential controls are placed on the operations of the unregulated hedge funds, the turbulence in the global financial markets cannot be contained. Like hedge funds, offshore financial centers (OFCs) have not only decisively contributed to the eruption of financial crises world wide, but these centers have also become conduits for laundering 'dirty money' on a mammoth scale. Chapter 5, therefore, draws attention to the urgent need for international regulation of OFCs in order to curb their dubious activities.

Chapter 6 highlights the rationale of capital controls, history of their use and the theoretical debates that have taken place on the efficacy of capital controls in minimizing volatility and curbing speculative flows. Two case studies, Malaysia and China, are discussed in great detail to emphasize the significance of capital controls. While favoring the imposition of capital controls, the chapter stresses the need for a transparent, rule based, accountable system of enforcement. It concludes that capital controls can only be effective if these are an integral part of government's developmental plans.

Chile is often showcased as a successful example of restricting 'hot money' inflows in the 1990s while the world was reeling under financial instability and crises. Chapter 7 describes at great length the history, policy response, effectiveness and shortcomings of the use of selective capital controls in Chile.

While acknowledging the positive features of the 'Chilean model' of restricting short-term inflows, the chapter points towards the need to examine the negative consequences of long-term capital inflows. This chapter also includes the experience of Colombia, which emulated the 'Chilean model.'

The recurring financial crises in both the developed and the developing countries have underscored the urgent need for radical reform of international financial system, often termed as 'international financial architecture'. Unless far reaching reforms are undertaken at various levels, the world would continue to witness financial crisis of one kind or the other. Chapter 8 enunciates certain guiding principles that could sustain a stable international financial architecture. The chapter also recommends nine steps to realize the same.

The concluding chapter deals with the peoples' response to the global financial issues. By citing the case of India, the chapter points out that earlier campaign strategies successfully employed against official capital flows (e.g, the World Bank-funded mega projects) and FDI (e.g, Cargill, Union Carbide, etc.) are unlikely to succeed in the case of global finance capital, as it is footloose in nature. In this chapter, broad contours of a new strategy that can be successfully deployed by peoples' movements to rein in the unwieldy nature of finance capital have been mapped out. The chapter underscores the need for campaigns in both the source and the recipient countries advocating transparent, rule based and accountable global financial system that serves the need of the real economy and people at large rather than a handful of speculators, institutional investors and currency traders.

Kavaljit Singh

To My Mother, Fabby and Ishu

1

Recent Trends in Global Financial Flows

SINCE the breakdown of the Bretton Woods system of fixed exchange rates in the early 1970s, the phenomenal increase in global financial flows is the most significant development in the world economy. Globalization of finance is not a new phenomenon as there was massive cross border movement of capital without any restrictions for 50 years prior to the First World War (1914-18). But the stupendous increase in global financial flows in both absolute terms and pace of movement in the post-Bretton Woods period has been unparalleled and as such has given rise to serious concern among policy makers and observers. The growing global financial integration could be gauged from the exponential rise in the volume of foreign exchange trading. According to the BIS, which monitors transactions in the world's foreign exchange markets, $1.49 trillion ($1490,000,000,000) is traded on an average every single day.

Box 1.1
Bretton Woods System

In July 1944, the procedure for fixing exchange rate and managing international financial system was worked out at a conference held in Bretton Woods, a town in New Hampshire in the US. The Bretton Woods system was designed to ensure that domestic economic objectives were not subordinated to global financial pressures. Under the Bretton Woods system, all countries were required to fix exchange rate to the US dollar, and the dollar was fixed in terms of gold at $35 an ounce.

Since the US emerged as the leading power after World War II, the dollar replaced the sterling as the dominant currency for exchange. Under this system, private financial flows were regulated by capital controls and an international institution, IMF, was set up to monitor the international financial system that was largely dominated by official capital flows. The Bretton Woods system was not universal in its outreach as the communist bloc was not part of it.

However, the rise of Eurocurrency market in the 1960s put strains on the Bretton Woods system. The system suffered a major breakdown on August 15, 1971 when the US — which was unable to deal with a massive speculative attack on the dollar in the wake of growing balance of payments deficit largely caused by the protracted Vietnam War — unilaterally declared that it would no longer honor its commitment to exchange dollars for gold at $35 per ounce. For some time, a few countries attempted to create alternatives (e.g., the Smithsonian Agreement) to the defunct Bretton Woods system. But on February 12, 1973, Japan decided to float the yen against the dollar, and on March 16, 1973, the European Community followed suit. Thereafter, the remaining countries took recourse to either floating or flexible exchange rate system.

Undoubtedly, this system was based on the hegemony of the US as it served the country's foreign policy and economic interests. Surely, the motive was not altruism on the part of the US but was based on the expectation that the country had much more to gain from managing international financial system. Despite its several shortcomings, this system provided adequate financial stability and economic growth for a considerable period.

In the initial years of the Bretton Woods system, international flow of capital was heavily controlled. For instance, it was not possible for a British investor to buy American stocks or bonds. The bulk of external capital available to developing countries was in the form of official aid and grant. FDI flows to developing countries, other than for exploitation of natural resources, were extremely low while commercial bank lending and portfolio investment flows were almost nonexistent. By the early 1960s, markets had found ways for circumventing some of these controls through the growth of 'Euromarkets,' where banks located in one country could take deposits and make loans in the currencies of other countries. After the collapse of the fixed exchange rate system in the early 1970s, the developed countries led by the EEC and the OECD countries gradually started dismantling controls on capital movement. The US soon followed suit to attract capital inflows, particularly from Germany and Japan.

The oil shock of 1973-74 soon followed leading to heavy surpluses in oil-exporting countries and corresponding deficits in oil-importing countries. Many oil-exporting countries preferred to keep surplus funds in Western commercial banks, which then needed investment outlets. They turned to the developing countries (particularly the Latin American countries) that were anxious to borrow funds to tide over balance of payments deficits. Thus, the recycling of 'petrodollars' from the surplus to deficit countries via the Eurocurrency market created a significant surge in global financial flows. Net flows to developing countries from commercial banks reached their peak by the late 1970s.

The excessive build up of external loans in the developing countries coupled with higher interest rates in the developed countries triggered the debt crisis as many developing countries were unable to service their huge external debts. There is no disagreement with the observation that several countries had mismanaged the use of external funds so much so that a major chunk of these funds were diverted towards conspicuous consumption or simply disappeared into the pockets of politicians and officials. Only a minor proportion went into productive investments. But, at the same time, international banks cannot be absolved of their role in perpetuating the debt crisis as they relaxed their credit criteria in order to reap huge profits from the recycling of 'petrodollars.' In 1982, when Mexico announced a moratorium on its repayment, the international banks realized that they were in thick soup as other developing countries in Latin America facing similar problems might follow suit. As heavy exposures to indebted countries was posing a threat to the Western banking system, several debt management packages (e.g., Baker Plan and Brady Plan) were set in motion by the developed countries and international financial institutions and groupings, particularly the IMF and the Paris Club, to rescue commercial banks. Consequently, the developing countries were net recipients of global financial flows in the early 1980s. In other words, new loans to the developing countries exceeded interest payments and repayments of principal. However, with the beginning of debt crisis in 1982, this pattern was completely reversed, as there were substantial net transfers from the developing to the developed countries. During the latter half of the 1980s, foreign capital flowed mainly within the developed countries.

In the aftermath of the debt crisis, the implementation of structural adjustment programs in several Latin American countries led to large-scale private capital inflows. With emphasis on privatization, liberalization and removal of controls on capital account, adjustment programs facilitated a renewed surge in global financial flows to several Latin American countries, particularly Mexico and Chile. In the case of Mexico, NAFTA also played a crucial role in facilitating capital inflows. The region witnessed a sharp increase in capital inflows, from $53 billion in 1995 to $74 billion in 1996. A large part of this increase emanated from equity flows through depository receipts and investments by institutional investors.

Apart from the Latin American countries, the greatest recipients of financial flows were the Southeast Asian countries known as 'Asian Tigers.' However, the reasons for capital inflows in the Southeast Asian countries were entirely different from the Latin American countries, as much of the financial flows were directed towards setting up of assembling and manufacturing facilities in these countries. As the currencies of 'Asian Tigers' were generally pegged to the dollar, they benefited from the rise of Yen against the dollar following the Plaza Accord of 1985. The euphoria created by the global investment community in the 1990s was so high that countries previously known as developing or third world countries earned the epithet of emerging markets.

Global Financial Flows to the Developing Countries in the 1990s

One of the most striking developments regarding global financial flows is the radical change in their configuration in the 1990s, particularly in the context of developing countries. Based on the data published by the World Bank in its various publications including *Global Development Finance 1999*, some of these trends and developments are summarized here.

Table 1.1: Net Long-term Resource Flows to Developing Countries
(1990-98) *($ billion)*

	1990	1994	1995	1996	1997	1998*
Net long-term resource flows	100.8	223.6	254.9	308.1	338.1	275.0
Official flows	56.9	45.5	53.4	32.2	39.1	47.9
Private flows	43.9	178.1	201.5	275.9	299.0	227.1
From international capital markets	19.4	89.6	96.1	149.5	135.5	72.1
Private debt flows	15.7	54.4	60.0	100.3	105.3	58.0
Commercial banks	3.2	13.9	32.4	43.7	60.1	25.1
Bonds	1.2	36.7	26.6	53.5	42.6	30.2
Others	11.4	3.7	1.0	3.0	2.6	2.7
Portfolio equity flows	3.7	35.2	36.1	49.2	30.2	14.1
Foreign direct investment	24.5	88.5	105.4	126.4	163.4	155.0

Note: Net long-term resource flows are defined as net liability transactions of original maturity greater than one year. Although the Republic of Korea is high-income country, it is included in the developing country aggregate since it is a borrower from the World Bank.
* Preliminary.

Source: World Bank, *Global Development Finance 1999*, 1999, p. 24.

■ Net long-term financial flows to the developing countries, both pri-vate and official, increased from $100 billion in 1990 to $338 billion in 1997. However, it declined to $275 billion in 1998 due to the Southeast Asian financial crisis and its contagion effects (see Table 1.1). In 1997, the developing countries made a net transfer of financial resources abroad to the tune of $27 billion — the first negative transfer since 1990.

■ Private capital flows dominate the total financial flows to the develop-ing countries. Out of the $338 billion of total financial flows in 1997, private flows accounted for $299 billion, nearly 88 per cent of the total flows.

■ Official capital flows, both bilateral and multilateral, are on the de-cline, from $56 billion in 1990 to $39 billion in 1997. Official flows are, however, critical to the economies of several African countries. Most of them still remain dependent on official capital flows to meet their re-quirement of external finance.

■ The bulk of private capital flows are highly concentrated, with a dozen countries receiving nearly three-quarters of capital inflows during the period 1990-97, while 140 of the 166 developing countries accounted for less than 5 per cent of total flows during the same period. China is the leading developing country which has attracted substantial amount of private capital flows, particularly FDI, in the nineties. As mentioned earlier, the recent surge in private capital flows which occurred in Latin America and Southeast Asia has largely bypassed Sub-Saharan Africa (except South Africa).

■ In the 1990s, a substantial part of private capital flows has gone to the private sector as compared to the governments just a decade ago.

■ FDI flows have emerged as the most important component of private capital flows and remains predominant despite several financial crises in the 1990s.

■ Flows from international capital markets (portfolio investments, bonds and bank loans) have increased considerably in the 1990s, from $19 billion in 1990 to $149 billion in 1996. Portfolio investment (PI), which was negligible during the 1970s and 1980s, became sizeable in the early 1990s. From $3 billion in 1990, PI flows increased to $49 billion by 1996. Borrowings through commercial bank loans have also registered an increase. It was $43 billion in 1996, an increase of $12 billion from 1995. The majority of borrowers of commercial bank lending belong to the private sector, accounting for nearly 60 per cent of all new loans during 1995-96. Another noticeable aspect of commercial bank lending is that nearly half of it is used to finance mega infrastructure projects like power, highways, etc. Given the extreme volatility associated with such financial flows, the flows from international capital markets declined from $135 billion in 1997 to $72 billion in 1998 in the wake of the Southeast Asian financial crisis.

■ Flows from international capital markets have been highly concentrated in the middle-income countries, which received more than 90 per cent of these flows during the 1990s.

Factors Behind the Surge in Global Financial Flows

A number of factors, both external and internal, have contributed to the increase in global financial flows. Some of the key factors are discussed in the succeeding pages. Needless to add, these are the contributory factors, which have engendered volatility and instability in the global financial system.

Global Financial Liberalization

Financial liberalization in both the developed and the developing countries is perhaps the most important factor behind increased capital mobility on a global scale. Although a detailed analysis of financial liberalization and its consequences is given in the next two chapters, a brief introduction may suffice here. Financial liberalization has two interrelated components, domestic and international. Domestic financial liberalization encourages market forces by reducing the role of the state in the financial sector. This is achieved by removing controls on interest rates and credit allocation as well as by diluting demarcation lines between banks, insurance and finance companies.

International financial liberalization, on the other hand, demands removal of controls and regulations on both the inflows and outflows of capital. By allowing cross border movement of capital, it promotes global financial integration. Due to increased global financial integration, the flow of funds is no longer unidirectional. Capital is not only flowing from the developed to developing countries but also from the developing countries (e.g., Mexico, Chile and Thailand) to the rest of the world.

Developed countries were the first to embark on the process of financial liberalization. Foreign exchange markets took the lead to liberalize in the late 1970s. The liberalization of capital account was followed by liberalization of bond markets in the 1980s, and equity markets in the 1990s. In addition, the growing institutionalization of savings in the developed countries has given rise to institutional investors who are both willing and able to invest in global financial markets. Much of financial assets in developed countries are now finding their way into mutual funds, hedge funds, pension funds and investment trusts rather than banks. For instance, in 1980, banks handled 58 per cent of savings and investment transactions in the US economy, and institutional investors held a 31 per cent market share. By 1994, the banks' proportion had fallen to 33 per cent and that of institutional investors had jumped to 44 per cent.[1]

Since the 1980s, the size and the structure of financial markets of developing countries have also undergone rapid changes. Deregulation of domestic financial markets along with liberalization of capital account have been important components of the adjustment programs supported by the World Bank and the IMF. During 1991-93, 11 developing countries undertook full or extensive liberalization of their exchange restrictions; 23 liberalized controls on FDI flows; 15 eased controls on portfolio inflows; and 5 eased restrictions on portfolio outflows. By the end of 1995, 35 developing countries had fully open capital accounts. A significant part of the surge in foreign equity financing has been associated with the privatization of public sector companies in the developing countries (e.g., Argentina), which also happens to be an important component of the adjustment programs. The number of countries that are classified as highly integrated increased from 2 in 1985-87 to 13 in 1992-94, whereas the number of countries classified as moderately integrated increased from 24 to 26.[2]

Apart from the structural adjustment program, several international agreements have also promoted financial liberalization in the developing countries. For instance, financial liberalization is an important component of the WTO agreement on financial services concluded in 1997 and the IMF's Article VIII obligations of convertibility of currencies for current account transactions. Under the WTO agreement on financial services, which came into effect from March 1998, 70 of its member-countries agreed to open up their financial services sector. This agreement brings trade in financial services — worth trillions of dollars — under the WTO's rules on a permanent and full most favored nation (MFN) basis. By this agreement, countries representing over 95 per cent of the trade in banking, insurance, securities, asset management and financial information, have brought financial services into the realm of international rules. While the number of countries which have accepted the IMF's Article VIII has increased sharply from 35 in 1970 (which was only 30 per cent of the membership of the IMF) to 137 in early 1997 (76 per cent of its membership).[3]

Over-capacity and Overproduction

From the beginning of the 1980s, the economies of the developed countries are suffering from over-capacity and overproduction in manufacturing. Their problems have been further compounded by the intrusion of the 'Asian Tigers' into the world markets during the 1980s and the 1990s. With no major expansion in the world's markets taking place, capital is looking for alternative profitable opportunities. As mentioned earlier, the global financial markets are expanding exponentially. Since profits can be made quickly in financial markets, much of the capital is shifting away from investment in production to investment in financial markets and speculative financial instruments. This shift in international economy has become more apparent in the 1990s.

Historically, wealth was created when income was diverted from consumption into investment in machinery, buildings and technological change. Nowadays, securitization — the issuance of stocks and bonds — has become the new instrument of wealth creation. As financial logic becomes more important than productive logic, the managers and owners of business corporations are more concerned with rewarding their shareholders in order to boost the value of shares in the financial markets. Many tend to sacrifice long-term investment goals for short-term profits and higher stock prices. In fact, several manufacturing firms have also started financial subsidiaries in order to benefit from finance capital. The General Electric Capital Services (GE Capital) — a subsidiary of the world's largest TNC, General Electric (GE) — is a classic example of this trend. With $255 billion in assets worldwide, GE Capital is a major player in global financial markets. In 1997, it contributed as much as 40 per cent to the parent company's total income.[4] A recent entrant into financial services is UPS Capital, a subsidiary of United Parcel Service, the world's largest courier company.

Low International Interest Rates

Among the external factors, perhaps the most important one is the relatively low real rates of return available on investments in the major developed economies from where large funds originate. For the past so many years, the interest rates are extremely low in the developed countries as compared to the developing countries. For instance, interest rates on treasury bills in the US are in the range of 4 to 5 per cent while long-term interest rates in Japan are perhaps the lowest in the world, i.e., less than 1 per cent. This prompts investors in developed countries to seek alternative markets for their investments in the developing countries where the interest rates are much higher.

Technological Advances

Major advances in the technological field, especially in communications and information, have played a supportive role in the globalization of financial markets. The influence of technological advances has broken the natural barriers of space and time as twenty-four hours trading is possible now, which was not the case a decade ago. Virtual stock exchanges are no longer a dream, thanks to advances in Internet technology. The 'electronic money' has added momentum to capital mobility as funds can be transferred globally with much ease and speed with the help of globally linked electronic monitors. With the help of SWIFT payments system, billions are transferred every day.[5] The advances in communications have drastically reduced the costs in moving money around the world. Wire-transfer systems such as FedWire and CHIPS (Clearing House Interbank Payments System) are also commonly used worldwide. With the adoption of International Accounting Standards (IAS), uniformity in accounting standards will soon become a reality thereby further facilitating the cross border movement of capital. However, technological advances have also increased the speed at which market shocks are transmitted nationally and globally. Earlier, market shocks used to take days and weeks to spread from one country to another, now they can be transmitted instantly.

The Domination of Finance Capital over the Real Economy

Due to the cumulative impact of the factors cited above, the global financial system has undergone tremendous change and has become much more complex and unruly than it was twenty years ago. New financial instruments and financial intermediaries have not only drastically changed the landscape but also the basic function of the global financial system. Much less regulated than the real economy, the financial economy has outgrown the real economy and has considerably blurred the existent relationship. The global financial markets have moved beyond their original function of facilitating cross border trade and investment. The financial markets are no longer a mechanism for making savings available for productive investments. Nowadays, global financial flows are less associated with the flows of real resources and long-term productive investments.

As the value of global foreign exchange trade is many times more than the value of annual world trade and output, much of global finance capital is moving in search of quick profits from speculative activities rather than contributing to the real economy. Since 1980, the global stock of financial assets (shares, bonds, bank deposits and cash) has increased more than twice as fast as the GDP of rich economies, from $12 trillion in 1980 to almost $80 trillion today.[6]

The swift cross border movement of capital has very little to do with the national or the world allocation of capital funds. Every day, trillions of dollars move in the world's financial markets in search of profit making opportunities from speculative investments. These flows are largely liquid and are attracted by short-term speculative gains, and can leave the country as quickly as they come. It has been calculated that over 80 per cent of spot forex turnover have a maturity of less than seven days.[7] Commercial and merchant banks, in addition to hedge funds, carry out most of the arbitrage and speculative dealing in foreign exchange and money markets.

Although not much attention has been paid, the globalization of finance can give rise to serious social, economic and political problems. According to Phil Cerny, the global finance capital "calls the tune for the real economy... it has developed its own autonomous structural dynamic, a dynamic with regard to which international politics has yet to find a workable consensus on objectives or a feasible method of control."[8] There are several ways in which the domination of finance capital negatively affects the real economy. Firstly, by providing economic incentives to gamble and speculate on financial instruments, the global finance capital diverts funds from long-term productive investments. According to Susan Strange, the real economy of manufacturing, services like entertainment, tourism, transport, mining, farming and retailing — all of it dances to the fast or slow rhythms of financial markets.[9] Secondly, it encourages banks and financial institutions to maintain a regime of higher real interest rates which significantly reduces the ability of productive industries and enterprises in terms of access to credit. Thirdly, finance capital (because of its speculative nature) brings uncertainty and volatility in interest and exchange rates. This volatility is extremely harmful to various sectors of the real economy, particularly trade. Lastly, it undermines efforts by governments to support full employment and reduce inequality.

In order to arrive at a better understanding of the operations of global finance capital, some of its key features as well as recent developments are outlined here.

Foreign Exchange Trading: Scaling Unprecedented Heights

The foreign exchange market is the largest market in the world today. As mentioned earlier, over $1.49 trillion is traded on an average every single day, whereas in 1977, the daily turnover in forex markets was just $18 billion. Since the breakdown of Bretton Woods system in the early 1970s, forex transactions have increased several times (see Table 1.2). Quite often, analysts tend to underestimate the significance and power of foreign exchange and money markets. It would be a serious mistake to underestimate the importance of these markets because the price at which

Table 1.2: Daily Global Forex Turnover, 1977-98

($ billion)

Year	Daily Turnover
1977	18.3
1980	82.5
1983	119.0
1986	270.0
1989	590.0
1992	820.0
1995	1190.0
1998	1490.0

Source: Bank for International Settlements.

Box 1.2
Foreign Exchange Trading

Foreign exchange is traded over-the-counter (OTC) twenty-four hours a day. OTC transactions are those that take place between two counterparties located anywhere in the world via a telephone or electronically rather than traded on an exchange. The main methods of forex trading are via direct interbank using systems (e.g., Reuters Dealing 2000-1), voice brokers and electronic broking systems (e.g., Reuters Dealing 2000-2). Some forex instruments are also traded on exchanges such as currency futures at the Chicago Mercantile Exchange and currency options at the Philadelphia Stock Exchange.

There are three broad categories of instruments and transactions in forex trading — spot transactions, forward transactions and derivatives (see diagram below). **Spot transaction** is a deal in which two counterparties exchange two different currencies at an agreed exchange rate for settlement

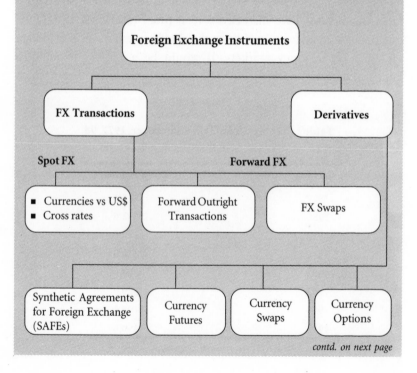

contd. on next page

in two-business days time. In 1998, spot transactions amounted to 40 per cent of the daily turnover of foreign exchange, down from 44 per cent in 1995. **Forward transactions** involve purchase or sale of foreign exchange established now but with payment and delivery at a specified future date. These transactions are derived from spot forex and money market interest rates. The two types of forward forex transactions used widely in the markets are forward outright transactions and forex swaps. In the past few years, forward transactions have grown in importance relative to spot transactions. Of the $1.49 trillion daily turnover in foreign exchange in 1998, nearly $900 billion was traded in forward transactions, approximately 60 per cent of the market. In 1995, its market share was 56 per cent. **Derivative instruments**, which are concerned with forward transactions of forex, include currency futures, currency swaps, currency options and Synthetic Agreements for Foreign Exchange.

Forex markets are driven by a number of factors including relative interest rates, balance of payments, money supply, political factors and market sentiments. Rumors have a powerful impact on the forex market. The way the forex markets react to rumors could be summarized by the phrase: Buy the rumor, sell the fact! Speculation makes up the largest portion of trading in the forex market. The major participants in the forex market are banks as nearly two-thirds of daily foreign exchange transactions take place through interbank trading. Only a small portion of foreign exchange transactions directly involve non-financial customers who import and export goods and services. The rest of the transactions involve forex traders, forex dealers and securities firms.

Although participants in the foreign exchange markets are spread all over the world, London is the largest foreign exchange trading center, followed by New York, Tokyo and Singapore. The most actively traded currencies in the forex markets are US Dollar, Deutsche Mark and Japanese Yen. These three currencies together constitute 69 per cent of the global forex trade. Much of forex trading is carried out by a handful of dealers consisting of banks and institutional investors. According to *Euromoney*, the top 10 dealers are Citibank, Deutsche Bank, Chase Manhattan, Goldman Sachs, HSBC Midlands, JP Morgan, SBC Warburg Dillon Read, Merrill Lynch, Netwest and Industrial Bank of Japan.

money is bought and sold dictates the economic policies of national governments and therefore affects the lives of billions of people.

Why do we need forex markets? The main function of forex markets is to facilitate cross border trade and investment. As different countries use different currencies, forex markets convert one currency to another currency for cross border deals. Another function could be to hedge against the risk. Historically, much of the trading in foreign exchange was the result of international trade, as buyers and sellers of foreign goods and services needed another currency to settle their transactions. In the early 1970s, about 90 per cent of forex transactions were related to trade and investment. But now, forex trading has very little to do with international trade as most purchases and sales of forex are related to financial transactions rather than merchandise trade. In fact, forex trading has grown much faster than international trade in goods and services. In 1997, the global volume of exports of goods and services was $6.6 trillion ($5.2 trillion of goods exports and $1.3 trillion of services exports). This comes to only approximately 4 days of global forex trade. If one compares global forex trade with the world GDP ($29.2 trillion in 1998), it is more than ten times the world GDP. Hence, the forex market is much bigger than all the other markets put together. These comparative statistics bring out the fact that forex trading has gained a life of its own as there is a growing delinking between forex transactions and real economic activities, with the former far exceeding the financing requirements of the latter. These statistics also reveal that speculation makes up by far the largest proportion of trading in the forex market.

But the foreign exchange markets are very volatile and therefore pose a systemic risk. As banks are involved in much of forex trading, they are exposed to large amounts of cross border settlement risk. Given the fact that national payment systems operate in different time zones, it is possible that after the first counterpart has delivered one side of the transaction, the other counterpart may go bankrupt and fail to deliver the offsetting currency. Because of increased inter-bank lending by international banks, a default by one large bank may cause a second bank to fail which in turn may lead to a larger systemic upheaval in the international banking system. Thus, any debacle in the settlement of foreign exchange transactions could have serious negative implications for the global financial system.

The Emergence of Securities

Besides global foreign exchange trade, the other important factor that has contributed to the spectacular growth in finance capital is the emergence of securities. Since 1980, the volume of trading in financial securities has increased phenomenally. The value of global financial securities is more than the value of annual world output. The total dollar value of all investment-grade securities worldwide that could potentially be issued is upward of $150 trillion, roughly five times the value of annual world output.[10] The growth of new financial instruments, such as derivatives, has further increased the volume of trading. As there are no reliable statistics of financial derivatives, it is estimated that the total outstanding notional value of derivative products was over $80 trillion in 1997. The world bond market has grown from $2 trillion in 1980 to $25 trillion in 1998.[11] According to Capital DATA (a company which monitors financial

Table 1.3: US Institutional Investment

Proportion of US equity market (in percentage) owned by institutional investors		Proportion of US equity market (net worth) owned by institutional investors (1997)	
Year	%		$bn
1950	6.1	Private pension funds	1709
1960	12.6	Mutual funds	1586
1970	19.4	Public pension funds	1213
1980	33.9	Bank and trust companies	803
1990	47.2	Insurance companies	303
1997	48.0	Other institutions	614

Source: The Conference Board.

markets), 3850 international bonds were issued by the top 25 investment banks in 1998 alone.[12] Led by Merrill Lynch, the top five leading issuers accounted for 37 per cent of the value of these bonds.[13]

Mutual funds have also witnessed a massive expansion since the 1980s. Mutual funds represent the second largest pool of private capital in the world after the banking industry. It has been estimated that US will enter the 21st century with half of all households owning shares directly or through mutual funds, compared with 25 per cent in the mid-1980s and only 5 per cent in the 1950s.[14] While pension funds represent the third largest pool of private capital in the world, after the banking and mutual fund industry. The value of global pension assets grew by more than 60 per cent, from $6 trillion in 1992 to $9.7 trillion in 1997.[15] As far as hedge fund industry is concerned, they are estimated to be at least 5500, with $300 billion of funds under management, as of mid-1998. By and large, the increase in financial assets is more pronounced in the developed countries where the process of securitization has been accompanied with the development of international institutional investors. According to OECD data, the total institutional assets of the main regions in the OECD domain rose from $3.2 trillion in 1981 to $24.4 trillion in 1995.[16]

The rapid growth of financial securities, however, raises some critical issues. In the recent years, there has been no parallel rise in the real economy despite the rapid rise in the value of global financial securities. In fact, the opposite is true because the growth in real economy has been the slowest in the post war period. In the US, for instance, where stock markets have witnessed a massive boom in the 1990s due to massive inflow of funds, growth in market capitalization has far outstripped the growth in output. Similar trends have also been witnessed in the employment and productivity growth rates in the US.

The assumption that borrowers can raise funds directly from investors through securities rather than going to other sources is difficult to accept for two reasons. Firstly, the trillions of dollars flowing into financial markets account for resale or trading of stocks in secondary markets. The corporation issuing the stock does not get this money which goes to the last owner of the stock. For instance, when shares of Ford Motor are bought and sold, the company's capital and physical assets do not change and there is no increase in its profits. What has changed is the ownership of the company. That is why many market observers argue that a more apt definition of institutional investors in securities should be institutional traders because they basically trade financial instruments and know when to make a killing. Only a small part of these huge sums enters the corporate real economy in the form of new issues sold in primary markets. Even new issues may not contribute to additional investment if the proceeds are used to retire other domestic debt or fund current expenditures or are mobilized for speculative purposes by the corporation.

Secondly, it is an established fact that banks are much more important when firms are building up a reputation. Once firms have established a reputation, only then equity and bonds markets have some role as providers of investment finance. Even in countries with a high level of development, new equity finance plays a very minor role in providing finance for investment. A study of eight developed countries found that net financing raised through short-term securities, bonds and shares is extremely small — less than 5 per cent.[17] By and large, corporations in most of the developed countries raise their financial resources internally. From 1945 to 1995, US non-financial firms raised 75 per cent of their finances internally, 12 per cent from intermediaries such as banks and 13 per cent from the security market.[18] In the case of certain other developed countries, corporations raise fewer funds from the market, for instance, Germany 3 per cent and Japan 7 per cent.[19] In several studies, Ajit Singh of University of Cambridge has demonstrated that equity markets in the developed countries are not effective either in ensuring an efficient allocation of savings or in encouraging efficient decision making by entrepreneurs.[20]

In the case of India, new equity raised in the market has declined over the years. According to the data provided by Centre for Monitoring Indian Economy, new equity raised in the market declined from Indian Rupees (Rs.) 3470 million in 1994-95 to Rs.1150 million in 1998-99, even as market capitalization on the Bombay Stock Exchange registered an increase from Rs.43340 million to Rs.54290 million over the same period. It is highly unlikely that equity finance will play a significant role in the developing countries where equity markets are underdeveloped. Further, in several developing countries (e.g., India and China) where the financial markets had been liberalized in the 1990s, corporations have raised lesser amount of funds from the market. Singh found that "there is little or no evidence of an increase in aggregate savings for most developing countries as a result of greater new issues activity on the stock market. In some of the countries (e.g., Turkey and Malaysia) aggregate savings actually fell during the 1980s."[21]

Securitization poses new problems and threats to macroeconomic stability. Trading in securities is influenced more by speculation rather than by economic fundamentals. Rumors play an important role in the trading. Because of high liquidity, funds can move out quickly thereby causing a steep fall in the value of stocks, assets and exchange rates. A sudden loss of confidence among foreign investors can cause a dramatic outflow of funds thereby creating conditions of an imminent financial crisis. This is precisely what happened in the recent Southeast Asian financial crisis.

The Great Transformation of Global Banking

The global banking system has witnessed a radical paradigm shift in recent years due to financial deregulation and liberalization. Historically, banks were the leading intermediaries but now non-bank financial intermediaries play a major role in the global financial system. As financial markets led by non-bank financial institutions have become more dominant than money markets, the power and influence enjoyed by the banks in the past has drastically weakened. Nowadays, banks compete with mutual funds and other non-banking financial institutions to attract funds. Thanks to megamergers taking place in the global banking industry, a trillion-dollar bank has now become a reality (see Box 1.3). In 1998, 505 merger and acquisition deals transferred $285 billion in market value and $1.22 trillion of assets, including megamergers of Citicorp-Travelers

Box 1.3

A $1000,000,000,000 Bank on the Cards?

A trillion-dollar bank! In the past, it was almost impossible to imagine such a gigantic bank. Given the pace at which megamergers are taking place in the banking industry these days, the world will soon witness not one but several trillion dollar banks. The French bank, Banque Nationale de Paris (BNP) made a bid in early 1999 to buy two other French banks, namely, Societe Generale and Paribas. Interestingly, both Societe Generale and Paribas had just entered into a friendly merger when the BNP launched its bid. If the bid by BNP works out, it would create the world's biggest bank, with assets over $1 trillion. Some other recent megamergers include Swiss Bank with Union Bank of Switzerland; Citicorp with Travelers Group; Nations Bank with Bank of America; and Deutsche Bank with Bankers Trust. Except BNP, other megamergers could not produce a trillion-dollar bank though some are inching toward it. It appears that merger mania never stops, as it becomes a self-perpetuating cycle. One merger deal leads to rise in share prices, which in turn, further provides the fuel for the next merger deal and so on, ad infinitum.

In the race to the trillion dollar mark, Japanese banks are also not lagging behind. Under a major financial restructuring plan announced in mid-1999, several megamergers between Japanese banks are on the anvil. If these megamerger deals proceed smoothly, Japanese banks may again become the biggest banks in the world, as was the case a decade ago when they reigned. The proposed tie-up of three big Japanese banks — Fuji Bank, Dai-Ichi Kangyo Bank and Industrial Bank of Japan — would create the largest bank in the world in terms of assets worth $1.27 trillion. Similarly, the deal between Sumitomo and Sakura banks to merge by April 2002 will create an entity worth $934 billion in assets.

While megamergers provide fodder for front-page stories in the newspapers, a simple fact is often ignored that mergers pose new challenges to regulatory authorities in terms of moral hazard. The complexity of big banks makes the task of managing risk more difficult. This became evident in 1998 when UBS suffered huge losses on account of bad deals in financial derivatives and lending to a hedge fund, LTCM. Recently, the BIS has come out with a critical study which found that mergers have failed to boost profits. Further, job cuts are an imminent fallout of every merger deal. Deutsche Bank's merger, for instance, with Bankers Trust was accompanied by a staggering downsizing of 5500 jobs.

Group and Nations Bank-Bank of America.[22] With the emergence of universal banking, the trillion dollar banks would provide a range of financial services including stock brokerage, insurance, mutual funds and Internet banking. Megamergers of banks, in fact, have been facilitated by financial deregulation and therefore should be seen as an integral part of a bigger phenomenon.

Largely because of increased competition and low margins in retail banking, banks have expanded their businesses in the last two decades. As a result, the distinction between the operations of commercial banks and non-banking financial institutions is getting blurred with the emergence of investment banking and universal banking. Similarly, many non-banking institutions have now ventured into banking services. For

---

Box 1.4

Financial Intermediary is an agent who deals with the general public on the one side and the financial markets on the other. The important function of financial intermediary is to bring together economic agents who wish to save with those who wish to invest.

Commercial Bank is a commercial institution that accepts deposits and makes credit to private individuals, companies and other organizations.

Investment Bank helps firms raise money in the financial markets. They underwrite issues by agreeing to buy unsold securities. They also advise their clients on mergers and acquisitions.

Universal Banking involves not only services related to loans and savings but also those involved in making investments in companies. Well developed in Germany, the Netherlands and Switzerland, universal banking system allows banks to act as investment banks and to provide a very wide range of other financial services to clients.

UK Building Societies are involved in both lending and borrowing funds in the money markets since 1982. In their financial transactions, the building societies resemble high street banks. The first building society to become a bank in the UK was the Abbey National.

instance, building societies in the UK now offer cheque accounts. Likewise, the launching of financial and banking services by several business corporations (e.g., the General Electric of US and Tesco, a chain of departmental stores in the UK) has further intensified this trend.

In the past, several countries had adopted policy measures to prevent commercial banks from acting as universal banks providing different financial services such as investment banking and underwriting insurance. In the US, for instance, the Glass-Steagall Act of 1933 was enacted in the wake of the Great Depression of the 1930s to prohibit universal banking. Under the Act, commercial banks were prohibited from investment banking activities, such as underwriting corporate securities. However, under pressure from market forces, the US repealed the Glass-Steagall Act in 1999. With massive financial deregulation, the original separation between commercial and investment banking has been drastically eroded in recent years as banks now take up discount brokerage operations, sell mutual funds and provide underwriting and other investment services. Rapid changes in the financial sector (e.g., emergence of financial derivatives) have also facilitated the diversification of banks into various non-fund businesses. Some banks have even diversified into the insurance services through mergers and acquisitions. In Germany, for instance, a new type of banking called Allfinanz has emerged which offers life insurance, pension schemes and traditional bank deposits. The list of universal banks includes Citigroup, Deutsche Bank, Dresdner Bank, Commerzbank and HSBC.

On the other hand, investment banks (e.g., Morgan Stanley Dean Witter and Co., Merrill Lynch, Goldman Sachs and Credit Suisse First Boston) help corporations to raise funds in financial markets. They also advise their clients on mergers and acquisitions. Much of the income earned by investment banks comes from fees and commissions. As investment banks indulge in heavy risk businesses (such as financial derivatives), their profits are relatively higher. Notwithstanding the growing trend of commercial banks taking on investment banking services, there are few success stories. In fact, several big banks such as Citicorp and

NatWest have abandoned their investment banking operations.

Recent experience, particularly in the context of the Southeast Asian financial crisis, also raises critical issues about the operations of investment banks. When the crisis broke out, several investment banks were blamed for speculating on Asian currencies and thereby causing the crisis. But curiously, some of them have become advisors to the crisis-ridden countries. Goldman Sachs, for instance, is advising Thailand and Indonesia on bond issues and privatization while Lehman Brothers is a consultant to the Financial Restructuring Agency of Thailand that is selling off assets of closed finance companies. It is ironical that while advising the Thai authorities on restructuring, Goldman Sachs in collaboration with GE Capital was busy bidding to buy up the assets of 56 defunct finance companies. Since these banks have commercial enterprises in Thailand and Indonesia, analysts have pointed out that banks are pursuing their own business interests without any compunction. None other than Thailand's Finance Minister, Tarrin Nimmanahaeminda, has echoed this concern:

> These banks have an advisory side and a wheeler-dealer commercial side...They always say they maintain Chinese walls between them. I rather doubt it. How else would they be proving to their board that they are maximizing profits?[23]

Financial Derivatives: The Source of Systemic Risks

Another major development in the global financial system is the explosive growth of financial derivatives in the 1980s and the 1990s. In fact, the growth in derivative markets has been more dramatic in comparison with the equity and bond markets. Trading of derivatives in raw minerals and goods dates back to the nineteenth century, while financial derivatives started in 1972 with currency trading. Stock-index futures trading began in 1982, and trading in interest-rate futures commenced in 1988. The derivative markets are not restricted to developed countries alone. A number of developing countries allow trading in derivative instruments. There are no reliable statistics pertaining to financial derivatives. From the end-March 1995 to the end-June 1998, notional amounts outstanding in the OTC markets rose by 52 per cent touching $72 trillion, compared with $13.2 trillion outstanding in exchange traded foreign exchange and interest rate derivatives which grew by 34.2 per cent, according to the latest estimates published by the IMF.[24]

While financial derivatives are supposed to help reduce risk, they have become one of the biggest sources of volatility and instability in the global financial markets. Derivatives pose additional risks because many of the contracts are highly speculative thereby increasing the chances of heavy losses if a bet goes sour. Speculators play an important role in the trading of financial derivatives. They keep buying and selling contracts

Table 1.4: Markets for Selected Derivative Instruments, 1991-96

	Estimated amounts outstanding at year-end ($bn)					
	1991	**1992**	**1993**	**1994**	**1995**	**1996**
Exchange traded instruments	3519	4634	7771	8863	9188	9885
Interest rate futures	2157	2913	4959	5778	5863	5931
Interest rate options[a]	1073	1385	2362	2624	2742	3278
Currency futures	18	27	35	40	38	50
Currency options	63	71	76	56	43	47
Stock market index futures	76	80	110	127	172	199
Stock market index options	133	159	230	238	329	380
Over the counter instruments	4449	5346	8475	11303	17713	24292
Interest rate swaps	3065	3851	6177	8861	12811	
Currency swaps[b]	807	860	900	915	1197	
Other swap-related derivatives[c]	577	634	1398	1573	3705	
Total	**7968**	**9980**	**16246**	**20166**	**26901**	**34177**

[a] Calls and puts.
[b] Adjusted for reporting of both currencies.
[c] Caps, collars, floors and swaptions.
Source: *Annual Report*, Bank for International Settlements, 1996-97.

Box 1.5

Derivatives: Trader's Dream, Regulator's Nightmare

A derivative product is a contract, the value of which depends on (i.e., 'derived' from) the price of some underlying asset (e.g., an interest level or stock market index). Financial derivatives are financial contracts whose value is based upon the value of other underlying financial assets such as stocks, bonds, mortgages or foreign exchange. They are contractual agreements for future exchange of assets whose present value are equal. However, the value of the derivatives will change over the term of the contract as market valuation change the value of each side of the contract. The key element in these derivatives is that one can buy and sell all the risk of an underlying asset without trading the asset itself.

Trading in financial derivatives is also distanceless and borderless. Financial derivatives are either transacted OTC or traded at exchanges. There are specialist exchanges (e.g., London International Financial Futures Exchange) in which financial derivatives are traded. However, in recent years, the value of OTC instruments has increased sharply as compared to exchange-traded instruments. While exchange-traded instruments are strictly regulated, OTC contracts are informal agreements between two parties and therefore carry heavy risk. The main users of financial derivatives are banks, forex dealers, corporate treasurers, institutional investors and hedge funds.

Recent experience shows that financial derivatives are largely used as tools to make profits from speculation and arbitrage rather than to reduce exposure to risk. From the nineties onwards, trade in derivatives has registered a rapid growth in terms of volume of trading and in the evolution of new and far more sophisticated instruments, giving rise to what is known as the 'derivatives of derivatives' syndrome. Due to these developments, it becomes a difficult task to regulate financial derivatives both at the company's as well as state regulatory levels. Financial derivatives, therefore, are going to pose one of the greatest challenges for regulatory bodies in the 21st century. It is high time that regulatory bodies pay adequate attention so that an effective strategy to deal with the systemic risks posed by the financial derivatives can be chalked out.

contd. on next page

The three forms of financial derivatives are options, futures and swaps. **Options** are the rights (without obligation) to buy or sell a specific item — such as stocks or currency — for a preset price during a specified period of time. The option can be freely exercised or disregarded, with no obligation to transact. Where the right is to buy, the contract is termed a **Call Option**; where the right is to sell, it is termed a **Put Option**. The holder of the option is able to take advantage of a favorable movement in prices, losing only the premium payable for the option should prices move adversely. Trade in option contracts was long practiced between banks but developed after these began to be traded on the Philadelphia Stock Exchange in 1982. Currency options were introduced on the London International Financial Futures Exchange (LIFFE) and the London Stock Exchange in 1985. Options on three-month sterling futures were introduced on LIFFE in November 1987; trade in Japanese government bond futures began in July 1987. Chief centers for trade in options are the Chicago Board Options Exchange, the American Stock Exchange, and the European Options Exchange in Amsterdam and markets in Australia, France, Sweden and Switzerland.

Futures are contracts that commit both parties to a transaction in a financial instrument on a future date at a fixed price. Unlike an option, a futures contract involves a definite purchase or sale and not an option to buy or sell. Often futures are used to speculate in the financial markets and therefore considered risky. A forward contract differs from a futures contract in the sense that each forward contract is a once-only deal between the two parties, while futures contracts are in standard amounts traded on exchanges. Unlike forward contracts, futures are traded face to face at exchanges and are regulated by the authorities.

Swaps are agreements in which two counterparties undertake to exchange payments within a specified time period. For example, a UK company may find it easy to raise a sterling loan when they really want to borrow Deutsche Marks; a German company may have exactly the opposite problem. A swap will enable them to exchange the currency they possess for the currency they need. Recent years have witnessed explosive growth in currency swaps and interest rate swaps. The first currency swap was between the World Bank and the IBM in 1981.

depending on their perceptions of the movements of financial markets. Rumors also play an important role in their decision making. The risks posed by derivative markets are twofold: firm specific risks and systemic risks. Since derivatives are highly leveraged, a small change in the interest rates, exchange rates and equity prices can cause huge financial losses to the firm. Depending on the extent of integration with the larger financial system, firm specific risk can easily spread to the entire system. Systemic risk refers to the vulnerability of the financial system to shocks. The rapid growth of derivative markets has increased the threat of systemic failure. Since much of derivatives involve cross border trading, systemic failure can spread out on a global scale. By the time the firm or regulatory authorities are able to react and take appropriate steps, the damage is already done as the speed at which market shocks are transmitted globally has increased many times in recent years, thanks to technological innovations.

Due to rapid changes in the global banking system, derivative markets have come to be concentrated in the hands of a few banks. Increased concentration in OTC derivative markets highlights the potential adverse impact on the entire financial system. Large exposures to one another among these key market participants increase the repercussion effects of shocks if one of the key market players were to default on its obligation. Since many derivatives are off-balance sheet items, the ability of market participants to assess the risks faced by the counterparties is hampered. Such lack of disclosures leads to counterparties having no idea about the financial health of the firm with which they are dealing. The blurring of distinctions between banks and non-bank financial institutions has expanded the scope of systemic failures.

Notwithstanding the brief history of financial derivatives, they have played havoc in the world financial markets. Derivatives trading played a key role in the stock market crash in the US on 'Black Monday' on October 19, 1987. Some disasters have come out in the open while others remain buried. Perhaps the most surprising disaster was the $1.2 billion derivative loss by the Belgian government in currency swaps in the late

1990s. Another notable disaster was suffered by a hedge fund, LTCM, in 1998. The near collapse of LTCM brought the financial crisis of Southeast Asia and Russia to the doors of Wall Street. To highlight the risks associated with financial derivatives, some of the major disasters are delineated below.

■ In 1992, Showa Shell Seikiyu, a Japanese subsidiary of Royal Dutch Shell, lost $1.1 billion. The company bet $6.4 trillion in the currency future markets assuming that the dollar would strengthen against the yen. Instead the dollar weakened, and as a result, the trading loss cleaned up 80 per cent of the company's capital.

■ In 1994, the Government of Orange County, California, suffered a loss of $2 billion in its fund by trading in financial derivatives. By pooling the funds of school districts and government agencies within the county along with $14 billion of short-term borrowing, the managers of Orange County gambled in the derivatives thinking that the interest rates would

Table 1.5: Billion Dollar Losses in Derivatives Deals

Organization	Instruments	$bn
Kidder Peabody	Oil futures	4.4
Schneider Property Group	Derivatives speculation using inflated assets as collateral	4
LTCM	Interest rate spreads	4
Sumitomo Corp.	Copper futures	2.6
Metallgesellschaft	Oil forwards	1.9
Orange County	Interest rate mismatching using structured notes	1.7
Kashima Oil	Oil forwards	1.5
Barings	Japanese equity index financial futures	1.4
Belgian government	Currency swaps	1.2
Daiwa Bank	US Treasury bond futures	1.1
Balsam Group	Deferral accounting	1

fall or remain stable. Instead the interest rates soared. Suffering huge losses, the Orange County defaulted on its loan and went bankrupt. In addition, there was a $40 million cut in the county budget and consequently the government had to drastically slash the budget earmarked for social welfare programs for low-income population. Thousands of workers, as a result, lost their jobs in Orange County.

- Have you ever heard of losing $157 million on a deal involving $200 million of borrowing? In 1993, Proctor and Gamble (P&G), a US conglomerate entered into a deal to reduce the interest costs on $200 million of loans. Under the deal, P&G's interest rates would vary according to a complex formula based on the yields of US Treasury bonds of different maturities. The nominal value of contracts that P&G had entered into was $3800 million. Rather than falling, the interest rates in the US rose. By the time the management of the company decided to extricate itself from the deal, it had suffered a whopping loss of $157 million.

- In 1995, Barings Plc., Britain's oldest merchant bank, suffered a loss of $1.4 billion when its Singapore based derivatives trader Nick Leeson built up large but uncovered positions in Nikkei 225 (Japan's leading share index) futures contracts on the Osaka and Singapore futures exchanges. Leeson was convinced that the Nikkei would rise and therefore he placed one-sided bets on the price movement of Nikkei 225. However, due to the Kobe earthquake in January 1995, Japanese share prices collapsed and Nikkei 225 fell sharply. Leeson continued trading and even increased his exposure after the earthquake. In February 1995, an inquiry ordered by the management to look into his operations found that the bank had suffered huge losses. Apart from the alleged fraud committed by Leeson, lax internal controls were found responsible for the huge losses. By forwarding nearly $890 million (more than half of its capital) to its Singapore subsidiary, Barings had violated the British and the European regulations which limit the funds to be used for any single purpose by a bank.

- The Daiwa Bank suffered losses totaling $1.1 billion when its New York-based branch's dealer Toshihide Iguchi carried out unauthorized trading in US Treasury bond futures. The problem started when Iguchi made a $200000 trading loss in 1984. For over 11 years, he continued accumulating $1.1 billion of losses by falsifying records in such a manner that neither the Daiwa Bank nor the US Federal Reserve had any clu about it. In July 1994, Iguchi finally informed the Daiwa Bank about his trading losses.

■ In 1998, Long-Term Capital Management (LTCM), a hedge fund, suffered a huge loss of more than $4 billion. With the notional value of derivatives contracts exceeding $1 trillion, LTCM was bound to make substantial profits if interest rate spreads on bonds narrowed. However, in the aftermath of the Russian crisis, there was a stampede to 'safety' and yield spreads widened instead of narrowing. By September 1998, LTCM lost 90 per cent of its equity. For details, see chapter 4.

Although much attention has been paid to the role of 'rogue trader' for incurring huge losses (e.g., Leeson of Barings and Iguchi of Daiwa), three underlying factors behind many of these financial disasters have been largely ignored. Since financial derivatives are very sophisticated, risky and highly leveraged instruments, a slight mishandling of trading can lead to huge losses. Secondly, there are serious weaknesses in the internal control and risk management systems within the banks and institutions involved in financial derivatives. Lastly, and perhaps more importantly, regulatory and supervisory authorities have lagged behind in foreseeing the risks involved in the derivatives trading particularly in the OTC derivative markets. There is no denying the fact that the central banks have intervened sporadically to avert the contagion effects of the financial disasters in the financial system. However, the real challenge before central banks and regulatory bodies is to curb speculative behavior and bring discipline in derivative markets so that financial disasters of such magnitude do not recur.

Offshore Financial Centers and the 'Dirty Money'

The world of offshore financial centers (which are also popularly known as 'tax havens') display the characteristic elements of 'casino capitalism.'

There is hardly any region in the world that does not have any offshore financial center. In total, there are over 69 offshore financial centers in the world and the funds routed through these centers are huge. A large number of hedge funds, trust companies, shell companies and brokerage houses are located in offshore centers. Central to financial liberalization, these centers originated primarily for avoiding foreign exchange and capital controls. Closely linked with corruption and crime, these centers are the natural destination of 'dirty money.' Often used for money laundering purposes, the offshore financial centers act as a tool to launder not only the proceeds of drug trafficking and other crimes but also aid and abet certain kinds of financial crime. The BCCI scandal is one of the glaring examples of this phenomenon that shook the world's markets in the early 1990s.

In a similar vein, the global hedge fund industry has witnessed tremendous growth in the past decade. The total number of hedge funds operating worldwide is estimated to be 5500, with $300 billion of funds under management, as of mid-1998. A substantial number of hedge funds operate from offshore financial centers. Since the issues related to hedge funds and offshore financial centers are of special significance and are integrally related to deregulation, they have been examined in detail in chapters 4 and 5 respectively.

Global Financial System: A Casino?

The recent trends and developments in global financial flows, as discussed above, corroborate the fact that international economy has moved away from productive pursuits to those of finance. As the value of global forex trade is many times more than the value of annual world output or export of goods and services, the global financial system resembles a casino in which assets are traded primarily for speculative profit rather than for the benefit of the real economy. That is why, many analysts have described this phenomenon as 'casino capitalism.'[25] In fact, it is 'casino capitalism' that very often perpetuates economic disasters thereby adversely affecting the lives of millions of ordinary people who have put their savings and assets at its disposal. Even those who are not part of 'casino capitalism' (e.g., poor people, workers, small traders, etc.) may not be able to escape from its machinations as witnessed in the wake of the Mexican and the Southeast Asian financial crises. As Susan Strange puts it succinctly:

> For the great difference between an ordinary casino which you can go into or stay away from, and the global casino of high finance, is that in the latter we are all involuntarily engaged in the day's play. A currency change can halve the value of a farmer's crop before he harvests it, or drive an exporter out of business. A rise in interest rates can fatally inflate the costs of holding stocks for the shopkeeper. A takeover dictated by financial considerations can rob the factory worker of his job. From school-leavers to pensioners, what goes on in the casino in the office blocks of the big financial centers is apt to have sudden, unpredictable and unavoidable consequences for individual lives. The financial casino has everyone playing the game of Snakes and Ladders.[26]

Notes and References

1. Peter Warburton, *Debt and Delusion*, Allen Lane The Penguin Press, 1999, p. 9.

2. For a detailed discussion on global financial integration, see World Bank, *Private Capital Flows to Developing Countries: The Road to Financial Integration*, Oxford University Press, 1997.

3. Kavaljit Singh, *Globalization of Finance: A Citizen's Guide*, Madhyam Books and Zed Books, 1999, p. 23.

4. James Rutter and Peter Lee, "GE Capital: Which Way After Wendt," *Euromoney*, January 1999 (via Internet).

5. Based in Belgium, Society for Worldwide Interbank Financial Telecommunications (SWIFT) is an international facility jointly owned by over 1000 banks dedicated to interbank funds transfer. In 1995, it had approximately 4700 users spread over in 124 countries and processed nearly 2.4 million messages per day.

6. "Finance: Trick or Treat?," *The Economist*, October 23, 1999, p. 101.

7. David Felix, "Statistical Appendix," in Mahbub ul Haq, Inge Kaul and Isabelle Grunberg, *The Tobin Tax: Coping with Financial Volatility*, Oxford University Press, 1996, p. 295.

8. P G Cerny (ed.), *Finance and World Politics: Markets, Regimes and States in the Post-Hegemonic Era*, Edward Elgar, 1993, p. 18.

9. Susan Strange, *Mad Money*, Manchester University Press, 1998, pp. 179-180.

10. John C Edmunds, "Securities: The New World Wealth Machine," *Foreign Policy*, Fall 1996, p. 120.

11. Peter Warburton, op. cit., p. 72.

12. *The Economist*, January 16, 1999, p. 105.

13. Ibid.

14. *The Economist*, October 23, 1999, op. cit.

15. *The Economist*, June 13, 1998, p. 101.

16. Hans Blommestein, "Impact of Institutional Investors on Financial Markets," in *Institutional Investors in the New Financial Landscape*, OECD, 1999, p. 30.

17. See C Mayer, "Financial Systems, Corporate Finance and Economic Development," in R G Hubbard (ed.), *Asymmetric Information, Corporate Finance, and Investment*, University of Chicago Press, 1990.

18. Patricia Cayo Sexton, "Con Games and Gamblers on Wall Street," *Dissent*, Winter 1999, p. 17.

19. Ibid.

20. Ajit Singh and J Hamid, *Corporate Financial Structures in Developing Countries*, Technical Paper No. 1, International Finance Corporation, World Bank, 1992; Ajit Singh, "The Stock-Market and Economic Development: Should Developing Countries Encourage Stock-Markets," *UNCTAD Review*, No. 4, 1993; Ajit Singh, *Corporate Financial Patterns in Industrializing Economies: A Comparative International Study*, Technical Paper No. 2, International Finance Corporation, World Bank, 1995; and Ajit Singh, *Pension Reform, the Stock Market, Capital Formation and Economic Growth: A Critical Commentary on the World Bank's Proposals*, Working Paper No. 2, Center for Economic Policy Analysis, New School of Social Research, 1996.

21. Ajit Singh, op. cit., 1996, p. 19.

22. "Financial Services: M&A Seen Rebounding in Year 2000," *The Hindu Business Line*, December 1, 1999.

23. Quoted in Michael Vatikiotis and Salil Tripathi, "Banking on Big Names," *Far Eastern Economic Review*, November 19, 1998, p. 50.

24. *International Capital Markets: Developments, Prospects and Key Policy Issues*, IMF, 1999, p. 22.

25. See, for instance, Susan Strange, *Casino Capitalism*, Blackwell, 1986.

26. Ibid., p. 2.

2

Financial Liberalization and
Financial Fragility

IMPLEMENTED in conjunction with other macroeconomic policy reforms, financial liberalization remains one of the most controversial issues in economic literature. Perhaps no other issue of economic reform has witnessed such wide variations and swings in the realm of economic theory as financial liberalization. After having swayed the imagination of neo-liberal economic thinkers for over two decades, the doctrine of financial liberalization is under thorough scrutiny, particularly in the wake of the Southeast Asian financial crisis.

What is Financial Liberalization?

Financial liberalization is a process in which allocation of resources is determined by market forces rather than the state. It minimizes the role of the state in the financial sector by encouraging market forces to decide who gets and gives credit and at what price. The much-touted benefits of financial liberalization include higher savings, enhancement of efficiency in financial intermediation by removing 'distortions' created by controls, greater competition in financial markets and improvement in monetary control. The key components of financial liberalization are the following:

- Deregulation of interest rates.
- Removal of credit controls.
- Privatization of government owned banks and financial institutions.

Box 2.1

Interest Rate Controls are those measures that are applicable on both deposit and lending rates. As economic and financial activity is greatly influenced by interest rates, governments usually keep interest rates low in order to encourage investment. On the other hand, higher rates of interest tend to discourage investment and reduce the demand for money, giving a downward impetus to both employment and prices.

Credit Controls are used by governments to ensure that credit is provided to key sectors of the economy (e.g., agriculture and export sectors in India). Credit controls can also be used to bar certain types of transactions such as real estate and stock market. In addition, banks and financial intermediaries are not permitted to decide freely to whom they wish to lend. Credit controls are exercised with the help of a variety of instruments including lending requirements and ceilings imposed on banks, compulsory loans at preferential interest rates and credit guarantees.

Monetary Controls are those measures that regulate the size of the money supply in a country. These controls can be implemented with the help of various instruments like instructing banks to hold a certain percentage of their deposits in government bonds or non-interest bearing reserves at the central bank. In some countries (e.g., India and the UK), monetary control is a matter of government policy and the central bank acts in accordance with this. In other countries (e.g., Germany and the US), the central bank is fully independent of government policy.

Box 2.2

Two Approaches: Sequencing and 'Big Bang'

Broadly speaking, there are two approaches towards implementation of financial reforms. One approach, which is popularly known as **sequencing**, gives more emphasis on the proper sequencing of financial liberalization. It focuses greater attention on the order of liberalization between the financial sector and the real sector as well as between the domestic and the external sector. Financial liberalization, according to this approach, should begin with domestic real sector reform, then moving on to domestic financial sector reform, followed by the external real sector (i.e., trade account), and finally to the external financial sector (i.e., capital account). This approach underscores the occurrence of market failures and calls for their correction before going full steam with financial liberalization. Sequencing of financial liberalization appears to be the preferred mode as compared to the 'big bang' approach, but with powerful interest groups and lobbies inhabiting the real world, issues pertaining to the pace and sequencing of reforms are often put in the backburner. There are several instances (e.g., Chile, Argentina, Mexico, New Zealand and Turkey) where financial sector reforms were implemented very rapidly with little regard to requisite pace and sequencing. The consequences were disastrous.

In contrast, the other approach gives credence to a more rapid process of liberalization. Popularly known as **'big bang'**, this approach was followed in stock market reforms in the UK in the late 1980s. The 'big bang' approach justifies the economic costs (in terms of severe financial shocks and crises) associated with rapid financial liberalization on the assumption that the long-term benefits from liberalization outweigh these 'short-term' costs. It outrightly rejects the need for state intervention in the financial markets believing that markets have an innate capacity to attain equilibrium sooner or later. This approach was strongly advocated by Jeffrey Sachs for implementation in the East European countries to facilitate their transition from socialist economies to market economies. In 1998, the Japanese authorities favored the adoption of 'big bang' approach to carry out radical financial reforms. The successful examples of 'big bang' approach are very few. Even in UK where the 'big bang' approach was considered successful, it was only limited to the securities market.

- Liberalization of restrictions on the entry of private sector and/or foreign banks and financial institutions into domestic financial markets.
- Introduction of market-based instruments of monetary control.
- Liberalization of capital account.

Since the issues related to liberalization of capital account and capital controls are of considerable significance, they are discussed at great length elsewhere in the book (see chapters 3 and 6).

Till the 1960s and the early 1970s, the dominant thinking in both the developed and the developing countries was in favor of economic planning with credit and interest rate controls. In the late 1970s, the neo-liberal thinking on financial markets became the dominant paradigm in the developed countries which was subsequently to be embraced by the developing countries. The most well known advocates of neo-liberal thinking were Ronald McKinnon and Edward Shaw. In 1973, McKinnon and Shaw published their works in which they delineated the distortions created by governments (particularly through interest rate controls) in the economy and vigorously advocated the case for financial liberalization.[1] Coining the term 'financial repression' to describe the financial system of the developing countries where the government exercised credit and interest rate controls, McKinnon and Shaw argued that full liberalization of financial sector is a necessary precondition for successful economic development.

For almost 25 years after the publications of McKinnon and Shaw, the neo-liberal outlook on financial liberalization held sway in both theory and practice. Most developed countries had liberalized their financial sector by the end of the seventies, but the process took a considerable time to take root in certain others. For instance, the process of interest rate deregulation in the UK and the Scandinavian countries took several years to complete. The financial systems in the developing countries (except Hong Kong and Singapore) were largely 'repressed' till the late 1970s. The Latin American countries were the first to introduce financial liberalization. Chile began with a rapid liberalization approach in the late 1970s followed by Argentina and Uruguay. Financial reforms in Asia commenced in the mid-1980s in the East Asian countries initially and then spread to other countries in the region. Several African countries have initiated or are in the process of initiating financial liberalization in the 1990s. It needs to be emphasized here that financial reforms in the developing countries were not introduced as isolated policy measures but were important components of the Washington Consensus.[2]

Financial Liberalization: Some Critical Issues

While making a strong case in favor of financial liberalization, its proponents downplay the positive contribution made by 'financial repression' in ensuring financial stability and an enhanced economic performance. Generally speaking, the periods marked by financial liberalization have witnessed financial fragility and deterioration in the economic performance in both the developed as well as the developing countries. It is to be noted that countries such as South Korea and Japan enjoyed rapid economic growth and financial stability under a regime of 'financial repression.' In the case of South Korea, the success of its industrial policy and growth would not have occurred without 'financial repression.' The Korean authorities promoted their long-term industrial policy of export oriented industries by targeting financial resources at industrial projects while providing credits at preferential rates of interest to such projects. Japan and Taiwan also maintained interest rate and credit controls that contributed towards higher growth rates. The policy of 'strategic planning' in Japan was supported by credit controls which ensured that sufficient credit was available for priority areas. However, when South Korea and Japan introduced financial reforms, not only their economic performance deteriorated but their financial systems also became much more fragile. Taiwan, to a considerable extent, has been able to maintain its economic performance even in the 1990s because its financial sector is still not fully liberalized. This had also helped Taiwan to protect its economy from the contagion effects of the Southeast Asian financial crisis.

Analysts have pointed out that financial liberalization has led to a steep fall in revenue because in the course of regulating interest rates or steering credit to various sectors of the economy, governments occasionally make a profit or are able to borrow at subsidized rates.[3] By imposing taxes or other regulations (such as cash reserve ratios), a 'financial repression' regime is instrumental in creating substantial governmental revenues. The total revenue from 'financial repression' has been estimated on an average at 9 per cent of the total government revenue or 2 per cent of the GDP.[4]

It must be admitted that a 'financial repression' regime is not beyond reproach as there are problems in terms of its outreach and the potential for corruption and cronyism to thrive. In spite of these and other administrative problems, it is an undeniable fact that a financial system under such a regime is seriously engaged with the real economy. In contrast, financial liberalization delinks financial sector from the real economy and encourages flow of funds for speculative purposes, both at the national and global levels. And due to inherent problems associated with financial markets (e.g., asymmetric information, herd behavior and self-fulfilling panics), discussed in detail later, financial liberalization further enhances the capacity of speculative funds to destabilize the real economy which otherwise may be sufficiently sound. Although this problem becomes more acute in those countries where adequate regulatory mechanisms are not in place, but even in countries with adequate regulatory mechanisms, the authorities find it extremely hard to cope with massive inflows and outflows of speculative funds.

There is little evidence to demonstrate that low or negative interest rates discourage savings and hence growth. Several studies have proved that there is hardly any correlation between interest rates and savings.[5] Despite large hike in real interest rates in Chile during the liberalization period, savings did not increase. In fact, the average national savings rate in Chile was 10.7 per cent during the liberalization period (1974-83), down from 12.6 per cent during the 'financial repression' period (1966-73). Further, there was no substantial increase in investment. As far as the quality of investment in Chile is concerned, a substantial part went into speculative activities in the real estate and stock market.

Higher interest rates, on the contrary, adversely affect investment in the real economy. Higher interest rates also have an adverse indirect impact as noted by Prabhat Patnaik, "it makes the servicing of public debt more expensive and hence squeezes the public exchequer, leading to lower public investment and, via the demand and supply constraints it causes, to lower private investment as well. The squeeze on the public exchequer also affects welfare expenditures adversely."[6] It has also been observed that no substantial change in aggregate savings occurs even if higher interest rates encourage shifting of funds from informal to formal savings institutions. However, the shift to formal savings institutions has serious negative implications for small farmers, small producers and traders because it reduces the amount of finance they can avail.[7]

Another serious repercussion of financial liberalization pertains to the loss of autonomy in the management of monetary policy. The 'impossible trinity' (fixed exchange rates, capital mobility and monetary autonomy) is an indication that national authorities have lost autonomy in monetary policy. In a financially liberalized environment, the government is unable to use direct instruments of monetary control such as required reserve ratios. The survey on financial liberalization carried out by John Williamson and Molly Mahar found that several countries (e.g., New Zealand, Indonesia and Korea) suffered loss of monetary control following liberalization.[8] Further, by providing autonomy to the central bank, the liberalization process poses grave threat to the legitimacy of the political process and the state itself.

The proponents of financial liberalization tend to underestimate the risks associated with it. When interest rates rise, both lenders and borrowers tend to favor risky projects with potentially higher returns. This makes adverse selection and moral hazard worse and if the regulatory and supervisory mechanisms are weak, a financial crisis becomes imminent. Rampant competition in the financial sector may also prove counterproductive as it enhances the risks. Fearing erosion of the franchise value because of increased competition, banks and financial institutions have a natural tendency to lend more money to risky projects. A study by

Table 2.1: A Glossary of Capital Markets

Types of Markets	Examples
Money and foreign exchange markets	Currency (notes and coins) Deposits with banks and other financial institutions Loans from banks and other financial institutions
Securities markets	Certificates of Deposit (CDs) Commercial bills Government debt (e.g., Treasury bills) maturing within one year Bonds issued by governments and their agencies Bonds issued by industrial, commercial and financial corporations Bonds issued by banks Bonds issued by supra-national organizations (e.g., the World Bank, the European Investment Bank) Equities issued by industrial, commercial and financial corporations Equities issued by banks Equities issued in the context of the privatization of state-owned assets Loans which have been 'securitized' (that is, repackaged as bonds) Derivatives (forwards, futures, options and swaps) Interest rate (money market) derivatives Bond derivatives Equity derivatives Credit derivatives Commodity derivatives
Financial markets	All of the above
Capital markets	All of the above, plus the markets in residential, industrial and commercial property

Source: Peter Warburton, *Debt and Delusion*, Allen Lane The Penguin Press, 1999, p. 4.

Andrew Sheng of the World Bank found that increased competition was responsible for bank failures in Chile, Argentina, Spain and Kenya.[9] Increased competition may not always lead to more investment in the real economy. Fierce competition in the banking sector has given rise to a situation where banks are increasingly resorting to speculative activities (e.g., foreign exchange speculation) to reap higher profits. Besides, it has been observed that rapid credit expansion in a liberalized environment increases the exposure of banks and financial institutions to boom-bust prone activities.

It must be emphasized here that financial liberalization poses risks not only to individual banks or institutions but also to the entire financial system itself. The failure of a large bank can lead to collapse of other banks — which may be otherwise fundamentally sound — which in turn, could trigger a larger systemic risk. Systemic risk in financial markets is much greater than any other markets due precisely to inter-bank payment and settlement system. Banks are exposed to large amounts of cross border settlement risk because settlement of transactions take place in different time zones. Because two national payment systems (for instance, of Japan and Switzerland) are never open at the same time, it poses the risk in the sense that if the first counterparty has delivered one side of the transaction, the other counterparty may go bankrupt and fail to honor the contract.

This kind of risk is also known as 'Herstatt risk.' In June 1974, the Bundesbank closed down Herstatt Bank after business hours when it suffered huge foreign exchange losses. Several banks who had paid out Deutsche Marks to Herstatt suffered losses because its closure at this time of the day prevented them from receiving US dollars in return. Andrew Crockett of BIS has estimated that in two and a half business days the inter-bank settlement systems of Switzerland and Japan generate a turnover equivalent to those countries' annual GDP. Given the fact that large amounts are transacted through the inter-bank system, participants can pull out from it anticipating any problem, thereby triggering a liquidity crisis that can further lead to a systemic crisis.

Financial Markets are Different from Commodity Markets

Arguments in favor of financial liberalization are largely based on an analogy between commodity and financial markets. This analogy is fallacious because commodity markets are different from financial markets.[10] The differences are not merely restricted to the nature of goods and services transacted in these markets. In fact, they differ in terms of their operations. In commodity markets, one good is exchanged for another but in financial markets a real good is exchanged for a future promise. That is the reason why banks and financial institutions are hesitant in lending, as they want loans to be repaid.

The fallacy of this line of thinking can be illustrated by drawing a comparison between financial markets and fish markets. If a fish shop fails, it will not have a wider impact either sectorally or on the national economy. But if one bank fails, other banks are likely to face problems because of heavy inter-bank lending and other interlinkages through the payment and settlement system. Besides, a bank failure gives an indication to other banks to ration credit supply even to good borrowers, which can negatively impact the real economy. Thus, credit rationing remains a problem even in a fully liberalized financial market. Since finance plays a crucial role in economic development, the impact of failures in financial markets is much more widespread and damaging. In addition, the banking system becomes more vulnerable to contagion effects because of the mismatch between the liquidity and maturity profiles of bank assets and liabilities. Consequently, a crisis in one financial market has a spread out effect on other financial markets.

Asymmetric Information, Herd Behavior, Self-fulfilling Panics and Market Failures

Although all markets are imperfect and liable to fail, financial markets are more prone to failure because they are afflicted with asymmetric information, herd behavior and self-fulfilling panics. These factors make financial markets more inefficient and volatile. Market failures generate instability in the financial system with large social costs. One of the main obstacles in the efficient functioning of the financial markets is asymmetric information, a situation in which one party to an economic transaction does not know enough about the other party to make accurate decisions. In most financial markets, asymmetries of information exist between lenders and borrowers. For instance, a borrower who takes a loan has much better information about the potential returns and risks associated with the investment financed by that loan, as compared to the lender. Precisely because of rapid transnationalization of financial services in recent years, the problems related to information asymmetries have increased manifold as the geographical and cultural spread make the task of acquiring and analyzing relevant information much more difficult and expensive.

Asymmetric information further gives rise to two problems — adverse selection and moral hazard. Adverse selection is a problem that occurs before a financial transaction takes place. Adverse selection occurs when the parties who are most likely to produce an adverse result enter into a financial transaction. Moral hazard is an asymmetric information problem that occurs after the financial transaction. This happens when the borrower engages in undesirable activities (for instance, high-risk investments) consequently creating a situation in which s/he does well if the project succeeds. But in case the project fails, the entire loss is borne by the lender. There are also instances of moral hazard where lenders indulge in indiscriminate lending presuming that the governments or international institutions will bail them out if things go awry. This scenario was quite evident in the case of the Mexican and the Southeast Asian crises.

Decisions in financial markets are not primarily influenced by 'economic fundamentals' or developments in the real economy but by expectations concerning the selling and buying behavior of other participants in the financial market. In financial markets, investors do not decide by rational analysis or objective realities. Rather, they decide on the basis of average opinion, that is, what everybody else believes. For instance, if everybody believes that investment in a particular country or a region is rewarding, you are also supposed to invest in that particular country or region irrespective of the fact whether you agree or not. Similarly, if everybody believes that investment in a particular stock or sector is profitable, you are also supposed to invest in that particular stock or sector. Keynes had compared this phenomenon of herd behavior in financial markets to that of a beauty contest run by newspapers in the 1930s. In these contests, the judges did not choose the contestants closest to his or her preference but ranked the contestants according to what they believed average opinion to be. This, according to Keynes, was how financial markets behaved as they reacted to perceptions of how others perceived the likely behavior of the markets. In the real world, average opinion or confidence can change quickly thereby inducing herd behavior as observed in several financial crises in the 1990s. The herd behavior among international investors was one of the principal factors that contributed to the sudden reversal of financial flows in the Southeast Asian countries in 1997.

The environment in which global financial markets function justifies the prevalence of irrational herd behavior on two counts. Firstly, obtaining appropriate information, correctly analyzing and regularly monitoring it, is an extremely expensive and time consuming process particularly when investments are carried out on a global scale. Therefore, it makes economic sense for fund managers and traders to follow the herd. Secondly, the competitive environment provides ample incentives for following the herd. For instance, if fund managers decide rationally and do not follow the herd, their competence will be seriously questioned. On the other hand, if fund managers follow the herd and in case the markets go bust (which is a regular phenomenon nowadays), no one will question their competence because others too have suffered losses. By following the herd, fund managers can blame the 'events' or other factors and thereby escape from individual responsibilities for potential losses.

In several cases, a financial crisis can be self-fulfilling. A rumor can trigger a self-fulfilling speculative attack (e.g., on a currency) which may be baseless and far removed from the economic fundamentals. This can

Box 2.3

What Caused the Southeast Asian Crisis: Crony Capitalism or Casino Capitalism?

There is no consensus on what really caused the Southeast Asian financial crisis. One school of thought holds domestic factors responsible for propelling the crisis. According to its proponents, the Southeast Asian crisis was an outcome of 'crony capitalism' that led to widespread political interference with market processes by cronies of political leadership. They argue that 'crony capitalism' not merely resulted in corruption and inefficiency, it also induced fragility in the financial system in terms of misallocation of investments and moral hazard.

Although one is critical of 'crony capitalism' since it works against the spirit of public interest and the rule of law, it would be a serious mistake to blame it solely for creating the crisis for various reasons. Firstly, in the case of Korean crisis, it is difficult to prove the role of 'crony capitalism' because large enterprises had been allowed by the government to go under in the pre-crisis period and much of foreign borrowings went into the tradable sector rather than fuelling asset bubbles in the non-tradable sector.[12] Secondly, cronyism in the crisis-affected countries is not a recent phenomenon as it had been prevalent for the last four decades or so. Therefore, it does not explain why the financial crisis occurred as late as in 1997. Further, there is no evidence to prove that cronyism had suddenly cropped up in the years immediately preceding the onset of the crisis. Thirdly, there are many countries in the Asian region and elsewhere where large-scale corruption and cronyism exist (e.g., China and India) but were not affected by the financial crisis. Lastly, similar financial crises have occurred in countries that are supposed to be free from crony capitalism. Can one argue that the financial crisis in the ERM in 1992 or the crisis in the Scandinavian countries in the early 1990s was the result of crony capitalism?

There cannot be unicausal explanation because a host of factors worked together in triggering the Asian crisis. The prime culprit is none other than financial globalization that facilitated massive and abrupt flight of capital almost to the tune of $105 billion in 1997.

cause a sudden shift in the investors' predilections, which in turn, can lead to unanticipated market movements and in certain cases may precipitate severe financial crisis as demonstrated by the Mexican and the Southeast Asian financial crises in the 1990s. In fact, it may well be argued that unregulated financial markets have the capacity to provoke financial crises of one kind or the other.

Good-bye Financial Repression, Hello Financial Crash[11]

Financial crisis is not a new phenomenon in the world of finance. The world has witnessed a number of banking and currency crises in the past 100 years. In his classic book, *Mania, Panics and Crashes*, Charles Kindleberger provides an exhaustive account of recurring financial crises. He provides a historic overview of financial crises starting with the crisis in the 'Holy Roman Empire' between 1618 and 1623, which was related to the 30-year war in Europe. Kindleberger also recounts 35 episodes of financial crisis before the Great Depression.

Since the breakdown of Bretton Woods system, various types of financial crises (banking crises, currency crises, or both) have occurred in both the developed and the developing countries. The first major financial crisis occurred in Chile in the early 1980s. The second crisis erupted in 1992-93, when several currencies in the ERM of the European Monetary System experienced speculative attacks. Because of the attacks, the UK and Italy were forced to abandon the ERM and allow their currencies to depreciate in 1992. Likewise, Sweden followed suit as its currency was pegged to the ERM currencies. In the following months, other ERM currencies also experienced depreciation and consequently the ERM exchange rate bands had to be widened in 1993 to cope with speculative pressures.

Then came the Mexican crisis in 1994, which affected the currencies of other Latin American countries through what is known as the 'tequila effect.' By the time these countries could recover from the 'tequila effect,' the world witnessed the eruption of the Southeast Asian financial crisis. Triggered by the devaluation of the Thai currency in July 1997, the

Southeast Asian crisis was the third major financial crisis in a short span of five years. This crisis soon spread tô other Southeast Asian countries and was transformed into a regional financial crisis by the end of 1997. Unlike other recent crises, the Asian crisis took the form of a global financial crisis by the summer of 1998 when the Czech Republic, Russia and Latin America came under its sway. The contagion effects from Russia and Latin America were so severe that they even affected the financial markets of the US and Europe. By the end of 1998, there was hardly any region in the world that was not adversely affected by the contagion effects of the Southeast Asian financial crisis. There is a growing debate as to the plausible causes which led to the Asian financial crisis (see Box 2.3).

Although the characteristics displayed by various financial crises that occurred in the 1990s may appear to be different, there are several common strands other than excessive buildup of short-term foreign debt. Firstly, the frequency of financial crisis has increased sharply all over the world. Secondly, the cumulative costs of these crises are enormous in terms of bank defaults, closures, loss in output, unemployment and poverty. Needless to add, the costs of crises are much greater in the developing countries because of their heavy external indebtedness in comparison to the developed countries. In terms of social costs, the World Bank in a recent report stated that Indonesia, Thailand and South Korea have experienced significant increase in poverty levels after the financial crisis. In Indonesia alone, the proportion of people forced to live on less than $1 per day increased from 11 per cent in 1997 to 19.9 per cent in 1998, implying a staggering increase of 20 million in the ranks of the poor.[13] Thirdly, a common feature of these crises is that a crisis that had initially started in one country was soon to spread to other countries. In certain cases, the victims of contagion effects were the neighboring countries while in others the victims were either trade partners or those who suffered shocks due to the sudden withdrawal of funds by international investors.

Lastly, and perhaps more importantly, in all these episodes, financial liberalization (both domestic and external) preceded the crisis. For instance, Italy and France had liberalized their capital account just before the ERM crisis. Similarly, Mexico and the Southeast Asian countries had embarked upon financial liberalization in the 1990s. This reinforces the conviction that financial liberalization is one of the causative elements that precipitated the financial crises. Carlos Diaz-Alejandro was perhaps the first analyst who exposed the linkages between financial liberalization and financial crises by analyzing the experience of financial liberalization in the Southern Cone countries, namely, Argentina, Chile and Uruguay, during the late 1970s and the early 1980s.[14] It should be noted that these countries (Chile in particular) had expected that financial liberalization would bring in much sought after efficiency in the financial sector; however, their expectations were belied as they were to be hit by one of the worst financial disasters in the annals of neo-liberal history. In the mid-1970s, rapid financial reforms were introduced in Chile by the Pinochet government. Within a short span of time, interest rates were freed, reserve requirements were reduced, banks nationalized by the Allende government were privatized and the newly created non-banking financial intermediaries (*financieras*) were allowed to operate without any restrictions.

In addition to domestic financial liberalization, capital account was also liberalized in Chile. But the consequences were devastating. For instance, higher interest rates had no positive effects on savings. Rather, hike in interest rates created macroeconomic imbalances. Over a long period, the persistence of high interest rates and the 'bubble' of asset prices were facilitated by capital inflows. Once the inflows reduced, companies could not repay their debts, and their asset value collapsed. The financial reforms in Chile not only contributed to heavy external indebtedness, but also led to rampant bankruptcies and high inflation. The real costs of financial crisis to the economy were so high that the government had to re-intervene in the financial system to bailout the ailing banking system. In fact, the financial system was re-nationalized. Chile also undertook several policy measures such as re-imposition of capital controls, promulgation of new regulations on interest rates and financial intermediaries to deal with the financial crisis. A detailed account is given in chapter 7.

Like Chile, financial liberalization in Uruguay and Argentina had no positive impact on savings and investment. In both the countries, economic power was concentrated in the hands of a few large conglomerates, which owned both banks and industrial units. Taking advantage of lax regulatory environment, conglomerates borrowed heavily from their own banks and invested in risky businesses. Consequently, the financial system of these countries soon collapsed. Nigeria is another example where the consequences of rapid financial liberalization were disastrous. As part of a broader structural adjustment program prescribed by the World Bank, Nigeria began to liberalize its financial sector in 1986. Under the program, financial services were opened to new entrants, interest rates were liberalized and restrictions on bank ownership and capital movements were eased out. Banks and insurance companies were privatized, number of private banks tripled, and a host of ancillary finance, mortgage, insurance and brokerage houses mushroomed. Attracted by quick and heady returns, investors, entrepreneurs and professionals rushed to the banking sector, real estate and retail trade to make a kill. In the aftermath of financial liberalization, while the financial sector registered a surge; savings, lending and investments were to touch an all time low. By the early 1990s, there were signs of an impending financial collapse and the bubble burst in 1993 amidst a political crisis.

Turkey and Bolivia also faced similar consequences with financial liberalization. In Turkey, financial reforms were first introduced in 1980 as part of structural adjustment program. These reforms made no positive impact on the efficiency of the financial system. Within two years, Turkey faced a major financial crisis. In Bolivia too, financial liberalization launched in 1985 did not lead to increased savings and investment or higher economic growth. Rather, it is considered to be the main factor behind the banking crises in 1987 and 1989.

In recent years, several studies have also corroborated the fact that there is a direct linkage between financial liberalization and the onset of financial crisis. In 1996, Graciela L Kaminsky and Carmen M Reinhart carried out an empirical investigation to detect links between banking crises, balance-of-payments crises, and financial liberalization.[15] Their sample consisted of 20 countries that witnessed a total of 76 currency crises and 26 banking crises between 1970 and 1995. They concluded that banking and currency crises are the inevitable outcome of unfettered financial liberalization. They also found that when currency and banking crises occur jointly, they are far more severe than when they occur in isolation. In 1998, Asli Demirguc-Kunt and Enrica Detragiache of the World Bank and the IMF respectively carried out a study which looked into the relationship between banking crises and financial liberalization in a panel of 53 countries for the period 1980-95.[16] Their study concluded that banking crises are more likely to occur in liberalized financial systems. In addition, a survey on financial liberalization conducted by John Williamson and Molly Mahar presented a long list of countries where a majority of financial crises were associated with financial liberalization.[17] According to the survey, financial liberalization was a major contributory factor in financial crises in Argentina, Chile, Mexico, the Philippines, Thailand, Turkey, the US and Venezuela.

Two broad conclusions can be drawn from the case studies related to global financial liberalization cited above. That there is enhanced financial fragility, and without exception, the real economy is the worst victim.

Good-bye Financial Liberalization, Hello 'Mild Financial Repression'!

In the aftermath of the Southeast Asian financial crisis, several important events took place in the global financial markets that have turned the tide against unbridled financial liberalization. During August 1998, Russia — the darling of foreign investors — sharply devalued the rouble and unilaterally defaulted on its domestic debt. In addition, Russia also imposed severe capital controls. In August 1998, the Hong Kong Monetary Authority (HKMA) intervened massively in the stock market.[18] This was the first major intervention in the financial markets by the authorities since 1987 when the global stock prices crashed and trading was stopped. Since foreign exchange controls in Hong Kong are banned

Box 2.4

Hong Kong: Disenchantment with Free Market?

For two weeks in August 1998, the HKMA intervened in the financial markets to wipe out short positions taken in equities by speculators. The HKMA had found that speculators and hedge funds were deliberately trying to crash the stock market by taking advantage of links between the Hong Kong dollar and interest rates. The Hong Kong dollar is pegged to the US dollar at a rate of around 7.80 under a currency board system since 1983. Under the system, Hong Kong dollar interest rates automatically rise if the currency comes under attack. Confident of the fact that the Hong Kong authorities would not intervene in the markets (given its history of free market policies), the speculators were playing a no-loss game, which is also known as 'double play.' After betting that the entire market will fall, the speculators used tactics such as short selling, which in simple terms means that they were selling borrowed shares in the hope of buying them back later at a lower price. After shorting shares, they were selling Hong Kong dollars — as per the currency board rules — which automatically shrinks the money supply and pushes up interest rates. The higher rates would have sucked money out of the stock market, which in turn, would have led to a rapid fall in securities so that speculators could reap a bonanza from stock index futures.

According to market sources, nearly 20000 futures contracts expiring on August 28, 1998 were sold at an average of 8600 on the benchmark Hang Seng index. The government would have had to boost the market to that level or higher, if it wanted to inflict heavy losses on the speculators. By pumping billions into the markets, the HKMA shored up the share prices and a number of speculators suffered losses. Realizing the loopholes in the financial system, the HKMA has also announced a series of policy measures which include tightening of regulation and disclosure norms, mainly of short selling; stiff penalties for violators; enunciation of criminal legislation against unreported short selling; and enhancement of prison sentence for illegal trading. It is still too early to conclude that by intervening in the financial markets, the Hong Kong authorities have renounced their free market credentials. Nonetheless, the moves certainly suggest its growing disenchantment with free market policies.

under the post-handover constitution, the HKMA spent an estimated $15 billion (out of its $96 billion reserves) to purchase the stocks. On August 28 alone, the authorities poured an estimated $9 billion into the stock market. Such a large-scale intervention in the financial market by the authorities was unparalleled in the recent history of *laissez faire* Hong Kong (see Box 2.4). In August 1998, the Indian authorities also announced various policy measures to curb speculative attacks on its currency.

In order to restore autonomy in economic management, Malaysia imposed wide-ranging capital controls on September 1, 1998 (for details, see chapter 6). Besides, Ukraine suspended trading in its money and Singapore drafted tough measures against stock market manipulations. Taiwan also banned all trading of funds managed by US financier George Soros after local dealers blamed those funds for the stock market's plunge. And the Chinese authorities promulgated new controls on outflows.

These events, perhaps for the first time after the end of the Cold War, have seriously challenged the hitherto undisputed ideology of neo-liberal financial liberalization and globalization. Even those economists, who have been vocal supporters of the free market ideology, are arguing for an extremely cautious approach towards financial liberalization. Increasingly, financial analysts are veering towards a regime marked by 'mild financial repression.' Nowadays, there is wider acceptance of the salient role played by regulatory and supervisory institutions in a liberalized environment. Analysts have also called for an alternative strategy that integrates some aspects of liberalization with the development of appropriate financial institutions designed to serve the needs of the real economy.[19] It remains to be seen where this shift ultimately leads to in the near future. Given the fact that these developments have serious economic and political implications for the world economy, they are being monitored closely by the governments and global institutions alike.

Notes and References

1. For a detailed analysis of this line of thinking, see Ronald I McKinnon, *Money and Capital in Economic Development,* Brookings Institution, 1973; and Edward S Shaw, *Financial Deepening in Economic Development,* Oxford University Press, 1973.

2. The term 'Washington Consensus' was first coined by John Williamson of the Institute for International Economics. The term was used to describe the institutions based in Washington — the IMF and the World Bank, the US Treasury, the US Federal Reserve and several like minded lobby groups and think tanks (e.g., Heritage Foundation) — which have been supporting the neo-liberal thinking on economic reforms.

3. Isabelle Grunberg, "Double Jeopardy: Globalization, Liberalization and the Fiscal Squeeze," *World Development,* No. 4, 1998, p. 594.

4. Alberto Giovannini and M de Melo, "Government Revenue from Fiscal Repression," *American Economic Review,* No. 83, 1993, pp. 953-963.

5. See, for instance, Alberto Giovannini, "Saving and the Real Interest Rate in LDCs," *Journal of Development Economics,* Vol. 18, No. 2/3, 1985, pp. 197-217; Roland Clarke, "Equilibrium Interest Rates and Financial Liberalisation in Developing Countries," *The Journal of Development Studies,* Vol. 32, No. 3, February 1996, pp. 391-413; Gulnur Muradoglu and Fatma Taskin, "Differences in Household Savings Behavior: Evidence from Industrial and Developing Countries," *The Developing Economies,* Vol. 34, No. 2, June 1996, pp. 138-153; and F M Mwega, "Saving in Sub-Saharan Africa: A Comparative Analysis," *Journal of African Economies,* Vol. 6, No. 3, October 1997, pp. 199-228.

6. Prabhat Patnaik, "The Real Face of Financial Liberalisation," *Frontline,* February 26, 1999, p. 102.

7. Henk-Jan Brinkman, "Financial Reforms in Africa and the Lessons from Asia," in Barry Herman (ed.), *Global Financial Turmoil and Reform: A United Nations Perspective,* the United Nations University Press, 1999, p. 218.

8. John Williamson and Molly Mahar, *A Survey of Financial Liberalization,* Essays in International Finance, No. 211, International Finance Section, Department of Economics, Princeton University, November 1998, p. 62.

9. See Andrew Sheng, *Bank Restructuring: Lessons from the 1980s,* World Bank, 1996.

10. For more details on how financial markets are different from other markets, see Joseph Stiglitz, "The Role of the State in Financial Markets," *Proceedings of the World Bank Annual Conference on Development Economics 1993,* World Bank, 1994, pp. 19-52; Jagdish Bhagwati, "The Capital Myth: The Difference Between Trade in Widgets and Dollars," *Foreign Affairs,* Vol. 77, No. 3, May/June 1998, pp. 7-12; and Henk-Jan Brinkman, op. cit.

11. This phrase is taken from an article by Carlos Diaz-Alejandro titled, "Good-bye Financial Repression, Hello Financial Crash," *Journal of Development Economics*, Vol. 19, No. 1/2, September-October 1985, pp. 1-24.

12. Eddy Lee, "The Debate on the Causes of the Asian Crisis: Crony Capitalism Versus International System Failure," *International Politics and Society*, No. 2, 1999, p. 164.

13. Nick Beams, "'Free Market' Program Boost World Poverty," June 8, 1999, International Committee of the Fourth International (via Internet).

14. Carlos Diaz-Alejandro, op.cit.

15. Graciela L Kaminsky and Carmen M Reinhart, "The Twin Crises: The Causes of Banking and Balance-of-Payments Problems," *The American Economic Review*, Vol. 89, No. 3, June 1999, pp. 473-500.

16. Asli Demirguc-Kunt and Enrica Detragiache, "Financial Liberalization and Financial Fragility," *Working Paper WP/98/83*, IMF, 1998.

17. John Williamson and Molly Mahar, op. cit.

18. For a detailed analysis, see Todd Crowell and Law Siu-Lan, "War Against Speculators," *Asiaweek*, September 11, 1998, pp. 30-31; and Kavaljit Singh, *Capital Controls, State Intervention and Public Action in the Era of Financial Globalization*, Occasional Paper No. 4, Public Interest Research Group, 1998, pp. 7-9.

19. For the important role of institutions and a detailed survey of domestic financial liberalization, see Heather D Gibson and Euclid Tsakalotos, "The Scope and Limits of Financial Liberalisation in Developing Countries: A Critical Survey," *The Journal of Development Studies*, Vol. 30, No. 3, April 1994, pp. 578-628.

3

Capital Account Liberalization: Benefactor or Menace?

CAPITAL account liberalization (CAL) is the process through which countries liberalize their capital account by removing controls, taxes, subsidies and quantitative restrictions that affect capital account transactions. It involves the dismantling of all barriers on international financial transactions and the purchase and sale of financial or real assets across borders. With full CAL, companies and individuals (both residents and non-residents) can move their financial resources and assets from country to country without any restrictions.

Until the eruption of the Southeast Asian financial crisis in 1997, there was a broad consensus among international fund managers, financial institutions, experts and officials that the benefits of free flow of international capital are enormous. The benefits, touted by the supporters of free movement of capital include the increased availability of investment, efficient allocation of savings into more productive use on global scale, diversification of risky assets and healthy discipline for governments that encourage better economic policies. Liberalization of capital account was proclaimed as the quintessential measure for countries to benefit from global capital mobility. According to Stanley Fischer, Deputy Managing Director of the IMF:

> Put abstractly, free capital movements facilitate a more efficient global allocation of saving and help channel resources into their most productive uses, thus increasing economic growth and welfare. From the individual country's perspective, the benefits take the form of increases in both the potential pool of investable funds and the access of domestic residents to foreign capital markets. From the viewpoint of the international economy, open capital accounts support the multilateral trading system by broadening the channels through which developed and developing countries alike can finance trade and investment and attain higher levels of income.[1]

Eruption of the Southeast Asian crisis was, however, a turning point that impelled a dramatic shift in public opinion on CAL. The crisis has emphatically demonstrated to the world that CAL is a vexatious issue with numerous reverberating effects. An open capital account is perceived as a source of risk rather than benefit. Particularly in the case of the developing countries, the costs of an open capital account are enormous because volatile capital flows can cause sharp swings in real exchange rates and financial markets thereby engendering instability in the financial system and the real economy.

Even before the eruption of the Southeast Asian crisis, many countries had experienced financial crisis because their capital account was open. Take the case of Australia and New Zealand which opened their capital account in the 1980s. With an open capital account, a large number of private sector companies as well as farmers borrowed money abroad in foreign currency. When the Australian dollar plunged, the crisis spread to the real economy. Both Australia and New Zealand's foreign debt rose considerably. It stands to reason that the probability of occurrence of a financial crisis is much higher in a regime of free capital movement.

A recent survey carried out by John Williamson and Molly Mahar found that the liberalization of capital account led to financial crisis in a number of countries such as Argentina, Chile, Mexico, Brazil, Turkey, South Africa, Australia, New Zealand, Egypt, Indonesia, South Korea, Malaysia, Sri Lanka, and Thailand.[2] In the majority of cases the capital

Table 3.1: Capital Account Liberalization and Financial Crises

Country	Capital Inflows	
(First year of financial crisis)	**Short-Term**	**Portfolio**
Argentina (1980)	Open	Open
Argentina (1995)	Open	Open
Australia (1989)	Open	Open
Brazil (1997)	Open	Open
Chile (1981)	Open	Open
Finland (1992)	Open	Open
France (1991)	Open	Open
Indonesia (1992)	Open	Open
Indonesia (1997)	Open	Open
Italy (1990)	Open	Open
Japan (1992)	Open	Open
Malaysia (1985)	Open	Open
Malaysia (1997)	Open	Open
Mexico (1994)	Open	Open
New Zealand (1989)	Open	Open
South Africa (1985)	Closed	Open
South Africa (1998)	Open	Open
South Korea (1997)	Open	Open
South Korea (1997)	Open	Open
Sri Lanka (early 1990s)	Closed	Open
Sweden (1992)	Open	Open
Thailand (1997)	Open	Open
Turkey (1991)	Open	Open
Turkey (1994)	Open	Open

Source: John Williamson and Molly Mahar, *A Survey of Financial Liberalization*, Essays in International Finance, No. 211, International Finance Section, Department of Economics, Princeton University, November 1998 (updated by the author).

account had been opened recently (within the preceding five years).[3]

The contagion effects of the Asian crisis have led many developing countries to re-evaluate the so called benefits and their commitments to CAL. Increasingly, countries are paying more attention to financial policy instruments to deal with the vagaries of global finance capital. Given the fact that capital controls can be helpful in dealing with destabilizing financial flows, developing countries are likely to adopt a cautious approach towards CAL in the coming years.

Nowadays, there are few takers of newly founded buzzwords such as 'sequencing' and 'orderly capital account liberalization.' These approaches emphasize the timing and sequencing of capital account liberalization and identify the real cause of financial crises in the weak domestic financial system, particularly the banking system.[4] Therefore, these approaches advocate a rapid reform of the banking system beforeliberalizing the capital account. But such approaches suffer from serious limitations in terms of application for various reasons. There seems to be no consensus on what is an 'orderly capital account liberalization' — what may be an appropriate timing of capital account liberalization in one country may not be for another. Besides, a significant amount of global capital is passing through stock markets and is not intermediated through the banking system. Many domestic firms also borrow funds directly from international banks and financial institutions. Therefore, banking sector regulations alone cannot deal with the problems associated with such financial flows. Add to that, in the real world, powerful interests and lobbies see to it that issues pertaining to pace and sequencing of reforms are consigned to the backyard.

Increasingly, financial institutions (e.g., the World Bank and the ADB) are recommending a more cautious approach towards CAL. This trend has been accompanied by a sudden change in the positions of economists who otherwise are vocal supporters of free market ideology like Jeffery Sachs, Jagdish Bhagwati, Joseph Stiglitz among others. They are now vociferously advocating the need to enforce capital controls. However, these economists seem to have a constricted perspective on capital controls as they perceive controls as a transitory measure. Even the die-hard proponents of CAL find it difficult to advance the idea of global capital mobility. This is well captured in a recent statement by Helmut Reisen, "with virtually all emerging-market assets on fire sale, these are very hard times to 'sell' the gains from global capital mobility."[5]

Capital Account Liberalization: In Whose Interest?

In recent years, much attention has been focused on the IMF (perhaps rightly so) for its role in promoting capital account liberalization.[6] A number of powerful international financial institutions and lobbies have also been advancing CAL as part of the larger financial liberalization process. These institutions and lobbies have succeeded in institutionalizing capital account liberalization as a component of several multilateral and regional agreements. In the case of the developed countries, the process of CAL was carried out in the past through the OECD Code of Liberalization of Capital Movements and the EU Directives. While in the case of the developing countries, the conditionalities attached to the loans by the IMF still require countries to liberalize their capital account in order to enhance their attraction to private capital flows.

With the successful completion of Uruguay round of negotiations, a series of policy initiatives at the international level have been launched to remove restrictions on the capital account and ease cross border capital movements. Implemented without any concern for national sovereignty or public participation, these initiatives include the establishment of a Multilateral Agreement on Investment (MAI) at the OECD, which was subsequently shelved; preliminary discussions at the WTO on a similar instrument, the Multilateral Framework for Investment (MFI); the recently concluded WTO Agreement on Financial Services; and attempts by the IMF to include convertibility of the capital account in its Articles of Agreement.

Given the fact that these initiatives have the support of the TNCs, fund managers and governments of the developed countries, it becomes imperative to analyze them in relation to other major developments. In the

Box 3.1

Capital Account Liberalization and India

Capital controls in the form of exchange controls were introduced in India during the outbreak of World War II. After the war, controls continued and were given a statutory backing by the enactment of Foreign Exchange Regulation Act in 1947. This act was replaced in 1973 in the wake of sharp balance of payments crisis.

In tune with the liberal economic policy regime, the country introduced current account convertibility in 1994 and satisfied the VIII schedule of the IMF's Articles of Agreement. By and large, the capital account is convertible for foreign investors and non-resident Indians (NRIs). Except for a handful of sectors, FDI is allowed in most sectors of the economy and earlier restrictions (e.g., on ownership, payment of royalty fees, etc.) have been gradually reduced. Indian financial markets were opened to investment by FIIs in September 1992 with certain restrictions. However, these restrictions have been eased since then. Still, domestic residents and companies are not allowed to invest abroad without permit and cannot operate in currency, stock and gilt market abroad. Recently, domestic companies have been allowed to raise capital from abroad through the issuance of GDR, and other debt instruments, but with certain restrictions in the form of prior approvals and ceilings.

The move towards full capital account convertibility began with the setting up of a committee in 1997, headed by former RBI Deputy Governor, S S Tarapore. The report of the committee recommended sweeping changes and suggested a three-year road map towards achieving full CAL. However, with the eruption of financial crisis in Southeast Asia in 1997, the initial zeal to achieve full CAL subsided.

By facilitating outflow of capital legally from the country, CAL has the potential for creating a serious financial crisis. Thanks to controls on capital account, India was able to protect its economy from the contagion effects of the Asian crisis. Instead of learning lessons from the Southeast Asian crisis and consequently adopting policy measures to avert a similar crisis, the Indian authorities still appear committed to CAL.

present global context, investment liberalization (along with trade liberalization) has acquired top priority on the economic agenda of transnational capital. This is supported and facilitated by the G-7, OECD, IMF, and the WTO. Although investment liberalization and trade liberalization may appear to be two different phenomena, they complement and reinforce each other to strengthen economic globalization. They are two sides of the same coin — free trade tends to encourage foreign investment and foreign investments tend to boost trade. In a context where the TNCs dominate much of the world trade and investment, a combination of free trade and financial liberalization are sure enough prescriptions for expansion and restructuring of TNC's hegemonic global operations.

With the proposed amendment of the IMF's articles alongwith international proposals such as the MAI and MFI, new business opportunities were expected to unfold for the owners and managers of mobile capital to move funds from one country to another without any restrictions. By making capital mobility a legally enforceable global property rule through such agreements, global capital is all set to consolidate its power. On the other hand, in all likelihood, the developing countries are bound to lose control over their capital account thereby succumbing to volatile capital flows.

Analysts have pointed to the convergence of interests among Wall Street, TNCs, IMF and the US Treasury in promoting capital account liberalization. Jagdish Bhagwati has termed it the 'Wall Street-Treasury complex.' In his words:

> Wall Street's financial firms have obvious self-interest in a world of free capital mobility since it only enlarges the arena in which to make money. It is not surprising, therefore, that Wall Street has put its powerful oar into the turbulent waters of Washington political lobbying to steer in this direction... Wall Street has exceptional clout with Washington for the simple reason that there is a definite networking of like minded luminaries among the powerful institutions — Wall Street, the Treasury Department, the State Department, the IMF, and the World Bank most prominent among them... This powerful network, which may aptly, if loosely, be called the Wall Street-Treasury

complex, is unable to look much beyond the interest of Wall Street, which it equates with the good of the world.[7]

Robert Wade has gone a step further and rechristened Bhagwati's 'Wall Street-Treasury complex' as the 'Wall Street-US Treasury-US Congress-City of London-UK Treasury-IMF complex.' Wade is convinced that, "US and UK financial firms know they can gain hugely against all comers in an institutional context of arms-length transactions, stock markets, open capital accounts and the new financial instruments. Their respective Treasuries are deeply responsive to their needs and Jesuistic in their commitment to the neoclassical 'Washington Consensus'."[8]

Capital Account Liberalization and International Agreements

Let us examine in detail the role of important multilateral agreements and institutions that have been advocating the liberalization of capital account on a world scale.

OECD and Capital Account Liberalization

OECD Codes: Soon after its establishment in 1961, the OECD adopted the Code of Liberalization of Capital Movements and the Code of Liberalization of Current Invisible Operations. Both the codes fulfil the basic objective of the OECD which states that member countries agree "to pursue their efforts to reduce or abolish obstacles to the exchange of goods and services and current payments and maintain and extend the liberalization of capital movements." The codes commit member countries to eliminate any restrictions between one another on the current invisible and capital movement operations.

The Article 1 of the Code of Liberalization of Capital Movements states that "members shall progressively abolish between one another, in accordance with the provisions of Article 2, restrictions on movements of capital to the extent necessary for effective economic cooperation." Article 2 specifies that "members shall grant any authorization requested for the conclusion or execution of transactions and for transfers specified in any item set out in List A or List B of Annex to this Code" subject only to reservations and derogations granted in certain circumstances. The codes consist of a detailed list of transactions to be liberalized. It includes direct investments, portfolio investments, commercial credit, real estate operations and other financial instruments. Since these codes have a legal status equal to OECD decisions and are binding on all members, countries seeking to join the OECD are required to comply with the obligations of these codes prior to formal membership. Implementation of codes is the responsibility of OECD's Committee on Capital Movements and Invisible Transactions.

The OECD codes have been amended several times (1964, 1973, 1984 and 1989) to widen their coverage. However, a major push towards capital account liberalization was provided in the amendments in 1989 which included, amongst others, provisions for operations in money

Table 3.2: Comparison of the Percentage of Acceptance of Two Liberalization Regulations

	Current Trade/ Business Liberalization Regulations	Flow of Captial Liberalization Regulations
Average of OECD	88% (7 out of 57 clauses reserved)	89% (10 out of 91 clauses reserved)
Korea	81% (11 out of 57 clauses reserved)	55% (41 out of 91 clauses reserved)
Mexico	75% (57 out of 57 clauses reserved)	71% (26 out of 91 clauses reserved)
Czechoslovakia	82% (10 out of 57 clauses reserved)	65% (32 out of 91 clauses reserved)
Hungary	81% (11 out of 57 clauses reserved)	58% (38 out of 91 clauses reserved)
Poland	79% (12 out of 57 clauses reserved)	56% (40 out of 91 clauses reserved)

Source: Kwon Jae-Jung, "The Change in the System and Effect of the Acceptance of the Two Main Liberalization Regulations of the OECD," Foreign Economy Policy Research Institute, 1996, p. 18, cited in *96-97 Korean Situation*, Christian Institute for the Study of Justice and Development, 1998, p. 104.

markets including operations in securities and interbank markets; short-term financial credits and loans to both private individuals and financial institutions; foreign exchange operations, including spot and forward transactions; long-term commercial credits; and swaps, options, futures, and other innovative instruments.

Generally, there is wider acceptance of both the codes by the member countries of the OECD, 88 per cent in the case of Code of Liberalization of Current Invisible Operations and 89 per cent in the case of the Code of Liberalization of Capital Movements (see Table 3.2). Still, a number of member countries (e.g., UK, US, Denmark, France, Sweden, Austria, Australia and Japan) have used article 7 of the code which allows them to put restrictions — in the form of reservations and derogations — in response to balance of payment or exchange rate crises, or unfavorable monetary developments. The UK, which had no reservations as of the end of June 1981, made a partial reservation on direct investment related to investment in air transport, broadcasting, and acquisition of UK flag vessels by December 1, 1989.[9]

Similarly, the US that had only one reservation (regarding direct investment in atomic energy, broadcasting, air transport, domestic and coastal shipping, and thermal and hydroelectric power) introduced two more reservations related to operations in securities markets and operations in collective investment securities by June 30, 1993.[10] Luxembourg is the only member of the OECD that maintained neither reservations nor derogations under the code. The countries which became new members of the OECD in the 1990s (i.e., Mexico in 1994, Czechoslovakia in 1995, Hungary, Poland and South Korea in 1996) are maintaining a significant number of reservations, in comparison with older members. Table 3.2 reveals that in these five countries, the acceptance of Code of Liberalization of Current Invisible Operations is higher compared with the Code of Liberalization of Capital Movements.

To understand the wider implications of the OECD codes, let us examine the case of South Korea, which maintained tight regulations on financial flows particularly on foreign borrowings till the early 1990s.

South Korea is a classic example of external pressure being used for capital account liberalization under the OECD codes. It illustrates how an open capital account created conditions for an imminent financial crisis despite the fact that Korea accepted only 55 per cent of regulations and maintained reservations in 41 out of 91 clauses under the Code of Liberalization of Capital Movements. Korea formally became the 29th member country of OECD on December 12, 1996 and prior to its joining, removed substantial restrictions and controls on its capital account (although not full scale) in order to comply with the OECD codes. Korea removed restrictions on its domestic financial sector to borrow (short-term) abroad, opened up its domestic financial and capital markets to foreign investors, further liberalized foreign exchange regulations and abandoned investment coordination.

The new scenario gave ample opportunities to merchant banks to borrow from abroad and lend to domestic companies. According to Ha-Joon Chang, supervision of the merchant banks was lax and the government was apparently unaware of the huge mismatch in the maturity structures between their borrowings (64 per cent of the total $20 billion were short-term) and lendings (85 per cent of them long-term).[11]

The reliance on short-term borrowings was so excessive that 67 per cent of the total debt was short-term.[12] Coupled with the overall framework of neo-liberal sentiment and demise of five-year plans and selective industrial policy, the abandonment of investment coordination led to over-capacity. These policies led to a fall in export prices, low profitability and rise in non-performing loans in almost all major industries including semiconductors, automobiles, petrochemicals and shipbuilding. With negative sentiments prevailing in the entire Southeast Asian region as a result of the financial crisis, foreign banks and investors started withdrawing loans and investments from Korea. The massive and rapid capital reversals facilitated by the liberalized regime of capital account precipitated the Korean crisis.

OECD's Multilateral Agreement on Investment (MAI): The MAI, an international economic agreement, was first mooted in the OECD in

1995. Politically backed by the governments of the European Union and the US, the provisions under the MAI were aimed at removing controls and regulations on the capital account. Initially, the member countries of the OECD were supposed to adopt the agreement. Then other countries were expected to join it. Since most of the restrictions on capital account transactions happen to be in the developing countries, the critics argued that MAI would be used as an instrument to further open their capital account. But, there was no participation of the developing and other non-OECD countries in the negotiations which had been largely conducted in secrecy with no inputs from the public.

The MAI defined investment in these words: "Investment means: Every kind of asset owned or controlled, directly or indirectly, by an investor." In simple terms, it included FDI, portfolio investment and intellectual property rights such as patents and trademarks, contract rights and concession rights. Any move by national governments that could affect any of these 'assets' was covered by the MAI. Thus, regulations on labor, environment and repatriation of profits besides controls on 'hot money' flows would have to abide by the MAI.

This agreement was designed to remove all controls on the movement of finance capital and production facilities. The MAI was meant to weaken the bargaining position of governments to deal with foreign capital by placing all obligations on host governments and none on foreign capital concerning issues such as restrictive business practices, transfer pricing, working conditions, environment, observance of national laws, or contribution to development. The MAI proposed a ban on restrictions on the repatriation of profits or the movement of capital. Under it, countries were prohibited to delay or stop an investor from moving profits and assets from the operation or sale of a local enterprise to his/her home country. 'Roll-back' and 'standstill' provisions required countries to eliminate laws that violated MAI rules (either immediately or over a set period of time) and to refrain from passing any such laws in the future.

The MAI was based on two main principles — national treatment

(NT) and the most favored nation (MFN). The NT principle ensured that foreign investors would receive equal treatment to that granted to national investors. The MFN principle required countries to treat all foreign countries and all foreign investors in the same manner, preventing any country from using human rights, environmental or labor standards as investment criteria. Further, these principles were to be applied at the pre-investment phase, which meant that countries would have no right whatsoever to regulate foreign capital.

The discussions on MAI were supposed to be completed by May 1997. Due to the delay in reaching a consensus on all the provisions of the MAI coupled with strong protests by the NGOs, citizens' groups and others in the OECD countries, the negotiations were first extended to April and then to October 1998. By then negotiations at the OECD on the MAI had broken down. Nevertheless, it seems that many of the MAI provisions are likely to be pushed through other international agreements, including the WTO. Therefore, this process requires close monitoring by individuals and groups concerned with the implications of such an agreement.

IMF and Capital Account Liberalization

The IMF is an international institution that deals with the liberalization of global capital movements. Capital account liberalization was not the objective of the 1944 Articles of Agreement that established this institution. The obligations in IMF's Articles of Agreement are associated with only current account transactions. These obligations are set out in its articles VIII and XIV. Article VIII of the IMF's Articles of Agreement requires member countries to avoid imposing restrictions on current account transactions related to trade in goods and services and the remittance of profits and dividends.

Many member countries of the IMF have not accepted the obligations of Article VIII. It was only in the late 1980s and early 1990s that most of the countries began accepting these obligations. By June 1998, 145 members of the IMF had accepted them, with 70 countries accepting

Box 3.2

Interim Committee Statement on Liberalization of Capital Movements

Following are the excerpts from the statement of Interim Committee of the IMF, as adopted in Hong Kong on September 21, 1997.

It is time to add a new chapter to the Bretton Woods agreement. Private capital flows have become much more important to the international monetary system, and an increasingly open and liberal system has proved to be highly beneficial to the world economy. By facilitating the flow of savings to their most productive uses, capital movements increase investment, growth, and prosperity. Provided it is introduced in an orderly manner, and backed both by adequate national policies and a solid multilateral system for surveillance and financial support, the liberalization of capital flows is an essential element of an efficient international monetary system in this age of globalization. The IMF's central role in the international monetary system, and its near universal membership, make it uniquely placed to help this process. The Committee sees the IMF's proposed new mandate as bold in its vision, but requiring cautious implementation.

... The IMF will have the task of assisting in the establishment of such a system and stands ready to support members' efforts in this regard. Its role is also key to the adoption of policies that would facilitate properly sequenced liberalization and reduce the likelihood of financial and balance of payments crises.

... The Committee invites the Executive Board to complete its work on a proposed amendment of the Fund's Articles that would make the liberalization of capital movements one of the purposes of the Fund and extend, as needed, the Fund's jurisdiction through the establishment of carefully defined and uniformly applied obligations regarding the liberalization of such movements.

... In view of the importance of moving decisively toward this new worldwide regime of liberalized capital movements... the Committee invites the Executive Board to give high priority to the completion of the required amendment of the Fund's Articles of Agreement.

only since 1993. Article XIV specifies transitional arrangements for member countries not yet willing to accept the obligations of Article VIII. These arrangements allow a country to maintain the restrictions on payments and transfer for current transactions in force on the date it becomes a member of the IMF.

Under Article VI.3 of the IMF, member countries can exercise controls to regulate international capital movements so long as they do not restrict payments for current transactions or unduly delay transfers of funds in settlement of commitments. Section 1 of this Article also gives the Fund the authority to request a member country to impose controls to prevent the use of resources from its General Resources Account to finance a large or sustained capital outflow. Further, the right of member countries to impose capital controls was duly recognized in a decision of the Executive Board in 1956, which stated that, "subject to the provisions of Article VI, Section 3, concerning payments for current transactions and undue delay in transfers of funds in settlement of commitments: (a) Members are free to adopt a policy of regulating capital movements for any reason, due regard being paid to the general purposes of the Fund and without prejudice to the provisions of Article VI, Section 1; (b) They may, for that purpose, exercise such controls as are necessary, including such arrangements as may reasonably be needed with other countries, without approval of the Fund."[13]

However, for the past few years, the IMF itself is violating its original mandate (as mentioned in the Articles of Agreement) by advocating removal of controls and regulations on capital movements. This is evident in the IMF's loan agreements with its member countries where the removal of controls on capital movement is put forward as a necessary precondition to attract foreign investment. In several cases (e.g., Mexico and South Korea), assistance was provided by the IMF explicitly to enable countries to withstand capital flight without imposing controls.

In the past two years, the IMF has become a vocal supporter of capital account liberalization. In its meeting of April 28, 1997, the Interim Committee of the IMF "agreed that the Fund's Articles should be amended to make the promotion of capital account liberalization a specific purpose of the Fund and to give the Fund appropriate jurisdiction over capital movements." At its Annual Meeting in Hong Kong in September 1997, the Interim Committee of the IMF issued a Statement on the Liberalization of Capital Movements (see Box 3.2). This statement was issued at a time when the Asian countries were reeling under severe financial crisis. The statement invited the Executive Board to complete its work on a proposed amendment to make liberalization of capital movements one of the purposes of the IMF and to extend, as needed, the IMF's jurisdiction in this area. The IMF's Board of Directors endorsed this proposal and included it in the Hong Kong declaration.

But the fervor subsided in 1998 once the impact of the Southeast Asian crisis took on alarming proportions. The World Bank was the first to change its position on liberalization of the capital account while the IMF continued with its earlier position of promoting CAL which was reiterated at the seminar hosted by it in Washington on March 9-10, 1998. "The trend towards capital account liberalization is irreversible," said IMF Managing Director, Michel Camdessus, in his address to the seminar. Perhaps, realizing that not many will follow its blanket approach towards CAL, the Fund started using terms such as 'sequencing' and 'orderly capital account liberalization.' But, as evidence shows, this was not the first time that the IMF was using such buzzwords. In early 1980s when a number of Southern Cone countries encountered financial crises, the IMF used similar terms then also. It is ironical that after more than two decades, the IMF is back to square one.

However, given the sharp criticism evoked by its multi billion-bailout programs in Thailand, Indonesia and South Korea and subsequent opposition to its proposed hike in quotas, the Fund has slightly modified its approach by publicly accepting that controls on inflows could be useful for some countries. In its annual report on international capital markets in September 1998, the IMF suggested that countries could consider imposing temporary measures to control certain types of inflows. It should be emphasized that the IMF is only supporting price-based controls on inflows (e.g., as in Chile) rather than other types of controls.

The amendment in the IMF's Article will have serious repercussions on the world economy. There is no doubt that by enlarging its jurisdiction over capital account, the IMF's power and authority will increase tremendously. But the worst affected would be the developing countries who will find capital account liberalization in the list of IMF conditionalities.

WTO and Capital Account Liberalization

Established in 1995, the WTO provides a common institutional framework for the conduct of trade relations among its members as contained in the associated agreements dealing with the trade in goods and services and intellectual property. Although various agreements under the WTO are aimed at liberalizing services rather than capital transactions, the General Agreement on Trade in Services (GATS) forbids certain restrictions on capital transactions related to the provision of services identified in such agreements. The GATS clearly expresses the commitment to liberalization of capital movements associated with cross border transactions.

The WTO's all out endorsement of capital account liberalization finds explicit expression in the Financial Services Agreement (FSA), concluded on December 13, 1997, after two years of negotiations in the midst of the severe financial crisis in Asia. The FSA, which came into force from March 1, 1999, extends the GATS to financial services and includes market-opening commitments by 102 WTO members. The FSA replaces an interim agreement concluded in 1995 at the initiative of the European Union. In that agreement, the US withdrew most favored nation treatment in financial services and committed itself only to granting market access and national treatment to the existing operations of foreign service providers. The FSA works basically on the principle of a positive list that means that only those services will be liberalized which are specified unlike the MAI under which everything is liberalized unless specifically excluded.[14]

Under the FSA, member countries of the WTO agreed to a legal framework for cross border trade and market access in financial services, and in addition, to a mechanism for dispute settlement. Nearly 95 per cent of the world trade in banking, insurance, securities and financial information now comes under the WTO's jurisdiction, on the basis of broad MFN and under the auspices of the dispute settlement mechanism.[15] The cross border trade of financial services will require removal of restrictions on capital transactions. As exchange controls are often cited as barriers to international trade in financial services and are largely maintained in the developing countries, FSA will serve as an effective tool to remove these. The extension of the WTO jurisdiction to financial services is of grave concern as it is not the appropriate forum for discussing capital transactions and financial liberalization.

The Benefits of Capital Account Liberalization: Six Myths

There is a seeming paradox between the gains of capital account liberalization in theory and in practice. The arguments supportive of CAL are highly overstated and backed by very little evidence. On the contrary, evidence shows that the benefits of free capital movements are much fewer in comparison with the costs. Let us examine six myths associated with the benefits of CAL.

Myth 1: Free flow of capital across national border offers immense benefits to countries as it leads to increased investment.

Reality: There is no evidence to prove that by achieving CAL, countries attract massive foreign investment. Nor does it enhance the prospects of obtaining investment in future. Since the 1980s, a large number of developing countries have liberalized their capital account but only a dozen received about 80 per cent of net private capital flows during 1990-95. According to the *Human Development Report 1999*, 85 per cent of the FDI and 94 per cent of portfolio and other flows to the developing and transition economies went to just 20 countries in 1997 (see Table 3.3). The fact that nearly 140 developing countries account for a mere 15 per cent of the FDI and 6 per cent of portfolio investment demonstrates that there is no positive correlation between capital account liberalization and increased investment. The report further notes that for 100 countries the FDI has averaged less than $100 million a year since 1990, and for nine countries net flows have been negative.[16]

A close look at several countries in Africa confirms that CAL does not guarantee increased investment. Since the early 1980s, many African countries have opened up their capital account and carried out financial and the real sector reforms but get only a fraction of the global private capital flows. According to a 1997 survey by UNCTAD, 26 of the 32 least

Table 3.3: Top 20 Recipients among Developing and Transition Countries

Foreign Direct Investment (1997, current $ millions)		Portfolio and other Flows (1997, current $ millions)	
China	45300	Brazil	18495
Brazil	16330	Mexico	16028
Mexico	12101	Thailand	11181
Singapore	10000	Argentina	10132
Argentina	6327	Indonesia	10070
Russian Federation	6241	China	9920
Chile	5417	Malaysia	7596
Indonesia	5350	Russian Federation	4975
Poland	5000	Turkey	4913
Venezuela	4893	Colombia	4417
Malaysia	3754	India	3817
Thailand	3600	Czech Republic	3459
India	3264	Philippines	3192
Hong Kong	2600	Chile	2712
Colombia	2447	Venezuela	2411
Korea, Rep. of	2341	Peru	2273
Taiwan	2248	Romania	1551
Hungary	2085	South Africa	1281
Peru	2000	Pakistan	1246
Kazakhstan	1320	Slovenia	1033
Totalling 85% of FDI		**Totalling 94% of flows**	

Source: *Human Development Report 1999*, UNDP, 1999, p. 27.

developed countries in Africa had liberalized regulations related to repatriation of dividends and capital. It is to be noted that Africa's share of FDI flows to the developing economies declined from 9 per cent in 1981-85 to only just about 4 per cent in 1996-97. During the period 1990-96, Sub-Saharan Africa (except South Africa) received negligible net portfolio flows, while FDI flows were concentrated in a few countries such as Nigeria, Botswana, Ghana, Mozambique and Uganda. Among the major reasons that prevent the flow of investment to Africa include small size of domestic markets, poor infrastructure and locational disadvantages. In addition, civil unrest and political instability have impeded foreign investment. The African experience clearly indicates that countries wishing to attract investment will have to be more concerned about economic and political factors rather than capital account liberalization.

In the case of Latin America, there is no denying that it witnessed a surge in financial flows in the 1990s. The capital inflows touched between 5 and 10 per cent of the GDP in several countries including Chile, Argentina, Brazil and Mexico. But it will be incorrect to attribute this to capital account liberalization because these countries had opened up their capital account much earlier, in the mid-1980s, as part of the structural adjustment program. The surge was primarily due to a sharp decline in interest rates in the US and the new interest shown in emerging markets by institutional investors of the developed countries.

Analysts have also found that the ratios of investment to GDP have been lower in countries that have adopted capital account liberalization. John Eatwell has examined the changes in the share of investment to GDP in 54 countries as between the Bretton Woods era of fixed exchange and capital controls (1960-71) and the current regime of open capital account.[17] He discovered that the predominant tendency has been for investment to fall as a share of GDP. "The decline is more pronounced in the period 1982-91 as capital liberalization has become more widespread, with two-thirds of the countries in the sample experiencing declines," notes Eatwell.[18]

On the contrary, one finds that several countries without CAL are receiving substantial foreign investment. China is a prime example of this. After the US, China is the top recipient of foreign investment in the 1990s. In 1997 alone, China attracted over $63 billion worth of foreign investment, most of it was in the form of FDI. China's currency, the yuan, is not convertible except for its current account. Taiwan is also receiving significant investment without CAL. With only current account liberalization, India is emerging as an important destination of foreign investment in South Asia. On the other hand, Malaysia, which re-imposed controls on its capital account in 1998, continues to receive substantial amounts of FDI. These examples suggest that increased investment is neither automatic nor a necessary outcome of CAL.

CAL, on the other hand, can significantly contribute to capital flight by legalizing capital outflows. This was a persistent problem in many Latin American countries in the 1980s. In Sub-Saharan Africa, where profit remittances exceed net inflows of FDI since 1984, there has been an estimated net transfer of $20 billion in the last decade. The openness of capital accounts in the Southeast Asian countries contributed substantially to capital flight following the Thai currency crisis in mid-1997.

Myth 2: Free movement of capital is vital for higher economic growth.

Reality: This is an erroneous assumption on two counts. Firstly, a positive correlation between CAL and higher economic growth is yet to be firmly established because growth is a complicated process, subject to a wide range of factors. Further, there is no empirical evidence to prove that the free flow of speculative funds contributes to the development of the real economy, rather there is considerable evidence to the contrary. What is the connection between portfolio investment and short-term lending with productivity and growth? Even the link between FDI and economic growth is hard to establish if other factors such as competition policy, labor skills and policy intervention are not taken into account.

Take the example of the US that has been a net importer of capital since the 1980s. It has been estimated that the inflows were roughly 20 per cent of gross private domestic investment in the US economy in 1996 and 1997.[19] But where is the evidence to prove that this large increase in the inflows contributed significantly to the growth of productivity in the US economy in these years. In fact, over half of these inflows went into US Treasury bonds, considered to be the safest in the world. A significant portion of this foreign capital went to the stock markets, which to a large extent, contributed to the boom. As a result, stock prices have increased by roughly 50 per cent over the last two years.[20]

Secondly, if one tries to match the periods of CAL with the economic performance of countries the results are contradictory. Growth began to deteriorate around the 1970s when many countries started moving toward capital account liberalization. The 1980s and the 1990s witnessed sharp deterioration in economic performance of many countries including those belonging to the G-7, the OECD and a number of developing countries. The worst decadal-growth performance has occurred in the 1990s. According to the IMF's *World Economic Outlook,* average annual world output growth in the 1990s is now estimated at only 3.1 per cent, which is below the average growth rates in the 1980s (3.4 per cent) and the 1970s (4.4 per cent).[21]

Some recent studies have found little empirical evidence regarding the claim that countries without capital controls have grown faster than countries with capital controls. An interesting study by Dani Rodrik points out that free capital mobility has had no significant impact on the economies of almost 100 countries (developing and developed) during 1975-89 which had no restrictions on the capital account.[22] Comparing the growth performance of countries that have liberalized capital accounts and those that have not, this study found no evidence of the former having performed better. Furthermore, countries without capital controls have neither grown faster nor invested more and have not experienced lower inflation.

On the contrary, restrictions on capital account have not necessarily led to poor economic performance. Many countries enjoyed high growth without liberalizing their capital accounts. China and Korea are prime examples of this. The experience of China demonstrates that high growth rates can be achieved without liberalizing capital account. Can anyone buy the argument that growth rates in China could have been much higher than the present ones (9 to 10 per cent), had it adopted capital account liberalization. In the 1970s and 1980s, Korea reported extraordinary economic growth when the government strictly controlled its capital account. The growth prospects were put in jeopardy in mid-1990s when Korea accepted CAL as a precondition to join the OECD. This paved the way for reckless borrowing and lending by the Korean commercial banks, merchant banks and other financial institutions that subsequently precipitated the financial crisis of 1997.

It holds true for Chile, Uruguay and Argentina that rapidly liberalized their capital account in the mid-1970s. In these countries, CAL led to rapid capital flight, banking crises, large scale bankruptcies, falling output and massive unemployment. In a like manner, the eruption of financial crises in the Scandinavian countries, Mexico and the Southeast Asian countries in the 1990s had significantly lowered growth and raised unemployment on a global scale.

Myth 3: Free movement of capital results in efficient allocation of world savings for the most productive investment.

Reality: There is no evidence to prove it. A majority of financial flows have tenuous linkages with production or trade and are speculative in nature. Since portfolio investment, short-term lending and other speculative funds are prone to reversals with changes in the international interest rates, the movement of capital per se does not lead to productive investment. Even in the case of FDI flows, cross border mergers and acquisitions — which have been the prime movers behind the surge in the 1990s — have little to do with productive investment.

As mentioned earlier, financial markets, through which allocation of capital occurs, are not perfect. They are prone to asymmetric information, moral hazard and herd behavior. Investors and lenders are driven more by herd instinct than rational analysis. Following the herd is the norm, rather than an exception in the financial markets. Further, the risk-reward relationship is loaded in favor of following the herd.[23] For instance, if a greater number of investors are putting money in East Asia, you are also expected to invest in the region, otherwise your competence will be open to question. Conversely, if you suffer heavy losses along with other investors in Indonesia, there will be fraternal acceptance since others have suffered losses as well. Therefore, it is incorrect to assume that free movement of capital through financial markets will result in efficient allocation of world savings for the most productive investment.

Moreover, capital flows not used judiciously pose grave problems for recipient countries as witnessed in many Latin American countries in the 1990s, which could not cope with the surfeit of foreign capital. In Latin America, the increase in real investment has been only about one third of the net capital inflow.[24] The surge in foreign capital in most Latin American countries has not led to increased investment. Rather, it has depressed domestic savings (e.g., Mexico). In fact, if one takes the Latin American region as a whole, external savings have crowded out the national savings. Analysts have estimated that financial deregulation in the United Kingdom resulted in a decline in the personal savings ratio of 2.3 percentage points over the 1980s.[25] In New Zealand, both household and corporate savings have fallen since liberalization.[26] There is ample evidence of lower private savings rates following liberalization in Argentina, Chile, Colombia and the Philippines.[27]

In addition, there are cases where CAL has contributed to a consumption boom. In Mexico, the inflows sustained a boom in private consumption after its capital account was liberalized in the late 1980s. In 1992-93, capital inflows were estimated to be about 8 per cent of the GDP. With higher interest rates in Mexico, the international investment banks and fund managers invested billions of dollars in the financial markets and real estate, and consequently, a sharp real estate and stock market boom ensued. The higher but unrealistic valuation of stocks and real estate coupled with the appreciation of the exchange rate fuelled the consumption boom in Mexico. There was a substantial hike in consumer lending after liberalization in Mexico as banks rapidly expanded credit card businesses and loans for consumer items. As a result, investment stagnated and foreign savings crowded out domestic savings. In Mexico, national savings as a ratio of the GDP came down by more than 4 percentage points between 1989 and 1994. Mexico paid a high price for financial liberalization. In 1995, its GDP contracted by 7 per cent and inflation soared above 50 per cent.[28] By all accounts, the evidence militates against conventional thinking that financial liberalization will increase savings.

Table 3.4: Net Capital Inflow into the US, 1983-1997

($ million)

Year	US Capital Outflow	Foreign Capital Inflow	Net Capital Inflow
1983	-61573	83380	21807
1984	-36313	113932	77619
1985	-39889	141183	101294
1986	-106753	226111	119358
1987	-72617	242983	170366
1988	-100087	240265	140178
1989	-168744	218490	49746
1990	-74011	122912	48181
1991	-57881	94241	36360
1992	-68622	154285	85663
1993	-194609	250996	56387
1994	-150695	285376	134681
1995	-307207	451234	144027
1996	-352444	547555	195111
1997	-426938	690497	263559

Source: *Survey of Current Business*, July 1998, cited in Fred Moseley, "The United States Economy at the Turn of the Century: Entering a New Era of Prosperity?," *Capital and Class*, No. 67, 1999, p. 35.

Myth 4: A regime of free capital mobility would simply mean flow of savings from a region where they are surplus to a region where they are in deficit. In other words, capital will flow from capital-rich countries to capital-poor countries.

Reality: Not true. The data shows that net transfer of financial resources has been predominantly towards the capital-rich countries, particularly the US. Despite the fact that global capital mobility has increased exponentially in the 1990s and real rates of return in the US are lower than other developed and developing countries, the US continues to absorb nearly two-thirds of the rest of the world's surplus savings. In the eighties, the US became the world's biggest debtor nation (a net importer of capital). Since then, the US economy has become increasingly dependent on foreign capital. From 1993 onwards, there has been a sharp increase in the net annual inflow of foreign capital into the US (see Table 3.4). The net inflow of foreign capital increased from $59 billion in 1990-93 to around $140 billion in 1994 and 1995 and then increased again to $195 billion in 1996 and again to $264 billion in 1997.[29] As mentioned earlier, much of the recent increase in foreign capital has gone into the purchase of treasury bills and to the stock market. Net foreign purchases of US stocks rose rapidly from $12 billion in 1996 to $66 billion in 1997.[30] In the aftermath of the Asian financial crisis, the US is increasingly being perceived as a 'safe haven' by the investors and is receiving large inflows of foreign capital. Due to CAL in several capital deficient countries (e.g., Mexico, Chile, Korea and Thailand), financial resources are flowing from these countries to capital surplus countries.

In the case of the developing countries, financial resources were transferred out in the 1980s, and by and large, net flows were almost zero. However, between 1991 and 1996, some Southeast Asian and Latin American countries started receiving positive net transfers. Initially, the positive transfers to Asia were considered beneficial but this enthusiasm subsided soon when these financial flows sharply reversed in the wake of the Southeast Asian currency crisis in 1997. According to the estimates of Institute for International Finance, five Asian economies, namely, South

Korea, Indonesia, Malaysia, Thailand and the Philippines experienced —
in the aggregate — a total outflow of $105 billion in 1997; from an inflow
of $93 billion in 1996 to an outflow of $12 billion in 1997. Except FDI
(which remained constant), financial flows in the form of commercial
bank lendings and portfolio investments exhibited the sharpest decline.
There was an estimated outflow of $12 billion through commercial banks,
compared with inflows of about $56 billion in 1996; and portfolio invest-
ment suffered an outflow of $12 billion in 1997, in contrast to an inflow
of about $12 billion in 1996.

Thus, there is no evidence to support the view that free movement of
capital will simply mean the flow of savings from surplus to deficit
regions.

**Myth 5: Free movement of capital allows international diversification
of assets that enhances opportunities for savers and lowers costs for
borrowers.**

Reality: This argument is unconvincing on three grounds. Firstly, there is
no evidence to prove that CAL has contributed to the lowering of borrowing costs. On the contrary, real long-term interest rates are found to be
higher in the 1980s. "In all the G-7 countries, real interest rates have risen
sharply in the 1980s as compared with the Bretton Woods era of capital
controls," finds Eatwell's study.[31]

Secondly, the benefits of free movement of capital have accrued to
investors (particularly large institutional investors) in the form of higher
real interest rates. Given the minuscule number of 'global investors,'
these benefits have remained limited to a minority and have not trickled
down to the majority of the people in both the developed and the developing countries.

Lastly, such an argument is prejudiced in favor of private lenders and
borrowers. What is good for a private lender (to lend internationally at
higher returns) or a private borrower (to borrow cheaper funds from
abroad) may not be beneficial for a country's economy. The Mexican and

the Asian financial crises have shown how private lenders and borrowers can push economies into a precipice. In the words of Dani Rodrik:

> The greatest concern I have about canonizing capital-account convertibility is that it will leave economic policy in the typical 'emerging market' hostage to the whims and fancies of two dozen or so thirty-something country analysts in London, Frankfurt, and New York. A finance minister whose top priority is to keep foreign investors happy will be one who pays less attention to developmental goals. We would have to have blind faith in the efficiency and rationality of international capital markets to believe that the two sets of priorities will regularly coincide.[32]

Dalip Swamy voiced similar concern in the Indian context: "the globalizers who want full convertibility know what they are after... It [CAL] might be useful for a few hundred FIIs and forex operators whose influence in the stock market will increase, but to a vast majority of farmers, traders, small and medium industrialists, convertibility on capital account is fiction."[33]

Myth 6: Liberal capital account regime and open financial markets provide healthy discipline for governments, which encourages better economic policies and performance.

Reality: There are several inherent difficulties in managing an economy with an open capital account. Not only does an open capital account deprive countries of tools to pursue independent monetary policies, but also a sudden change in the perception of foreign investors can plunge the domestic financial system into a crisis. The sudden withdrawal of capital can have serious impact on the exchange and interest rates as well as the financial markets. The volatile capital inflows, easily subject to reversal, can substantially complicate economic management and threaten macroeconomic stability. Further, a domestic crisis can have a contagion effect due to a higher degree of global integration of financial markets, facilitated by CAL. The series of recent financial crises (e.g., in Scandinavia, Mexico, Southeast Asia, Russia and Brazil) are the outcome of volatile capital flows in open capital account regimes. Their costs in these countries are estimated to be between 10 and 20 per cent of the GDP.

In this context, it is worthwhile to examine the consequences of implementing rapid liberalization of capital account in Turkey in 1989 that even surpassed the parameters of the developed countries. Between 1990 and 1996, Turkey consequently suffered an excess of speculative capital inflows. Most of it was in the form of portfolio investment and short-term inflows. This surge in inflows deteriorated macroeconomic performance thereby leading to appreciation of the real exchange rate, increase in interest rates, growth of money supply and increase in current account and public deficits.[34] Unable to deal with volatile 'hot money' flows, Turkey was gripped by a severe financial crisis in 1994. The Turkish example amply demonstrates the vulnerability of the governments to grapple with excessive speculative capital inflows. The volatile and self-fulfilling behavior of foreign portfolio capital (and of domestic capital able to invest abroad) underscores the perils of CAL.

The recent financial crises seem to have demolished blind faith in market fundamentalism. In the aftermath of these crises, the dangers inherent in an unbridled CAL stand exposed. The role of capital controls in stemming financial crisis is being increasingly recognized and accepted. In the light of these crises very few can assert that global capital flows provide immense benefits to countries, particularly the developing ones. At the same time, the financial crises underscore the necessity for effective, constructive and well-coordinated regulation of financial markets by the state.

Notes and References

1. Stanley Fischer, "Capital Account Liberalization and the Role of the IMF," in *Should the IMF Pursue Capital-Account Convertibility?*, Essays in International Finance, No. 207, International Finance Section, Department of Economics, Princeton University, May 1998, pp. 2-3.

2. John Williamson and Molly Mahar, *A Survey of Financial Liberalization*, Essays in International Finance, No. 211, International Finance Section, Department of

Economics, Princeton University, November 1998, p. 54.

3. Ibid., p. 57.

4. See, for instance, Bernhard Fischer and Helmut Reisen, *Towards Capital Account Convertibility*, OECD Development Centre Policy Brief No. 4, 1992; Deena Khatkhate, "Timing and Sequencing of Financial Sector Reforms: Evidence and Rationale," *Economic and Political Weekly*, July 11, 1998, pp. 1831-1840; and Sebastian Edwards, "A Capital Idea?: Reconsidering a Financial Quick Fix," *Foreign Affairs*, May/June 1999, pp. 18-22.

5. Helmut Reisen, *After the Great Asian Slump: Towards a Coherent Approach to Global Capital Flows*, Policy Brief No. 16, OECD, 1999, p. 6.

6. The IMF is not the only international organization promoting CAL. Its twin, the World Bank too had been encouraging liberalization of capital markets through its affiliate, International Finance Corporation. However, in the wake of the Southeast Asian crisis, the Bank has done some rethinking on its previous position while the IMF continues to prescribe liberalization of capital account. Obligations regarding international capital transfers are also included in regional treaties such as the North American Free Trade Agreement (NAFTA) and in Treaties of Friendship, Commerce and Navigation (FCN Treaties).

7. Jagdish Bhagwati, "The Capital Myth: The Difference between Trade in Widgets and Dollars," *Foreign Affairs*, May/June 1998, pp. 11-12.

8. Robert Wade, "The Asian Debt-and-Development Crisis of 1997-?: Causes and Consequences," *World Development*, Vol. 26, No. 8, p. 1546.

9. Peter J Quirk and Owen Evans, *Capital Account Convertibility: Review of Experience and Implications for IMF Policies*, Occasional Paper No. 131, IMF, October 1995, p. 31.

10. Ibid.

11. Ha-Joon Chang, "Korea: The Misunderstood Crisis," *World Development*, Vol. 26, No. 8, 1998, p. 1556.

12. *Global Development Finance 1998*, World Bank, 1998, p. 34.

13. IMF's Executive Board Decision No. 541-(56/39), July 25, 1956.

14. Manuel R Agosin, "Capital-Account Convertibility and Multilateral Investment Agreements: What is in the Interest of Developing Countries?," *International Monetary and Financial Issues for the 1990s*, Research Papers for the Group of Twenty-Four, Vol. X, UNCTAD, 1999, p. 66.

15. Wendy Dobson and Pierre Jacquet, *Financial Services Liberalization in the WTO*, Institute for International Economics, 1998, p. 89.

16. *Human Development Report 1999*, UNDP, 1999, p. 31.

17. See John Eatwell, *International Financial Liberalization: The Impact on World Development*, Discussion Paper Series, No. 12, UNDP, 1997.

18. Ibid., p. 20.

19. Fred Moseley, "The United States Economy at the Turn of the Century: Entering a New Era of Prosperity?," *Capital and Class*, No. 67, 1999, p. 34.

20. Ibid., p. 36.

21. *World Economic Outlook*, IMF, 1999, p. 46.

22. Dani Rodrik, "Who needs Capital-Account Convertibility?," in *Should the IMF Pursue Capital-Account Convertibility?*, Essays in International Finance, No. 207, International Finance Section, Department of Economics, Princeton University, May 1998, pp. 55-65.

23. A V Rajwade, "Putting the Brakes on Capital Mobility," *Business Standard*, November 16, 1998.

24. Robert Devlin, Ricardo Ffrench-Davis and Stephany Griffith-Jones, "Surges in Capital Flows and Development: An Overview of Policy Issues in the Nineties," in Ricardo Ffrench-Davis and Stephany Griffith-Jones (eds.), *Coping With Capital Surges: The Return of Finance to Latin America*, International Development Research Centre, Lynne Rienner, 1995.

25. Tamir Bayoumi, "Financial Deregulation and Consumption in the United Kingdom," *Review of Economics and Statistics*, 75, 1993, pp. 536-539.

26. Simon Chappel, *Financial Liberalization in New Zealand, 1984-90*, Discussion Paper No. 35, UNCTAD, March 1991.

27. John Williamson and Molly Mahar, op. cit., p. 52.

28. Manuel R Agosin, "Liberalize, but Discourage Short-term Flows," in Isabelle Grunberg (ed.), *Perspectives on International Financial Liberalization*, Discussion Paper Series, No. 15, Office of Development Studies, UNDP, 1998, p. 5.

29. Fred Moseley, op. cit.

30. Ibid., p. 36.

31. John Eatwell, op. cit., p. 16.

32. Dani Rodrik, op. cit., p. 65.

33. Dalip Swamy, "Convertibility of Capital Account," unpublished, 1998, pp. 6-7.

34. Nurhan Yenturk, "Short-term Capital Inflows and Their Impact on Macroeconomic Structure: Turkey in the 1990s," *The Developing Economies*, No. 37-1, March 1999, pp. 89-113.

4

The Mysterious World of Hedge Funds

THE growing turbulence in the international financial markets in the 1990s has drawn attention to the existence and operations of hedge funds. There is no doubt that hedge funds have grown in popularity in recent years largely because of their outsized returns. But, simultaneously, hedge funds have been blamed for creating the ERM crisis in 1992, causing instability in the international bond market in 1994 and precipitating the Southeast Asian financial crisis in 1997. Due to lack of transparency in their operations very little information is available about them. The entire hedge fund industry is shrouded in mystery. In order to understand the intricacies of hedge funds, let us examine their basic characteristics.

What is a Hedge Fund?

There is no standard legal definition of a hedge fund. In fact, the term 'hedge fund' is a misnomer because a large number of hedge funds do not hedge against risk at all. In simple terms, a hedge fund is a private investment partnership wherein investor assets are pooled for the purpose of investing in a variety of securities and derivatives. As they are private investment partnerships in the US, the Securities and Exchange Commission (SEC) limits these entities to 99 investors, at least 65 of whom must be 'accredited.' Accredited investors are defined as investors having a net worth of at least $1 million. The minimum investment in a hedge fund is extremely high, usually not less than $1 million. Hedge funds are

Box 4.1

Absolute Returns Performance returns that are measured independently of a benchmark or index.

Accredited Investor According to the SEC of the US, this is a wealthy investor having a net worth of at least $1 million or an annual income equal to or greater than $200000. The investment must be at least $150000 and, at the same time, not exceed 20 per cent of his/her wealth.

Arbitrage Profiting from a price difference between securities in the same or different markets.

Hedging A process through which the risk of loss due to adverse price movements is transferred. Hedging one's bets means attempting to protect oneself from the ravages of the unexpected.

Leverage A company's long-term debt in relation to equity in its capital structure. The larger the long-term debt, the higher the leverage.

Limited Partnership A US vehicle for a collection of partners in a partnership that consists of 99 partners and one managing partner.

Program Trading Computer driven buying (buy program) or selling (sell program) of baskets of stocks by traders. 'Program' refers to computer programs that constantly monitor stock, futures and options markets, giving buy and sell signals when opportunities for arbitrage profits occur or when market conditions warrant liquidation transactions. Program trading has been blamed for excessive volatility in the markets, especially on 'Black Monday' in 1987.

open only to rich people who are also referred to as 'high-net-worth clients.'

By effectively using the existing loopholes in the regulatory system, many hedge fund managers structure the fund in such a way that they do not come under the purview of regulatory authorities. For instance, in the US, hedge funds are required to have less than 100 'high-net-worth clients' in order to make use of exemptions to regulations under the Securities Act of 1933, the Securities Act of 1934, and the Investment Company Act of 1940.

By and large, hedge funds are illiquid, requiring a commitment of money for a minimum period of one year with exit privileges thereafter on a quarterly basis. Unlike mutual funds, hedge funds are not regulated and are not publicly sold and purchased. Beyond a few disclosure and reporting requirements, hedge funds are largely unregulated investment instruments. By accepting investments only from institutional investors, companies and 'high-net-worth investors', hedge funds are exempted from various regulations. They are not required to publicly disclose data on their financial performance and transactions. There is no limit on the amount of leverage hedge funds can use or the size of any one investment.

While the size and number of hedge funds have increased by leaps and bounds in the 1980s and 1990s, they have existed since the late 1940s when A W Jones, a professor and *Fortune* magazine editor, founded the first hedge fund called A W Jones Group on January 1, 1949. The name, hedge fund, was derived from the fund's strategy of taking offsetting long and short positions in the stock of companies in the same industry, thereby hedging macroeconomic factors while benefiting from individual companies' specific performance. The Jones fund used a private partnership as a vehicle for flexibility, sold stocks short and employed leverage. Jones reasoned that having both short and long positions in a portfolio could increase returns and reduce risk due to lesser net market exposure. Many hedge funds still follow the structure and strategies of the Jones fund.

At present, nearly 90 per cent of hedge funds are located in the US and several offshore financial centers. According to the estimates of TASS Investment Research, 33.9 per cent of hedge funds are located in the US, 18.9 per cent in Cayman Islands, 16.5 per cent in British Virgin Islands, 11 per cent in Bermuda, 7.2 per cent in Bahamas and the rest in the UK, Switzerland and several offshore financial centers.[1] Further, 91 per cent of hedge fund managers are domiciled in the US.[2] The primary reason

---

Box 4.2

Hedge Funds vs. Mutual Funds: The Differences

■ Mutual funds have strict disclosure requirements and are relatively highly regulated. These regulations restrict the mutual funds from purchasing certain types of derivative instruments, leveraging, short selling, real estate and commodities. On the other hand, hedge funds are unregulated and therefore allow short selling and other strategies designed to accelerate performance.

■ Small investors can invest in mutual funds while hedge fund investors are only accredited investors, meaning folks with substantial assets. The minimum initial investment in a mutual fund ranges between $1000 to $2000 while hedge funds require a minimum investment of $1 million.

■ Mutual funds generally remunerate management based on a percentage of assets under management. Hedge funds always remunerate managers with performance related incentive fees as well as a fixed fee.

■ The future performance of mutual funds is dependent on the direction of the equity markets. While the future performance of hedge funds is not dependent on the direction of the equity markets. They make profits under all circumstances, whether markets rise or fall.

■ Mutual funds are measured on relative performance — that is, their performance is compared to a relevant index such as the Standard & Poor's 500 Index or to other mutual funds in their sector. While the performance of hedge funds is measured in terms of absolute returns.

behind the offshore location of hedge funds is to gain tax and regulatory concessions. The offshore havens allow the formation of hedge funds as long as they are not sold to citizens/taxpayers in the offshore jurisdiction. Offshore hedge funds are usually mutual fund companies that are domiciled in tax havens. They have no legal limits on the number of non-US investors. In the case of US investors, these funds are subject to the same legal guidelines as US-based investment partnerships.

There are two types of partners in a hedge fund — a general partner and limited partners. The general partner is the individual or entity who starts the hedge fund. The general partner handles all the trading activity and day-to-day operations of running a hedge fund. The limited partners supply most of the capital but do not participate in the trading or day-to-day running of the fund. For the services provided, the general partner receives an incentive fee that is usually 20 per cent of the net profits. The general partner also gets a fixed management fee amounting usually to 1 per cent of the assets under management. The earnings of hedge fund

Table 4.1: Number of Hedge Funds and Funds under Management
(1988-97)

Year	Number of Funds	Funds under Management[a]
1988	1373	42
1989	1648	58
1990	1977	67
1991	2373	94
1992	2848	120
1993	3417	172
1994	4100	189
1995	4700	217
1996	5100	261
1997	5500	295

[a] in $ billion.
Source: "Hedge Funds Worldwide Top 5,500 Mark," VAN Hedge Fund Advisors International, June 25, 1998 (via Internet).

managers are many times higher than those earned by mutual fund managers and investment managers. A typical hedge fund manager with modest funds under management can reasonably earn over a million dollars in a good year. Many hedge fund managers too put their own capital into the funds. Thirty hedge fund mangers were on the list of top paid Wall Streeters prepared by the *Financial World* in 1995. According to industry estimates, George Soros, Julian Robertson and Stanley Druckenmiller earned $1.1 billion, $300 million and $200 million respectively in 1996.[3]

According to a recent estimate, there are over 6 million millionaires in the world, holding nearly $17 trillion in assets.[4] Over 75 per cent of hedge funds investors are high-net-worth clients whose numbers have grown sharply in recent years. The rest include endowments, universities and foundations. Investors in many hedge funds have profited handsomely during the 1990s. There are hedge funds that have given returns of more than 40 per cent annually. According to MAR/Hedge *1997 Hedge Fund Profile*, the median returns of global macro managers have generated average returns of 19.4 per cent during 1992-96, against the Standard & Poor's return of 15.2 per cent and the US Treasury Bill rate of 4.4 per cent for the same period.[5] While another industry source, TASS Management Inc., calculated the average hedge fund returns at 17 per cent annually between January 1990 and August 1998.

Hedge Funds: A $300 Billion Industry

Given the lack of transparency in the operations of hedge funds, there is no exact figure on their numbers. As hedge funds are under no regulatory obligation to disclose their activities and trading strategies, much of the information available is through commercial data providers. According to a reliable industry source, VAN Hedge Fund Advisors International, the total number of hedge funds operating worldwide is at least 5500 with $300 billion of funds under management, as of mid-1998. Further, there are approximately 3800 US-based hedge funds managing $159 billion, while offshore hedge funds number approximately 1700 with $136 billion under management. The growth of hedge fund industry over time is given in Table 4.1. The largest and most famous funds, run by Soros Fund Management and Tiger Management, both of the US, approximate $11 billion each. There are another two dozen funds with assets exceeding one billion dollars.

In spite of the fact that investments in hedge funds are speculative and extremely risky, the hedge fund industry continues to grow. Even the pension funds — which are considered to be the most cautious — have invested substantially in hedge funds in recent years. Hedge funds currently represent one of the fastest growing segments of global finance capital in the 1980s and the 1990s. All new and existing hedge funds are benefiting substantially from the free flow of capital facilitated through the rapid deregulation and globalization of financial markets. Over the past 10 years, the number of funds has increased at an average annual rate of 25.74 per cent, showing a total growth of 648 per cent.[6] In 1998 alone, the industry witnessed an increase of 17 per cent in numbers, with no sign

Table 4.2: Hedge Funds: Style and Expected Risk

Style	Expected Risk
Short Sellers	Very High Risk
Emerging Markets	Very High Risk
Leveraged Bonds	High Risk
International	High Risk
Macro	High Risk
Market Neutral	High Risk
Distressed Securities	Medium Risk
Quantitative	Moderate Risk
Value	Moderate Risk
Growth	Moderate Risk
Opportunistic	Moderate Risk

Source: Alternative Investment Management Association.

of letting up despite the near collapse of a prominent US-based hedge fund, Long-Term Capital Management (LTCM), in late 1998. Earlier, hedge funds were primarily restricted to offshore financial havens and the US, nowadays hedge funds also originate in Europe, Latin America and Asia. A number of banks and brokerage firms have also started hedge funds in recent years. The list includes institutions like Alliance Capital Management, Swiss Bank Corporation, Daiwa Securities, State Street Global Advisors, among others.

Strategies of Hedge Funds

Hedge funds use a host of strategies. There are hedge funds for every category of equity, debt and money instruments. The strategies vary in terms of investment returns, volatility and risk. There are funds that specialize in currencies, futures, arbitrage, securities of distressed and bankrupt companies and funds that trade securities using computer models. Many hedge funds bet on foreign currencies, mergers and acquisitions and convertible securities. Others use short selling or bets, assuming that prices will fall to offset their securities holdings. They frequently use leverage in an effort to boost returns.

The basic problem with these strategies is the enhancement of risk factor because they are extremely volatile and unpredictable (see Table 4.2). Strategies such as short selling, program trading and arbitrage are highly speculative in nature and therefore pose very high risks. This problem is compounded by the fact that most hedge fund managers do not hedge their risks. As hedge funds move billions of dollars in and out of the markets quickly and potentially gain whether markets rise or fall, they have a significant impact on the daily trading developments in the global stock, bonds and futures markets.

Investment Style of Hedge Funds

Although there is no clear set of investment sectors in which hedge funds invest, following are some of the important sectors in which a majority of them invest.

Global Macro Funds: Although their numbers are small, global macro funds are the largest hedge funds in terms of assets under management. The most famous of the global macro hedge fund managers is George Soros. His Quantum Fund, established in 1969 with just $4 million, now has an estimated value of $18 billion.

Operating on a global scale, macro fund managers view the entire world as their playing field. They can invest anywhere and in any financial instrument — equities, bonds, currencies or commodities. They monitor changes in global economies and hope to realize profits from significant shifts in global interest rates, important changes in countries' economic policies, etc. A shift in government economic policy that affects interest rates, in turn, affects all financial instruments including currency, stock and bond markets. Macro fund managers speculate on such trends and profit by investing in financial instruments whose prices are most directly influenced by these trends. They extensively use leverage and derivatives to accentuate the impact of market moves. No doubt the returns can be high but so can the losses because leveraged directional investments (which are not hedged) tend to make the largest impact on performance. That is why macro funds are considered a very high risk and volatile investment strategy.

The most famous of Soros's activities was in September 1992 when he took on the Bank of England. He bet $10 billion worth of sterling (much of it was borrowed) on the speculation that sterling was overvalued and would be devalued. In a futile attempt to save the sterling, the Bank of England raised the interest rates several times and spent an estimated 15 billion sterling to defend the currency. Still, they could not prevent the dropping of the Pound and subsequent pull out from the European Monetary Union. It is estimated that Soros and his investors made a neat $2 billion on this bet.

But these macro managers many a times also cause abrupt fall in profits. For instance, during the first quarter of 1994, hedge fund superstar Michael Steinhardt (whose funds produced an average annual return of 24 per cent over several decades) placed huge unhedged bets thinking that the European interest rates would decline, causing bonds to rise. Instead, his funds lost 29 per cent when the Federal Reserve raised interest rates in the US, causing European interest rates to rise.

Global International Funds: Similar to the macro funds, these fund managers also invest in international equity markets of the US, Europe and Asia. They follow what is known as 'bottom up' approach — they stock pick individual companies, looking at what they have to offer in their sector or what opportunities there are for buying or shorting. These funds are also extremely volatile.

Emerging Markets Funds: These funds invest in equity or debt of emerging markets that tend to have higher inflation and volatile growth. The expected volatility of such funds is very high.

Short Selling Funds: This strategy is based on finding overvalued companies and selling the shares of those companies. The investor does not own these shares. Anticipating that the share price of the company will fall, the investor borrows the shares from his broker. Ideally, when the share price does fall, the investor buys shares at the new, lower price and thus can replace, to the broker, the shares sold earlier, thus netting a gain. This strategy is also employed where the investor believes that the share price will fall due to problems in the company, etc. These funds are extremely volatile and risky.

Market Neutral Funds: These funds tend to exploit perceived anomalies in the prices of different bonds by buying under-priced ones and selling short the overpriced ones. LTCM was a market neutral fund. These funds are also highly volatile.

Aggressive Growth Funds: Invests in equities expected to experience acceleration in growth of earnings per share. These funds tend to be highly volatile.

Event Driven Funds: Event driven managers take significant positions in a limited number of companies with 'special situations', that is, where companies' situations are unusual offering quick profit opportunities (e.g., depressed stock, an event offering significant potential market interest, mergers and acquisitions, etc.). This is one of the few investment sectors where economic or market conditions are of marginal concern.

Fund of Funds: This is a fund that mixes and matches the hedge funds and other pooled investments among many different funds or investment vehicles. These funds are the largest in number.

When Hedge Funds Shocked the Financial World

The collapse of the Russian rouble during August 1998 proved fatal to several global hedge funds. Although many hedge funds have failed in the past, the failures in the aftermath of the Russian crisis were across the board from global macro funds to event driven funds. The fund managers made a mistake by underestimating Russia's economic problems. Facing severe financial problems, Russia not only devalued the rouble but also defaulted on its debt. The hedge funds that had considerable exposure in the Russian financial markets suffered heavy losses. Hedge funds which did not have any exposure in Russia also suffered because the Russian turmoil sparked the 'flight to safety' syndrome among the investors. The Quantum Fund, owned by George Soros, reportedly lost almost $2 billion. Five prominent hedge funds went bankrupt including market leaders III's High Risk Opportunity Fund and the McGinnis funds run by San Antonio Capital Management. The average losses in 1998 for all hedge funds are estimated to be 50 per cent of their equity. The failure of LTCM was spectacular and brought the financial crisis of Russia to the center of Wall Street.

The Near Collapse of LTCM

Started in 1994, the US-based LTCM was headed by John Meriwether who had earlier worked with the Salomon Brothers. After being forced to resign for his involvement in illegal rigging of the US Treasury bond market, John founded the LTCM. John was a legend in the financial world of Wall Street known for his extraordinary skills. Same was the case with his other partners in LTCM which included David Mullins, former Vice

Chairman of the Federal Reserve Board; Myron Scholes, who won the Nobel Prize in economics for his work on the pricing of options; and Robert Merton, another Nobel laureate in economics.

Despite charging a higher fee (25 per cent of the profit), LTCM was able to raise billions of dollars from commercial banks and securities companies. The list of investors included the Rockefeller Foundation,

---

Box 4.3

LTCM: Long-Term or Short-Term!

December 1992: John Meriwether leaves Salomon Brothers in the wake of the 1991 Treasury auction scandal. Several of the firm's 'stars' join him at LTCM. So do David Mullins, former Fed Vice Chairman, and Nobel laureates Robert Merton and Myron Scholes.

February 1994: LTCM begins trading. In its first 10 months, its gross return is 28.49 per cent. In 1995, it returns 42.8 per cent after fees and 40.8 per cent in 1996, but slips to 17 per cent in 1997.

September 1997: LTCM surprises Wall Street by announcing it will return nearly half of its $6 billion capital to investors because "the fund has excess capital."

July 1998: Salomon, now owned by Travelers, closes its US bond arbitrage unit after suffering a $100 million reversal in the second quarter. The unit had engaged in similar trading like the LTCM.

August 16, 1998: Russia defaults on its debt, sparking global 'flight to safety' by investors.

September 2, 1998: LTCM tells investors that it suffered a 44 per cent drop in its net asset value in August and about 50 per cent in the year to date. It blames "sharp increases in volatility and widespread shifts toward greater liquidity in global fixed income and equity markets."

September 23, 1998: Federal Reserve of New York puts together a $3.75 billion bailout package for LTCM.

October 1999: New York Federal Reserve President announces that LTCM is very close to being out of business.

Dresdner Bank, Credit Suisse Group, UBS AG, Presidential Life Corporation and Bank Julius Baer. The heads of prestigious finance companies such as Merrill Lynch and Paine Webber had also put their personal wealth into the LTCM. Besides millionaires, investors in LTCM included the Italian central bank, Banca d' Italia, which had contributed $250 million to the fund. Investors were required to put in a minimum $10 million for a minimum period of three years. But they were kept in the dark about the trading strategy of the fund. In spite of being arrogant and secretive, LTCM was flooded with huge funds by investors much impressed by its extraordinary performance. The investors of LTCM earned returns of 42.8 per cent in 1995, after fees, 40 per cent in 1996 and 17 per cent in 1997.[7] In 1997, LTCM was flooded with so many funds that it decided to return $2.7 billion. That is why LTCM was often referred to as the 'Rolls Royce' of the global hedge fund industry.

With easy availability of funds at favorable terms, LTCM increased its leverage and exposure. With a capital base of $4.8 billion, LTCM borrowed money from banks and companies to purchase securities with an estimated value of $200 billion, a 50 to 1 degree of leverage, considered extremely high in the industry. Moreover, LTCM used these securities as collaterals to enter into speculative financial derivatives thereby increasing its exposure to $1.25 trillion.[8]

LTCM was involved in market neutral arbitrage. Most of LTCM's exposure was in the US, European and Japanese markets. By using sophisticated computerized models, LTCM placed highly leveraged bets on the interest rate spreads between risky bonds and safe US treasury bonds. Primarily because of large amounts of derivative contracts, LTCM was bound to make substantial profits or losses if yield spreads changed. This model worked successfully for three years but it changed suddenly in August 1998 when Russia defaulted on its debt. Although LTCM was not engaged in the Russian markets, the global 'flight to safety' that followed Russia's turmoil soured many of its bets which counted on interest rates on riskier bonds moving closer to the US and German government bonds. As a result of 'flight to safety', the prices of safe bonds rose and the yield differentials on which LTCM's bets were based, widened instead of narrowing. Because of the high degree of LTCM's leverage, it was faced with margin calls and was forced to liquidate at huge losses. Between August and September 1998, LTCM lost 90 per cent of its equity. By mid-September 1998, LTCM's equity had dropped to $600 million, a loss of more than $4 billion.[9]

In early September, LTCM informed the Federal Reserve Bank of New York of the problem it faced. In an unexpected move, the Federal Reserve quickly stepped in and organized a bailout package by persuading some of the big players in global finance capital such as Travelers Group, Bankers Trust, Barclays, Chase, Merrill Lynch, Goldman Sachs and other elite financial institutions to invest a total of $3.5 billion in LTCM. The fallout of the collapse of LTCM on global financial markets would have been disastrous. The fear of huge losses by banks and financial institutions would have triggered yet another chain of breakdowns. Because of their involvement with LTCM, two Swiss banks, namely, UBS and Credit Suisse Group, suffered huge losses. The top executives of UBS also resigned taking moral responsibility for their involvement with the fund.

Despite sharp criticism, the US authorities have defended the bailout program on the ground that the collapse of LTCM would have sparked a major crisis in Wall Street and the global financial system. In his testimony before the US House of Representatives Banking Committee, Federal Reserve Board Chairman, Alan Greenspan, said that the bailout program was necessary because of the fragility of international markets. "Had the failure of LTCM triggered the seizing up of markets, substantial damage could have been inflicted on many market participants, including some not directly involved with the firm, and could have potentially impaired the economies of many nations, including our own," observed Greenspan.[10]

The bailout program raises several questions. Firstly, LTCM is not the only hedge fund that went bust after the Russian turmoil. As mentioned earlier, there were five other hedge funds that failed along with LTCM but they had been allowed to go out of business without any support from the Federal Reserve. Critics argue that the sheer size of LTCM's trading position as well as its connections in Wall Street ensured its bailout. They view the bailout plan as a perfect example of Western style crony capitalism. Secondly, the bailout of LTCM militates against the recent US policy of "no bailouts" of financial institutions under any circumstance. By bailing out LTCM, the US Federal Reserve has done exactly the opposite of what it has been advising the rest of the world (e.g., Japan) against such bailouts. Thirdly, the Federal Reserve has no authority to bailout hedge funds that are beyond its jurisdiction. The role of the Federal Reserve is only restricted to banks. Lastly, although the bailout program provided 90 per cent of LTCM's equity to its rescuers there was no change sought in the top management of the fund. It is ironic that Meriwether and his team members were allowed to again run LTCM with a management fee of 1 per cent plus 12.5 per cent of profits.

In a nutshell, the bailout program of LTCM can be explained by quoting an old banking joke: "If you owe a bank 1000 dollars and can't pay, you are in trouble. But if you owe a billion dollars to the bank, and can't pay, the bank is in trouble!" However, recent media reports indicate that the Federal Reserve has decided to close down LTCM. According to reports, the New York Federal Reserve President, William McDonough, announced in early October 1999 that LTCM is "very close to being out of business."[11]

Emerging Issues

The LTCM episode has exposed the US's doublespeak and reaffirmed the need to regulate the hedge funds. But any move on the part of regulatory authorities to regulate hedge funds is likely to be resisted by the industry. Even a moderate call for greater transparency is opposed by the hedge funds industry on the ground that if the portfolio investment is "leaked" to the marketplace it can be used by other market participants against the fund managers and thereby against the best interests of the investors.[12]

There is an urgent need for greater regulation of hedge funds. In this regard, a beginning,could be made by imposing limits on their borrowings and making it mandatory for hedge funds to provide regular information about their activities and derivatives positions to not only creditors and investors but also to the regulatory authorities. Apart from regulating hedge funds, equal attention should be paid to banks that pump billions of dollars into hedge funds and other highly leveraged institutions without knowing exactly what these funds are doing with their money. Most of the money invested by hedge funds worldwide belongs to the banks but banks are under no regulatory obligation to disclose their exposure to hedge funds. With respect to hedge funds and OTC derivatives, bank regulation is fundamentally flawed. A significant restructuring is required to check the weaknesses in a bank's credit assessment process which allow very large exposures to hedge funds.

At the policy level, the recent busting of hedge funds and in particular the near collapse of LTCM has raised several important issues related to the systemic instability in the global financial system. One issue, which needs closer attention, is related to the financial system of source countries, where these funds originate in the first place. The near collapse of LTCM has significantly exposed the fragility and systemic instability in the so-called sound financial markets of the developed countries. Because of increased leverage and unhedged exposure, hedge funds can bring a financial crisis of a recipient country to the doors of a source country. It will be incorrect to assume that the source countries can remain insulated from negative externalities. In fact, it is in their self-interest to strictly monitor and regulate the operations of hedge funds. Unless hedge funds are regulated in source countries, the global financial system will remain unstable and recipient countries will have no other option but to keep away from such funds. Therefore transparency, regulation, supervision and prudential controls in source countries are as equally important. If the G-7 countries are really concerned about the growing instability of the global financial system, they can begin by dealing with these issues closer to home.

Notes and References

1. *The Case for Hedge Funds*, Tremont Partners, Inc. and TASS Investment Research Ltd., 1999, p. 8.

2. Ibid.

3. "Hedge Funds Worldwide Top 5,500 Mark," VAN Hedge Fund Advisors International, June 25, 1998 (via Internet).

4. Bethany McLean, "Everybody's Going Hedge Funds," *Fortune*, June 8, 1998, p. 182.

5. Beverly Chandler, *Investing with the Hedge Fund Giants: Profit Whether Markets Rise or Fall*, Financial Times Management, 1998, p. 71.

6. *The Case for Hedge Funds*, op. cit., p. 5.

7. Anita Raghavan and Mitchell Pacelle, "US Hedge Funds May Be Too Big to Fail," *Indian Express*, September 25, 1998.

8. Joseph Khan and Peter Truell, "Hedge Funds Are Now Estimated to Total $1.25 Trillion," *The New York Times*, September 26, 1998 (via Internet).

9. Franklin R Edwards, "Hedge Funds and the Collapse of Long-Term Capital Management," *Journal of Economic Perspective*, Vol. 13, No. 2, Spring 1999, p. 199.

10. Quoted in Nick Beams, "More Questions Than Answers on Hedge Fund Collapse," International Committee of the Fourth International, October 3, 1998 (via Internet).

11. Quoted in "LTCM May Go Out of Business," *The Hindu Businessline*, October 3, 1999.

12. *The Case for Hedge Funds*, op. cit., p. 25.

5

The Global Parasites:
Offshore Financial Centers

THE offshore financial centers (OFCs) are important constituents of the present global financial system in which 'megabyte money' (money traded through computer screens) moves around the world with incredible speed and ease. The OFCs, due to encouragement from political and business establishments and advances in telecommunications, have emerged as major centers for the operations of unregulated financial players such as trust companies, shell companies, hedge funds and brokerage houses. Development of OFCs is of grave concern because they are used not only to launder the proceeds of drug trafficking and other criminal activities but also aid and abet certain kinds of financial crime. The role of OFCs in catalyzing financial crises in the Latin American and the Southeast Asian countries in the 1990s is well documented. Attempts to regulate the global financial flows will remain incomplete without analyzing the role played by the OFCs in global finance capital.

What are Offshore Financial Centers?

In popular parlance, OFCs refer to those jurisdictions where banks and other financial institutions are exempt from a wide range of regulations that are normally imposed on onshore institutions. Financial transactions in OFCs are tax exempt and free of interest and exchange regulations. In many cases, offshore banks are exempt from regulatory scrutiny

Table 5.1: Countries and Territories with Offshore Financial Centers

Region	Offshore Financial Centers
Africa	Djibouti, Liberia, Mauritius, Seychelles, Tangier.
Asia and Pacific	Australia, Cook Islands, Guam, Hong Kong, Japan,[1] Macau, Malaysia,[2] Marianas, Marshall Islands, Micronesia, Nauru, Niue, Philippines, Singapore,[3] Thailand,[4] Vanuatu, Western Samoa.
Europe	Austria, Andorra, Campione, Cyprus, Gibraltar, Guernsey, Hungary, Ireland,[5] Sark, Isle of Man, Jersey, Liechtenstein, Luxembourg, Malta, Madeira, Monaco, Netherlands, Russia, Switzerland, UK.[6]
Middle East	Bahrain, Dubai, Israel, Kuwait, Lebanon, Oman.
Western Hemisphere	Antigua, Anguilla, Aruba, Bahamas, Barbados, Belize, Bermuda, British Virgin Islands, Cayman Islands, Costa Rica, Dominica, Grenada, Montserrat, Netherlands Antilles, St. Kitts and Nevis, St. Lucia, Panama, Puerto Rico, St. Vincent & the Grenadines, Turks & Caicos Islands, United States,[7] Uruguay.

[1] Japanese Offshore Market (JOM).
[2] Labuan
[3] Asian Currency Units (ACUs).
[4] Bangkok International Banking Facility (BIBF).
[5] Dublin
[6] London
[7] US International Banking Facilities (IBFs) are located in New York, Miami, Houston, Chicago and Los Angeles-San Francisco.

Source: Luca Errico and Alberto Musalem, "Offshore Banking: An Analysis of Micro- and Macro-Prudential Issues," *IMF Working Paper No. 99/5*, IMF, 1999.

in terms of liquidity, capital adequacy and disclosure requirements. It is not always necessary that offshore financing should take place physically 'offshore.' For instance, when a bank located in country A raises money in country B and then lends that money to clients in country C the transaction is considered 'offshore.' OFCs are also known as 'tax havens' or 'financial havens.' Most of the OFCs are countries but some are located within certain countries, for instance, the International Banking Facilities (IBFs) in the US, the Japanese Offshore Market (JOM), the Bangkok International Banking Facility (BIBF) in Thailand and the Labuan International Offshore Center in Malaysia (see Table 5.1).

It is important to note here that OFCs are inhabited by 'letterbox' or 'brass plate' banks and finance companies that exist only on paper, while the real activity takes place in financial centers such as London and New York. Thus, they are totally dependent on external financial flows. That is why OFCs are often referred to as parasites or 'paper tigers.' Most of the advertisement campaigns related to financial services available at the OFCs is carried out through business magazines and the Internet.

Often, analysts tend to underestimate the importance of OFCs because financial deregulation and liberalization have eroded the distinction between offshore and onshore financial operations. However, it would be a grave misjudgement to underestimate the importance of the offshore financial world for three reasons. Firstly, the world of OFCs and financial institutions that operate within their jurisdiction are multiplying. At present, there are 69 OFCs in the world and their number is likely to increase given the keen interest shown by several countries. There are news reports urging the government to make India's financial capital, Mumbai, an OFC.[1] In the case of British Virgin Islands, the number of new finance companies incorporated annually greatly exceeds the size of its population.

Secondly, the amount of money routed through the OFCs is staggering. For instance, 9 OFCs of the Caribbean are home to roughly half of the world's captive insurance companies and nearly 14 per cent of the world's merchant shipping.[2] OFCs such as the Cayman Islands are major centers of global finance. Cayman Islands is considered to be the fifth largest financial center in the world behind London, New York, Tokyo and Hong Kong.[3] Apart from mutual funds, hedge funds, offshore insurers and non-resident companies, there are over 570 banks with deposits of over $500 billion in the Cayman Islands alone.[4] Luxembourg, which has over 220 banks in the city is seventh in the world in terms of assets in foreign currencies.[5] Bermuda hosts about 40 per cent of the world's captive insurance companies.[6] During the period 1992-97, OFC cross border assets expanded at an average annual rate of 6.4 per cent, from $3.5 trillion to $4.8 trillion.[7] By the end of 1997, the share of OFC cross border assets in the total cross border assets stood at 54.2 per cent.[8] Further, over the period 1992-97, the outstanding amount of international money market instruments (bonds and notes) issued in OFCs grew at an average annual rate of 20.2 per cent.[9] At end-1997, they stood at $746.1 billion or 21.1 per cent of total international money market instruments.[10]

Thirdly, OFCs still remain attractive because they invite 'dirty money.' In Antigua, for instance, anyone with $1 million can open a bank (which requires just a brass plate or a room with a fax machine) with no reporting and regulatory requirements.[11] In 1995 itself, the number of banks shot up by 75 per cent in Antigua.[12] Luxembourg's secrecy laws have been the major factor behind attracting 'dirty money' from African dictators. It is the same country that hosted the BCCI.

On an average, over the period 1992-97, about 85 per cent of the assets of OFCs were bank assets.[13] Offshore banking is carried out through offshore branches or subsidiaries. Offshore branches are legally indistinguishable from parent banks onshore. While offshore subsidiaries are autonomous legal entities incorporated in OFCs and may be wholly or partially owned by parent banks onshore. Offshore banks engage in three types of transactions: Eurocurrency loans and deposits, underwriting of eurobonds, and OTC trading in derivatives for speculative purposes. Eurocurrency transactions happen to be the bulk of offshore banking operations. They include transactions between banks and original depositors, between banks and ultimate borrowers and between banks themselves on the inter-bank market.

Basic Characteristics of OFCs

Some of the main attributes of the OFCs include: no exchange controls; convertibility of foreign currencies; instant registration of corporations; banking and corporate secrecy laws; excellent electronic communications; a large tourist trade to explain major inflows of cash; a government relatively invulnerable to outside pressure; pronounced reliance on the financial services sector and a suitable geographic location to facilitate business travel.

Bank secrecy is a very important component of the OFCs. They attract funds largely because they promise anonymity. Primarily based on the Swiss banking laws, which put bank secrecy under official protection and grant foreign nationals the protection of Swiss criminal law, most OFCs possess secrecy laws which bar bank officials from revealing the identity and transactions of their customers, even to their own government. In fact, many Internet advertisements for banks emphasize the strictness of the jurisdiction's secrecy and assure the prospective customers that neither the bank nor the government will ever disclose bank data to another government. Although Swiss authorities have volunteered to provide information about their clients following a series of scandals and rumors (particularly the allegation that the former President of the Philippines, Ferdinand Marcos had deposited over $4 billion of his country's money in Swiss accounts), the OFCs continue to operate with bank secrecy laws.

OFCs: The Cornerstone of Financial Liberalization

Although OFCs have come to deal with substantial amount of global finance capital, they are of recent origin. Their outgrowth can be attributed to three main factors — the development of the Euromarkets, global financial deregulation and liberalization, and the 'dollarization' (the use of the United States dollar in transactions) of black markets. As part of the financial deregulation process, the OFCs have helped in the expansion of global financial industry through a variety of ways. On the one hand, they have been successful in putting pressure on governments to relax capital controls and other regulations on the banking sector, and on the other, they have impelled significant lowering of international standards and regulations.

Initially, the OFCs emerged as a conduit for circumventing strict financial regulations related to reserve requirements, interest rate ceilings, capital controls and financial disclosures. In the early 1970s, for instance, Luxembourg became the major OFC in Europe attracting funds from Germany, France and Belgium because of low tax rates and banking secrecy rules. Dismantling of capital controls coupled with financial liberalization in several developed countries during the 1970s led to significant proliferation of OFCs. When the Thatcher government abolished foreign exchange controls in 1979, London became an offshore financial center.

The US was under considerable pressure from the Swiss and Caribbean tax havens. Between 1964 and 1973, the number of foreign branches of US banks increased from 181 to 699 of which 181 were in Caribbean OFCs and 156 in European OFCs.[14] Between 1964 and 1970, the total overseas assets of US banks increased from $7 billion to $53 billion.[15] Unable to check the growing overseas assets of US banks, the US authorities established the New York IBF on December 1, 1980. In Asia, offshore inter-bank markets developed after 1968 when Singapore launched the Asian Dollar Market (ADM) and introduced the Asian Currency Units (ACUs) and Japan established the JOM. The cross border assets of Asian OFCs have, on an average, grown at a rate of 4.3 per cent over the period 1992-97, and by end-December 1997 accounted for 15.2 per cent of total cross border assets.[16]

The OFCs have imposed severe constraints on the developing countries by channeling out capital through dubious means. Because of strict secrecy laws, the elites of developing countries prefer to keep their capital often raised through illegal means in the OFCs. According to conservative estimates, about 30 per cent of the Third World debt has found its way into OFCs.[17] At least 40 per cent of foreign debt of Latin America, which witnessed a massive flight of capital in the 1980s, are estimated to be residing in OFCs.[18] With the removal of capital controls, governments are unable to regulate capital flows. This is ideal for money launderers who use OFCs to move their money around the world. When capital moves freely it becomes very difficult to trace its origins. The widespread development of black markets has been accompanied by dollarization of economy which provides the appropriate financial infrastructure to convert illegal transactions conducted in the local currency into US dollars. Easy availability and exchangeability of the dollar is borne by the fact that nearly $300 billion — out of the total $400 billion in circulation — is in circulation outside the US. This makes the dollar the preferred currency for illegal transactions.

Financial deregulation has further diluted the traditional barriers between financial institutions. As a result, various checks and balances which were regulating the nature and destination of financial assets have been removed in the process. Thus, once money passes the first barrier to gain entry into the 'financial supermarket,' there are no more layers of scrutiny.

OFCs and Financial Crises

The role of OFCs in catalyzing the financial crises in Latin America and Southeast Asia in the 1990s is well documented. Offshore establishments of Argentine banks were primarily responsible for the banking crisis in Argentina in 1995. Most of the losses were reported from the Caribbean OFCs. Conservative estimates put the losses from the failure of offshore establishments between $3 billion and $4 billion.[19] In order to benefit from lower taxation and higher returns, investors and onshore banks were lured by offshore establishments engaged in speculative investments in emerging markets as well as in real estate in Argentina. Due to the contagion effects of the financial crisis in Mexico in 1995, the offshore establishments of Argentine banks suffered a run. Because their exposures were unhedged, it led to massive failure of several offshore establishments and their onshore parents.

In Venezuela, a rise in real interest rates coupled with weak regulation of the offshore establishments of commercial banks and othe financial companies led to a severe banking crisis in 1994. Under the universal banking model adopted by Venezuela, the commercial banks were able to hide losses by shifting assets and liabilities around the groups' balance sheets with the help of offshore establishments. The weak position of some banks resulted in increased risk taking. Speculative investments in real estate, tourism and equities were made from offshore establishments.

In Asia, the OFCs were involved in the precipitation of the financial crisis in 1997. In Thailand, the establishment of the BIBF in 1993 was one of the major factors responsible for triggering the financial crisis in 1997.

Box 5.1

The Bangkok International Banking Facility

With the return of Hong Kong to China, the Thai authorities created the Bangkok International Banking Facility (BIBF) in the early 1990s ostensibly to relocate financial business from Hong Kong and make Bangkok as the major financial center in Asia. In March 1993, 46 domestic and foreign commercial banks were allowed to operate under this facility. Initially, this facility was meant to promote offshore transactions (called 'Out-out' lending) whereby banks borrow overseas and lend overseas, without having any relation to domestic transactions. However, in subsequent years, the BIBF-based banks were given special incentives and concessions (for instance, allowing foreign BIBFs to become full bank branches) and were also permitted to indulge in 'Out-in' lending , under which the liability side is offshore but the asset side is onshore. The 'Out-in' lending became the dominant channel through which the domestic financial sector was able to raise substantial short-term funds.

It has been estimated that nearly 65 per cent of all BIBF assets belonged to 'out-in' lending in early 1997. This led to a substantial increase in short-term offshore borrowings by domestic companies to invest in equity and real estate. Therefore, any analysis of the Thai financial crisis will remain incomplete without critically examining the key role played by the BIBF.

The establishment of the BIBF led to a substantial increase in short-term offshore borrowing by domestic companies to invest in equity and real estate. The BIBF altered the composition of foreign debt of Thailand in favor of short-term debt, which accounted for nearly 60 per cent of the total debt. In 1995, about two-thirds of short-term inflows were intermediated through the BIBF.[20] Over the period 1993-96, the total lending in foreign exchange by the BIBF increased on an average by 38 per cent annually, and at end-1996, stood around $32 billion.[21] Much of this lending was unhedged, which increased the banking system's vulnerability to foreign exchange risk.

In Malaysia, authorities found that offshore operations of one of its banks suffered substantial losses in the aftermath of the recent financial crisis. They also discovered that 52 offshore banks operating in its OFC, Labuan, had high short-term liabilities. In Korea, the liberalization of short-term international borrowings between 1993 and 1996 encouraged domestic corporations to tap international markets through offshore establishments of banks belonging to the same 'chaebol.'[22]

OFCs and 'Dirty Money'

The global financial system, which allows rapid capital mobility, is conducive to money laundering and various criminal activities. Because of strict secrecy laws, OFCs are the natural destinations of bulk of the 'dirty money' raised through illegal activities in the world. The best known scandal is the BCCI — the largest money laundering scam in the annals of financial history. The BCCI scandal, described in Box 5.2, shocked the global financial markets. The bank had operated for a long time without any interference from regulatory authorities. The collapse of BCCI was not an isolated phenomenon. Six years later, another prominent fraud came to notice following the bankruptcy of the Antigua-based European Union Bank (EUB). Founded by two Russians in 1994, this bank launched its website and claimed to be the first Internet bank which allowed clients to create and manage their accounts on line. The bank offered numbered accounts that operated by password rather than signature. With utmost

Box 5.2

The BCCI Scandal

BCCI was set up by a Pakistani businessman Agha Hassan Abedi in 1972 to serve clients in the developing countries. Among the prominent investors in BCCI were the Sheikh of Abu Dhabi and the Bank of America.

The bank performed quite well in earlier years because of the steep hike in oil prices that provided it plenty of money. But the lending was carried out without due diligence which led to large exposures to favored companies and individuals. Many of the clients were attracted to BCCI because of its secretive operations. BCCI was structured in such a way (for instance, it was registered in Luxembourg, headquartered in London but operated across the world through various OFCs) that it was not accountable to any particular jurisdiction or subject to any one set of regulations. By creating multiple layers of shell companies, subsidiaries, holding companies, affiliates and other entities in the OFCs, BCCI was able to evade restrictions on the movement of capital.

BCCI exploited to the hilt the inherent weaknesses of the global financial system by dividing its operations between two auditors, neither of whom looked at the totality of its activities, and therefore, had no clue about its involvement with money laundering and other corrupt practices. With much of the losses concealed in a Cayman Island subsidiary, the bank continued massive misappropriation of funds by showing largely fictitious profits.

To raise fresh deposits, BCCI turned to drug barons of Latin America who were themselves searching for opportunities to launder their 'dirty money.' One of the clients of BCCI was President of Panama, General Manuel Noriega, who opened an account with the bank in 1982 to route kickbacks received from the Colombian cocaine cartels for allowing them to use Panama as a transit point.

However, in the late 1980s, investigations by the US and the UK authorities revealed that BCCI provided services to a number of drug traffickers, dictators, arms traders and intelligence agencies. Finally, BCCI was closed down in July 1991 and more than $12 billion of its assets were seized.

privacy, confidentiality and security, clients of EUB received excellent interest rates. Soon the bank came to the attention of regulatory bodies and groups monitoring organized financial crimes and it was found that the bank was used to launder the illicit proceeds of Russian organized crime. Unlike BCCI, EUB officials disappeared with the deposits when it collapsed in July 1997. In addition, there are reports that the Russian central bank illegally diverted substantial IMF funds through an offshore company called Fimaco (see Box 5.3). Meanwhile, another major scandal related to money laundering in Russia broke out in mid-1999 when investigations were launched at the Bank of New York to examine the accounts of companies connected with the corporate giant Benex. Although investigators are still probing whether these accounts were used

Box 5.3

IMF Loans, Russia and Offshore Company

In early 1999, the Russian authorities launched investigations to find out how billions of dollars of the central bank's foreign currency reserves were funneled through an offshore company. According to *Washington Post* (March 23, 1999), $1.7 billion were transferred by the Russian central bank through a secret firm, Fimaco, based in the British island of Jersey in 1993. The IMF lent much of this amount to Russia. Part of this amount was reinvested in Russia's short-term treasury bills market. More funds were transferred through this route in 1994, 1995 and 1996. In the months preceding President Boris Yeltsin's reelection in 1996, hundreds of millions were pumped through this route back into the treasury bill market which was yielding more than 200 per cent annually. The central bank withdrew the money from Fimaco in 1997. Critics point out that these reserves were used for private gains because the profits earned from investing the overseas money are unlikely to return to Russia. The central bank of Russia defended the use of the offshore firm by claiming that no laws had been broken by it. It is ironical that though IMF professes the need to monitor and regulate OFCs through its surveillance and technical assistance programs, yet it singularly failed to keep a tab on its own funds clandestinely being routed through an offshore center!

for money laundering, there is enough evidence that nearly $200 million of IMF funds were diverted through the use of these accounts.

As a leading component of the white-collar crime of the 1990s, money laundering is carried out extensively through OFCs. Money laundering operations include diversion of the proceeds from various types of criminal and illegal activities ranging from drug trafficking to financial fraud. According to a report by the United States Office of Technology Assessment, 0.05 per cent to 0.1 per cent of the approximately 700000 wire transfers a day contain laundered funds up to a value of $300 million.[23] As $1.5 trillion is transferred by wire daily with little details about the senders and recipients, identifying the origins of laundered funds becomes an extremely onerous task. As far as global drug trafficking is concerned, the United Nations International Drug Control Programme (UNDCP) has estimated that the annual turnover is around $400 billion.[24] While the proceeds obtained from tax evasion, organized crime and financial frauds is expected to be several times more than drug trafficking.

There are various ways through which criminal organizations use OFCs as a conduit for money laundering. For instance, in Aruba, casinos are frequently used to launder money. The Russian criminal organizations send 'dirty money' to Israel via Antwerp, through Gibraltar and into Spain, into London's real estate market and into the Caribbean. The Italian mafia has been using banks and casinos in Nicaragua to launder money. Apart from criminals, legitimate business corporations also indulge in money laundering through transfer pricing. With the help of OFCs, corporations generate false invoices and documentation to legitimize various illegal transactions. The corporations often utilize the services of OFCs to route the payments for kickbacks. The existence of free trade zones and free trade agreements also create favorable conditions for money laundering. The main obstacle in containing money laundering is the absence of strict controls on capital movements. Removal of barriers and controls on trade and financial flows make it very difficult for regulatory authorities to scrutinize such transactions. This problem is further heightened by the development of Internet based banking that has no clear jurisdiction. Recent innovations and advances in the global financial system have, rather unwittingly, aided and abetted money laundering and financial crime.

Sovereignty for Sale?

The downright sway of OFCs raises critical issues related to the sovereignty of nations. The manner in which most of the countries have promoted and legitimized the operations of OFCs calls for serious debate about the intention and use of sovereignty. Self-determination and sovereignty of nations is a well established principle internationally. The problem arises when sovereignty becomes just another commodity to be bought and sold in the market. There are several instances in the past when countries and territories with OFCs have protected the privacy and secrecy of its rich clients in the name of sovereignty. The principle of sovereignty has been wielded by several countries as an excuse to attract investors to OFCs without delving into the negative consequences on the entire global financial system. It could be well illustrated by citing the example of Seychelles which passed an economic development act in mid-1990s offering citizenship (with no questions asked) to those who placed deposits of $10 million or more in the country. However, international pressure forced Seychelles to withdraw this offer.

In reality, since OFCs are largely dependent on onshore finance, they cannot be considered economically independent. For instance, Liechtenstein is dependent on Switzerland; Monaco on France; the US Virgin Islands on the US; Channel Islands on the UK; and the Dutch Antilles on the Netherlands. This shows that there is considerable amount of outside support to the OFCs. In several cases, the OFCs have been encouraged and established in the erstwhile colonies by the UK and other imperial powers. However, there are several instances in the past when onshore authorities have taken a tough stand against the operations of OFCs. In 1989, for instance, Britain forced Monsterrat to close down most of 300 odd 'brass plate' banks after a fraud scare.[25]

In the case of small countries, the development of OFCs and financial services in general require detailed investigation. The factors that have contributed to the growth of OFCs in several countries are basically local. Most of these countries have limited natural resources. Dumping of highly subsidized farm products from abroad has almost destroyed their traditional sources of livelihood such as agriculture. Only a handful of countries (especially in the Caribbean region) have been able to produce and export agricultural products. With little or no industry, financial services become the inevitable choice for many smaller countries. But the moot question is whether this is an ideal strategy of development for small countries? Are there no alternative ways of development?

In the past, the onshore regulatory authorities have, by and large, tolerated the evasive tactics of their banks and financial institutions and allowed them to establish offshore branches and subsidiaries with little or no regulation. However, the recent financial crises in Latin America and Southeast Asia have highlighted the dubious operations of OFCs and national authorities must take notice of this. Efforts have been made recently by the UN, Financial Action Task Force (FATF), the EC and other agencies to curb money laundering activities linked with drug trafficking. Some well-intentioned efforts towards regulating banks and financial institutions were also undertaken in the wake of the BCCI scandal. At the international level, strict international regulation and supervision of OFCs is imperative to curb tax and regulatory evasions. Otherwise, the world may continue to witness the mushrooming of OFCs with the active collusion of money launderers, financial fraudsters, drug traffickers and organized criminals.

Notes and References

1. See, for instance, J Rajagopal and Vineet Gupta, "Offshore Financial Centres: A Beacon on the Bay," *The Economic Times*, April 8, 1998; "A Case for Offshore Banking," *The Hindu*, October 5, 1998; and H P Aggarwal, "A Tax Haven Has its Good Points," *Business Standard*, September 17, 1999.

2. Ronen Palan, Jason Abbott and Phil Deans, *State Strategies in the Global Political Economy,* Pinter, 1996, p. 167.

3. *Financial Havens, Banking Secrecy and Money-Laundering,* UNDCP, United Nations, 1998, p. 28.

4. Ibid.

5. Ibid., p. 31.

6. Ibid., p. 29.

7. Luca Errico and Alberto Musalem, "Offshore Banking: An Analysis of Micro- and Macro-Prudential Issues," *IMF Working Paper No. 99/5,* IMF, 1999, p. 10.

8. Ibid.

9. Ibid., p. 14.

10. Ibid.

11. "Rum Sort of Banking: Drug Traffickers and Con Artists Vie in the Crowded Waters Offshore," *United States News and World Report,* October 28, 1996.

12. Ibid.

13. Luca Errico and Alberto Musalem, op. cit., p. 5.

14. Marcel Cassard, "The Role of Offshore Centers in International Financial Intermediation," *IMF Working Paper No. 94/107,* IMF, 1994.

15. Luca Errico and Alberto Musalem, op. cit., p. 16.

16. Ibid., p. 17.

17. Ronen Palan et.al, op. cit., p. 183.

18. R T Naylor, *Hot Money and the Politics of Debt,* Unwin Hyman, 1987.

19. Luca Errico and Alberto Musalem, op. cit., p. 36.

20. Ibid., p. 34.

21. Ibid.

22. Chaebol is a conglomeration of big Korean corporations.

23. *Financial Havens, Banking Secrecy and Money-Laundering,* op. cit., p. 20.

24. *World Drug Report,* UNDCP, Oxford University Press, 1997.

25. "Money Laundering: Cleaning Up?," *The Economist,* March 20, 1999, p. 86.

6

Capital Controls:
An Idea Whose Time Has Returned

IN an era where 'control' and 'intervention' have become synonymous with inefficiency and corruption, debates on the subject are beginning to suffer from severe buzzword fatigue. In this scenario, it is the need of the hour to re-examine some of the basic premises of neo-liberal policy and relate these to both economic theory and real world experiences. Capital controls, in this sense, provide an ideal setting for exploring the ramifications of the ongoing liberalization and globalization processes.

What are Capital Controls?

Capital controls may be defined as restrictions designed to affect the capital account of a country's balance of payments. Put simply, capital controls imply measures that restrict or prohibit the cross border movement of capital including restrictions on both inflows and outflows.

These would, in turn, include prohibitions; need for prior approval; authorization and notification; multiple currency practices; discriminatory taxes; and reserve requirements or interest penalties imposed by the authorities that regulate the conclusion or execution of transactions.[1] The coverage of the regulations would apply to receipts as well as payments and to actions initiated by non-residents and residents.[2]

Capital controls can be a combination of official, legal, and quasi-legal instruments. In the words of Jessica G Nembhard, capital controls

---

Box 6.1

Balance of Payments

Balance of Payments records the total movement of goods, services and financial transactions between one country and the rest of the world. The balance of payments record is divided into two heads, current account and capital account.

Current Account deals with the payments and receipts for immediate transactions, such as the sale of goods and rendering of services. It is further subdivided into the merchandise or visible account (also termed the trade account) comprising the movement of goods; and the invisible account, comprising the movement of services, transfers and investment income. Entries in this account are 'current' in nature because they do not give rise to future claims. The balance of payments on the current account is the broadest measure of a country's international trade because it includes financial transactions as well as trade in goods and services. A surplus on the current account represents an inflow of funds while a deficit represents an outflow of funds.

Capital Account deals with loans, investments, other transfers of financial assets and the creation of liabilities. Unlike current account entries, entries in the capital account indicate changes in future claims. It is further subdivided into long-term and short-term capital, the former relating to capital employed for investment purposes, the latter to bank advances, trade credit, etc. Long-term capital is again subdivided into direct investment capital and portfolio investment capital.

can be "legal restrictions, strictly or loosely enforced; bureaucratic restrictions left to the discretion or regulation of the administrative unit or agency in charge; or social, customary restrictions that are essentially 'gentlemen's' agreements or cultural mores between corporations, businesses and financial institutions, and the government."[3]

Capital controls can be quantity-based, price-based or regulatory. **Quantity-based controls** involve explicit limits or prohibitions on capital account transactions. Such quantity-based measures on inflows may include a ban on investment in money market instruments, limits on short-term borrowing, restrictions on certain types of securities that can be owned, etc. On outflows, quantity-based controls can take the form of an explicit moratorium. Malaysia has imposed quantity-based controls in September 1998. **Price-based controls** seek to alter the cost of capital transaction with a view to discouraging a certain class of flows and encouraging another set of flows. Price-based controls on inflows can take the form of a tax on stock market purchases, certain foreign exchange transactions, etc. Price-based controls on outflows can typically take the form of an exit tax. The imposition of capital gains tax in India is an example of price-based capital controls. **Regulatory controls** can be both price-based and quantity-based and such a policy package usually treats transactions with non-residents less favorably than with residents. An unremunerated reserve requirement is an example of regulatory controls on inflows. Reserve requirements can be imposed with differentiation between domestic and foreign currency to influence liquidity and to either encourage or discourage foreign currency deposits.

Jessica Nembhard has classified the entire range of capital controls into four distinct categories:

- Foreign exchange regulations (including exchange rate regime).

- Quantitative and tax policies.

- Investment and credit regulations.

- Trade (commercial) restrictions.[4]

Table 6.1: Categories of Capital Controls

Controls	Inward Movements	Outward Movements
Foreign Exchange and Exchange Rate Regime	Ceiling on incoming foreign currency; bank measures (reserve requirements on foreign liabilities, swaps between central bank and commercial banks, limits on banks' net foreign and net foreign currency position, restrictions on new foreign bank deposits, etc.); surrender of export proceeds, and/or any incoming foreign exchange.	Licenses for exporting currency and gold; licenses for owning or locally depositing foreign currency; import allowances; advance import deposits; bank measures (limitations on interest payments to foreigners, limits on banks' net foreign and net foreign currency positions). Multiple and special exchange rates.
Taxes, Surcharges	On incoming financial transactions; on earnings from residents' foreign investment earnings; on incoming direct foreign investment.	On international financial transactions; on remittance of dividends, principal and profits to foreign investors.
Investment/Credit	Direct foreign investment regulations (restrictions on percentage of equity, total amount per project, sectors allowed). Preferential allocation of and public guarantees on foreign credit; minimum maturity periods on foreign loans; interest rate restrictions on loans.	Restrictions on domestic firms' direct foreign investment and foreign lending. Credit controls (credit ceilings, preferential allocation, low interest rates or multiple interest rates).
Trade	Import tariffs; import licenses required.	Export incentives and subsidies; tariffs and licenses.

Source: Jessica Gordon Nembhard, *Capital Control, Financial Regulation, and Industrial Policy in South Korea and Brazil,* 1996, p. 12.

These categories of capital controls have different characteristics and are meant to restrict and regulate the inward and outward movements of financial flows (see Table 6.1).

Countries impose controls on inward and outward movements of capital to meet the wider objectives of economic policy, particularly those related to national development and macroeconomic policies. Controls on inflows are imposed to maintain autonomy in monetary policy. Controls on capital inflows include ceilings on investments and loans, capital gains tax, minimum period of stay and reserve requirements. Similarly, governments can put restrictions on foreign ownership of domestic assets and financial instruments. Controls on outflows are imposed when countries face dwindling foreign exchange reserves or to prevent speculative attacks on the currency. Controls on capital outflows include restrictions on citizens to own assets like stocks, bonds or property abroad. There are also restrictions (e.g., in India) on citizens regarding the amount of foreign currency they can carry abroad. Besides, countries can put limits on the amount of money that any investor can pull out of the country. In Thailand, for instance, investors were required to seek approval from the Bank of Thailand before moving any capital gains abroad till the early nineties. The use of differential exchange rates is another form of imposition of capital controls. For instance, in South Africa, a dual exchange rate policy was implemented during 1985-95 under which the authorities maintained a favorable exchange rate for foreign investment, called the 'financial rand,' and a less attractive rate for all other transactions called the 'commercial rand.'

Often, people tend to confuse capital controls with exchange controls. While capital controls include restrictions that only affect the capital account of a country's balance of payments, exchange controls include controls on foreign exchange transactions, both current and capital account. Exchange controls are meant to regulate the demand and supply of foreign exchange. Exchange controls are also associated with trade controls, as the latter cover the trade of goods and services, while the former regulate its financial transactions.

The type of capital controls in place will depend on the nature of financial flows and the institution through which the capital is flowing. For instance, capital controls on the banking sector will be different from the non-banking sector (e.g., capital markets), largely because of their peculiar characteristics and distinct regulatory agencies. Table 6.2 gives a listing of financial transactions that are subject to capital controls.

History of Capital Controls

Contrary to popular belief, both the developed and the developing countries have extensively used a variety of capital controls to restrict and regulate the cross border movement of money, credit, capital goods, direct investment, portfolio investment and other financial instruments. Although the types of capital controls and their implementation varied from country to country, it would be difficult to find any country in the world that had not used these at some point or the other. The significant decline in the use of capital controls (in both the developed and the developing countries) corresponded with the ascent of neo-liberal ideology in the late 1970s.

Capital controls were regarded as part of a solution to the global financial chaos in the 1920s and 1930s. Capital controls were widely used in the inter-war years and immediately after World War II. Given the fact that reconstructing economies and resuming foreign trade was the primary concern, most of the controls in the immediate post war period were associated with foreign trade. At that time, the basic link between capital controls and international trade was well acknowledged and the idea of cross border movement of capital through markets was almost inconceivable. During the post-war period, even the mainstream wisdom favored the imposition of capital controls. John M Keynes strongly advocated the use of capital controls to protect economies from negative external economic and political disturbances. The experience of the Great Depression led Keynes to argue, "above all, let finance be primarily national." He recommended that the use of capital controls be part of international economic agreements.

Table 6.2: Capital Transactions Subject to Controls

CAPITAL AND MONEY MARKET ■ Shares or other securities of participating nature ■Bonds or other debt securities ■ Money market instruments ■ Collective investment securities	INFLOWS Purchase locally by non-residents Sale/issue abroad by non-residents	OUTFLOWS Sale/issue abroad by non-residents Purchase abroad by residents
DERIVATIVES AND OTHER INSTRUMENTS	Purchase locally by residents Sale/issue abroad by residents	Sale/issue abroad by residents Purchase abroad by residents
CREDIT OPERATIONS ■ Commercial credits ■ Financial credits ■ Guarantees ■ Sureties ■ Financial backup facilities	To residents from non-residents	By residents to non residents
DIRECT INVESTMENTS	Inward direct investment	Outward direct investment Liquidation of direct investment
REAL ESTATE TRANSACTIONS	Purchase locally by non-residents	Sale locally by non-residents Purchase abroad by residents
PERSONAL CAPITAL MOVEMENTS ■ Loans, deposits, gifts, ■ Endowments, inheritances and legacies ■ Settlements of debts	To residents from non- residents Transfer by emigrants	By residents to non-residents Transfer abroad by emigrants
PROVISIONS SPECIFIC TO COMMERCIAL BANKS	Borrowing abroad Non-resident deposits Investments in banks by non-residents	Deposits overseas Foreign loans Investment abroad
PROVISIONS SPECIFIC TO INSTITUTIONAL INVESTORS	Limits on portfolio invested locally	Limits on securities issued by non-residents and on portfolio invested abroad

Source: *Annual Report on Exchange Arrangements and Exchange Restrictions*, International Monetary Fund, 1998.

In the negotiations for an international economic arrangement in the post-war period held at Bretton Woods, New Hampshire, in July 1944, the issue of capital controls was considered central to maintaining autonomy in policy making at the national level. The understanding that capital controls were necessary for autonomous national policy making was evident in both the UK and the US plans for international coordination. John M Keynes was the chief negotiator for the UK while his US counterpart was Harry Dexter White.

It is important to emphasize here that despite mainstream wisdom in favor of capital controls, the sentiments in favor of the free market approach to currency movements did not entirely disappear during the Bretton Woods negotiations. In fact, market liberalism was quite apparent when Keynes's proposal — which had the support of the UK Treasury and the Bank of England — that all currency be converted through official channels (i.e., through central banks) was rejected at the negotiations. Harry Dexter White and the US Treasury initially supported Keynes's proposal, but later changed their position largely under pressure from Wall Street. Given the strong US economic clout at that time and its key role in the negotiations, market convertibility became part of the Articles of Agreement of the IMF and attempts to control currency movements were further weakened by not accepting Keynes's proposal of official convertibility.

Similarly, no consensus could evolve on what kinds of controls would be appropriate, given the US animosity towards controls on the capital account. Consequently, a compromise was carved out with the establishment of the IMF, which provided freedom to its member countries to maintain or impose capital controls in order to achieve balance of payments and exchange rate stability. This understanding was firmly established in Article VI of the IMF which states that, "members may exercise such controls as necessary to regulate international capital movements," and the "Fund may request a member using its general resources to impose capital controls."

But the general approach at the Conference implied that member countries would progressively remove capital controls, as one of the purposes of the IMF was to assist in "the elimination of foreign exchange restrictions which hamper the growth of world trade." Nonetheless, maintenance of capital controls was not viewed as inconsistent with this objective because capital controls were considered necessary for supporting the system of fixed exchange rates and thus fostering trade.[5] Apart from establishing the IMF, the other key outcomes of the Bretton Woods agreement were the adoption of fixed, but adjustable, exchange rates; linking of US dollar to a gold reserve at a fixed price; and the creation of the World Bank to finance development projects initially in post-war Europe and then in the developing countries.

During the period 1945-60, capital controls remained largely unquestioned throughout the world as they contributed greatly in the achievement of two main objectives — an independent monetary policy and curbing destabilizing capital flows. The stable exchange rates accompanied by low and stable interest rates created positive financial conditions for long-term investment and rapid economic growth which occurred in many parts of the world. By 1959, 13 countries led by France and Germany dissolved the European Payments Union (EPU) and fully embraced the current account convertibility obligations outlined under Article VIII of the IMF.

However, with the establishment of the OECD in 1961, capital account liberalization became a part of international agenda. Article 2 of the OECD states that, "Members agree that they will, both individually and jointly... pursue their efforts to reduce or abolish obstacles to the exchange of goods and services and current payments and maintain the liberalization of capital movements." The member countries of the OECD (developed countries) were the first to remove capital controls over long-term capital flows in a decisive manner which was facilitated by its 'Code of Liberalization of Capital Movements' of 1961. Anticipating enormous benefits for its financial institutions and the TNCs, the US played a key role in pushing the removal of capital controls at the OECD. A detailed analysis of this Code is given in chapter 3.

Despite the OECD codes, removal of capital controls in the developed countries remained quite slow in the sixties. Although controls over long-term capital flows were gradually eased, policy makers were hesitant to remove controls on short-term flows. In fact, many member countries of the OECD either continued with their controls over short-term capital flows or further tightened them in order to pursue stable monetary policy. Even the US, a strong champion of free flow of capital imposed a variety of capital controls in the 1960s. For instance, the US introduced new controls in the form of an Interest Equalization Tax to curb capital outflows in 1963.[6] In a similar way, controls were also imposed by the US authorities on both short-term and long-term capital flows involving banks, portfolio investors and multinationals over the subsequent decade.[7] Germany too imposed a regulation called 'Bardepot' in the 1960s.[8]

In addition, the shortage of IMF funds coupled with the internationalization of the banking industry and the growth of the Eurocurrency market were important factors which led to the relaxation of capital controls in the late 1960s and the early 1970s. According to some estimates, the Eurodollar market witnessed a significant growth from $20 billion in 1964 to $305 billion in 1973. By 1973, a passive game of betting and speculating on currency devaluation turned into big business. A combination of these factors contributed to the collapse of the Bretton Woods regime and subsequent arrangements, perhaps the most significant systemic change since the re-establishment of the world economic order in the immediate post-war era. There is no denying that the Bretton Woods regime was troubled by some problems, and therefore, needed redesigning. But instead of rectifying the anomalies, the governments opted to dispense with the entire Bretton Woods system.

During 1971-73, the global financial markets were in a panic-like situation due to the collapse of the fixed exchange rates system and massive devaluation of currencies. This period also witnessed several negative external events such as the oil price shock and the subsequent global recession that precipitated instability in the international finance system. To mitigate some of the negative effects of these developments, capital controls were extensively resorted to by a number of developed countries during this period. During 1974-79, the role of capital controls was re-examined as a number of developed countries had abandoned fixed exchange rates in the early 1970s. Following Canada, Germany and Switzerland, the United States abolished all restrictions on international capital movements on January 1, 1974. Many other countries either floated their currencies or pegged it to a basket of currencies. Thus, the earlier strategy of using capital controls for realizing the objective of an independent monetary policy was abandoned by these countries.

A significant shift towards removal of capital controls occurred in the early 1980s when the deregulation and liberalization trend gained momentum in the developed countries. Dismantling of controls and regulations was considered a necessary precondition to usher in a new era of

Table 6.3: Controls on Capital Account Transactions (year end-1997)

	Total	Developing countries	Industrial countries
Number of IMF member countries	184	157	27
Controls			
Capital market securities	127	112	15
Money market instruments	111	102	9
Collective investment securities	102	97	5
Derivatives and other instruments	82	77	5
Commercial credits	110	107	3
Financial credits	114	112	2
Guarantees, sureties, and financial backup facilities	88	86	2
Direct investment	143	126	17
Liquidation of direct investment	54	54	0
Real estate transactions	128	115	13
Personal capital movements	64	61	3
Provisions specific to:			
Commercial banks and other credit institutions	152	137	15
Institutional investors	68	54	14

Source: *Global Economic Prospects 1998/99,* World Bank, 1999, p. 157.

market led growth. Financial deregulation and globalization were the essential objectives of this strategy. In 1979, the UK, which maintained comprehensive capital controls since the post-war period, took the lead when the new Thatcher government decided to remove all kinds of controls and regulations including capital controls. A year later, Japan also removed exchange controls. Subsequently, many other developed countries fell in line. Australia removed most controls in 1983. The Netherlands had adopted full capital account liberalization by 1986. While Denmark and France liberalized before the end of the eighties, Sweden and Norway liberalized in 1989 and 1990 respectively. By the end of the 1980s, there was a substantial decline in both the number and types of controls used by the developed countries. South Korea, which continued to maintain strict capital controls till the mid-nineties, removed these in 1995, as a precondition to become a member of the OECD. Needless to add, the move towards decontrol of the capital account was greeted with great relief by the international market players.

In Europe, the trend towards removal of capital controls gained further momentum with the adoption of the European Union's 'Second Directive on Liberalization of Capital Movements' in 1988. Despite the prevailing negative attitude towards the use of capital controls and the pressure exerted by the OECD and EU, some European countries (e.g., Spain, Portugal and Ireland) reintroduced capital controls for a short period in September 1992 to deal with extremely disturbed conditions in the European Monetary System.

Notwithstanding the dominance of the neo-liberal ideology in both the developed and the developing countries, the use of capital controls continues to be widespread (see Table 6.3). According to a recent document of the World Bank, most industrial and developing countries maintained some kind of capital controls at the end of 1997, mainly on direct investment (143 countries), real estate transactions (128), and capital market securities (127).[9] The number of developed countries with no restrictions on capital transactions increased from 3 in 1975 to 21 in 1995.[10] At present, only Luxembourg and the Netherlands have no capital controls among the developed countries while Armenia, Djibouti, El Salvador, Panama and Peru are the only developing countries which have completely dispensed with capital controls, states the document.[11]

On the other hand, the developing countries are found to be more consistent with the use of capital controls despite liberalization and deregulation of their economies — a process started in the 1980s and the 1990s. A variety of capital controls on both inflows and outflows have been used by the developing countries. For instance, conditions have been laid down for external bond and equity issues, and unremunerated reserve requirements on capital inflows have been imposed in Chile; limits have been imposed on domestic firms' issuance of securities abroad in Chile and India; limits have been put on banks' short-term obligations to non-residents in Indonesia; and capital gains tax has been imposed in India. Chile and Mexico have also widened the exchange rates band to increase risks for foreign investors.

In the fifties and the sixties, a large number of developing countries adopted capital controls in order to pursue a policy of import substitution. This trend was predominant in Latin America and Asia (e.g., Brazil and India) where a large number of countries adopted an import substitution policy soon after their independence. It is quite clear that without the use of capital controls, these countries could not have pursued an aggressive policy of industrialization through import substitution. The number of developing countries with neither separate exchange rates nor restrictions on capital transactions increased from 20 in 1975 to 31 in 1995.[12] China and India are still continuing with their erstwhile policy of controls on capital account, while Malaysia reintroduced these in September 1998 to protect its domestic economy from volatile capital flows. With the ascendancy of the so called export led growth strategy, based on the assumption of the reproducibility of the East Asian model, import-substitution as a strategy for industrialization took a severe beating.

Past experience of the use of capital controls in both the developed and the developing countries reveals interesting trends. Firstly, exchange controls have been more prevalent than trade controls. Secondly, a large number of controls are associated with the banking sector as compared to non-banking sectors. Controls on the banking sector, for instance, include putting limits on banks' net foreign currency position; reserve requirements on foreign liabilities; special provisions on central bank credit; limiting swaps between the central bank and commercial banks; and regulating interest payments to foreigners and new foreign bank deposits.[13] This is largely due to the fact that banks were dominating the global financial system till the 1990s. In addition, controls on the banking sector are relatively easy to put in place, as there are fewer players. The mandatory reporting by the banks on the compliance of controls further makes the task of regulatory and enforcement bodies easier.

Thirdly, over the years, there has been a marked shift in terms of preference over the types of capital controls, from the earlier quantitative restrictions to price-based mechanisms. The growing consensus in favor of using price-based mechanisms is largely in tune with the overall neoliberal and market-based approach towards financial liberalization and deregulation. Lastly, many recipient countries (for instance, Chile and Colombia) are increasingly in favor of controls on capital inflows, rather than on outflows. This preference is perhaps due to the fact that by putting controls on inflows, policy makers are able to prevent the occurrence of the problems associated with speculative financial flows, rather than allowing capital inflows to destabilize the economy. It is only in the wake of recent financial crises that developing countries have started paying attention to the destabilizing effects of 'hot money' flows.

Theoretical Debates on the Use of Capital Controls

Despite extensive use of capital controls by a large number of countries, the issues related to capital controls have not received adequate importance in economic theory. A large part of economic literature reveals a strong bias against capital controls.[14] This bias becomes explicit with the usage of an extremely harsh term, 'financial repression', by some economists to describe capital controls and other forms of state intervention in the financial system.

The argument that removal of capital controls will enhance economic efficiency derives from two basic propositions in economic theory — the 'Fundamental Theorem of Welfare Economics' (FTWE) and the 'Efficient Markets Hypothesis' (EMH). The FTWE deals with the efficiency of the real economy and presumes a perfectly competitive economy with no externalities while the EMH portrays that financial markets are efficient gatherers and transmitters of information. Together, they present a picture of economic efficiency being dependent upon free markets for goods, labor and finance, and a minimalist state. In these theoretical propositions, removal of capital controls (which by definition are contemplated as inefficient) is considered beneficial. Hence, a retreat by the interventionist state — under attack the world over — is a necessary prerequisite of this worldview which is in consonance with the neo-liberal ideology.

Conventional economic theories often tend to overplay the negative aspects associated with capital controls (such as evasion, corruption, etc.) while totally downplaying their benefits. These theories do not provide the tools to understand why a majority of countries in the world maintain some system of controls. Such analyses do not take into account the role of complementary policies, the reasons and purposes for their imposition, and the nature and role of state intervention. Further, the absence of class and welfare analyses in neoclassical theory restricts understanding about the use and effectiveness of capital controls as an integral part of state intervention strategy. Let us examine neoclassical economic theories. The neoclassical theories assert that capital controls are completely useless, ineffective and distortionary, and are used by rent seeking governments. Grounded on flawed assumptions that markets are perfect and financial and real assets are no different, the neoclassical theories conclude that capital controls cannot work. The ground reality is however quite different. The fact is that capital controls have been utilized at some point or the other in the modern history of almost every country, often for long periods of time and with success.[15]

In direct contradistinction to the theoretical positions, a number of empirical studies have reported the effectiveness of capital controls in controlling capital flight, curbing volatile capital flows and protecting the domestic economy from negative external developments.[16] The argument proffered by mainstream economists that countries with a history of capital controls have been less successful with their economies is backed by very little evidence. Rather, evidence suggests that successful economies such as Japan, Italy, France and South Korea have had success with long-term use of capital controls in conjunction with some form of national planning and development policy.[17] It is a misconception that economic success can only occur in countries with liberalized policies towards trade and capital flows. A study by Collier and Mayer found that economic development has occurred in the presence of tight controls on financial markets in the two most successful cases of the post World War II period, namely, Japan and South Korea.[18] Analysts have also pointed out that capital controls have been essential for the successful functioning of the European Monetary System.[19]

Although Keynesian theory recognizes the positive role of state intervention and use of capital controls, it considers them as 'second-best' solution. It justifies the use of capital controls as emergency measures to be used for short duration when the governments face specific problems. However, this analysis isolates capital controls from overall long-term government policy. Surprisingly, even the radical and Marxist economic theories have not adequately dealt with this issue. Jessica G Nembhard rightly notes that there seems to be a reluctance in the radical economic literature to take a direct stand in favor of capital controls and to spell out exactly what capital controls would entail in the financial sphere, how they are justified, what results to expect and why.[20]

The Rationale for Capital Controls

While making a strong argument against the use of capital controls and other forms of government intervention, an important issue that is often overlooked by neoclassical theories is that the consequences of financial deregulation and liberalization, by and large, have been disastrous. If too much government intervention in the financial system is considered ineffective, distortionary and expensive, too little government intervention or a rapid government withdrawal could also be problematic. Recent experience with financial deregulation and liberalization in many countries underlines this point. The occurrence of financial crises of various types in many countries (e.g., Chile in 1982 and Korea in 1997) were not the result of too much government intervention, rather, the opposite seems to hold true. These crises occurred because there was too little government regulation and supervision in the financial markets. In the case of Chile and Korea, the phase of sudden and rapid deregulation and liberalization of financial markets was immediately accompanied by increased capital flight, volatility and outflows thereby creating a severe financial crisis.

If effectively used as an integral part of a strategy of state intervention in conjunction with other complementary policy measures, capital controls can be beneficial to the economies in several ways. Some of the important objectives of capital controls along with their desired benefits are discussed below.

First and foremost, capital controls are the only effective and meaningful tools to protect and insulate the domestic economy from volatile capital flows and other negative external developments. This factor becomes more significant in the case of the developing countries and open economies that experience rapid capital flight, depletion of foreign exchange reserves and loss of autonomy in monetary policy in the wake of massive inflows and outflows of capital. Such countries, consequently, are unable to achieve the desired goals of economic development and increased national welfare. Sudden capital flight could lead to a severe balance of payments crisis, high inflation, decline in savings and resources for financing productive investments, and low economic growth. In the case of the developing countries, capital flight may fuel serious economic chaos as witnessed in many Latin American countries in the 1980s.

In the absence of capital controls, the authorities cannot pursue an independent monetary policy. Take the case of interest rates. Any attempt to change interest rates will bring undesired capital movements. If the interest rates are lowered in order to stimulate domestic investment, capital will move out to other countries offering higher interest rates. If the interest rates are kept high, domestic investment declines and a resource transfer to the rest of the world takes place. Whereas with the use of capital controls, countries can maintain differential interest rates, follow a relatively independent monetary policy, besides being able to defend their currencies from speculative attacks and devaluation.

Secondly, very few can disagree with the fact that capital is essential for development and some kind of social control over capital is not merely desirable but also critical for the enhancement of domestic savings and investment. With the use of capital controls, countries not only manage to keep domestic and foreign finances under national and social control, but also direct domestic savings (along with foreign borrowings) into productive domestic investment in accordance with their developmental plans. By restraining the private sector from investing abroad for higher short-term returns, capital controls retain domestic capital within national borders. This capital could either be used for productive or consumption purposes. In order to ensure that capital is used for productive purposes, complementary policy measures in the form of credit controls can be helpful. Credit controls provide tools to the authorities to direct credit to specific companies and sectors in order to promote economic development in accordance with their planned objectives. Capital controls, if used in conjunction with credit controls, can ensure that credit is created, accumulated and utilized productively. The best example of this approach is South Korea which maintained strict exchange and credit controls to fulfil its primary objective of planned development till the 1980s.

Several studies have also established that if capital controls are used in conjunction with credit controls and other policy measures, there is a substantial increase in domestic investment and government revenues. According to Jessica G Nembhard, the triad — capital controls, credit controls and an industrial strategy — can be successfully used in the developing countries to regulate productive investment, carry out industrialization, and to boost economic growth.[21]

Thirdly, capital controls enhance the bargaining power of countries to negotiate with their own private sector, foreign capital and multilateral financial institutions. Imposition of capital controls should be viewed as the beginning of a process whereby a country asserts its own right and ability to shape economic policy so that the ill effects of globalization and structural adjustment policies could be reversed. If judiciously used, capital controls can also become a vehicle to enhance the bargaining power of its citizens and the working classes. Particularly in the present context, when capital has become global and global capital mobility tends to favor the rich (both domestic and international), capital controls (e.g., taxes on global capital movements) can be useful to protect the interests of domestic labor. Used in conjunction with other policy measures, capital controls can be effective in achieving egalitarian economic development with better income redistribution, employment generation and increased public investment.

Fourthly, by influencing the exchange rate, the governments can maintain the desired level of foreign reserves and maneuver the terms of trade in order to protect domestic products from external competition. For instance, a country may devalue its exchange rate to make its exports competitive and to discourage imports. Alternatively, a country may overvalue its exchange rate to make needed imports less expensive. Quite often, countries have used exchange controls in combination with tariffs and trade controls. In addition, controls can also help a country to keep its real exchange rate relatively stable.

Fifthly, capital controls help countries to save foreign exchange for debt servicing, imports and capital goods. This has special significance for the developing countries whose foreign exchange reserves are relatively small. For instance, the removal of capital controls in Brazil led to a phenomenal increase in the remittances of profits, royalties and associated payments, from $73 million in 1993 to $8 billion in 1998. Similarly, the

Reserve Bank of India in a recent study covering 268 companies in the country, reported that the net forex outflows have increased by nearly 18 times between 1994-95 and 1996-97. Thus, granting unbridled freedom to the operations of foreign capital creates future payments problems.

Lastly, capital controls also help in generating government revenues through taxes, premia on controlled exchange rates, customs duties, etc.

In the present context, the use of capital controls becomes imperative because the regulatory mechanisms to deal with capital flows are national whereas the financial markets have become global. To protect economies from the vagaries of global finance capital, controls are the only effective tools available at the national level. This point has been stressed by the UNCTAD in its latest *Trade and Development Report 1998,* which states that, "in the absence of global mechanisms for stabilizing capital flows, controls will remain an indispensable part of developing countries' armoury of measures for the purpose of protection against international financial instability."[22] The Report further notes that, "capital controls are a tried technique for dealing with unstable capital movements."[23]

It is important to emphasize here that a transparent and accountable system of regulation and supervision is a necessary precondition for the effective use of capital controls. Otherwise, the tremendous potential for abuse of capital controls can make them ineffective as there are various legal and illegal means (including transfer pricing) to transfer capital. Moreover, hydra-headed evils like red tapism, corruption and black market are likely to take root in a non-transparent bureaucratic system, which can defeat the very purpose behind the imposition of capital controls. Therefore, it is imperative that a regime of capital controls is accompanied by a well-coordinated, rule based, transparent and accountable system of enforcement.

Recent Experiences with Capital Controls: Two Case Studies from Asia

In the aftermath of the Southeast Asian financial crisis in 1997, capital controls in Malaysia (which were reintroduced in 1998) and China have gained special significance. The following is a brief account of capital controls and their effectiveness in these two Asian countries. The use and effectiveness of capital controls in Chile and Colombia are discussed in the next chapter.

Malaysia

On September 1, 1998, the Malaysian government announced a series of policy measures in the form of strict capital controls on international trading and speculation in the Malaysian ringgit (RM) and stocks. These controls are designed to curb short-term speculative flows and their negative impact on the domestic economy while the long-term financial flows in the form of foreign direct investment as well as trade flows are not meant to be affected.

This is not the first instance in recent history when Malaysia imposed capital controls. During January-August 1994 too, the Malaysian authorities had imposed a series of selective, temporary controls to deal with discrepancies arising out of short-term speculative inflows. For instance, banks were subjected to a ceiling on their external liabilities not related to trade or investment and residents were barred from selling short-term monetary instruments to non-residents. However, these controls were gradually removed from 1995 onwards.

By imposing capital controls, the Malaysian authorities have now made it exacting for speculators to launch attacks on its currency, as they can no longer access the currency. The new capital controls include the following:

- The central bank pegged the RM exchange rate at 3.8 against the US dollar, about 10 per cent above the currency's recent levels.

- Offshore trading in the ringgit is banned. All ringgit held offshore had to be repatriated within a month, otherwise these would become worthless. Thus, from October 1, 1998, the RM held offshore has ceased to be legal tender. According to the government, the large quantity of the RM held offshore (unofficially estimated to be over $5 billion) was the major source of speculative trading. Transfer of the RM held offshore to resident accounts in Malaysia after September 30, 1998 required prior approval, and residents were no longer allowed to obtain RM credit facilities from non-resident individuals. The Malaysian stock exchange has also stopped share trading at the over-the-counter market in Singapore.[24]

■ There are strict restrictions on external accounts. Debits and credits into the external accounts (RM accounts maintained in Malaysian banks by non-residents), which had not been subjected to any restrictions, were henceforth subjected to the following controls: (a) payments for Malaysian exports can no longer be made in the RM from an external account; (b) funds in external accounts can only be used for purchasing the RM assets in Malaysia; and (c) sources of funding for external accounts were limited to certain specified transactions like sale of foreign currency, salaries, dividends, etc., or as proceeds from the sale of RM instruments, securities registered in Malaysia, or other assets in Malaysia.

■ Regarding payment restrictions, the RM would continue to be convertible for current transactions. However, residents travelling abroad can pay in foreign currency through their credit cards only up to a limit of RM10000; a resident traveler can carry a maximum of RM1000 and foreign currency equivalent to RM10000; and prior approval requirements are needed for payments by residents to non-residents for investments abroad in excess of RM10000.

■ Foreign institutional investors were required to keep the sale proceeds for a year, thereby discouraging short-term financial flows. However, in February 1999, the government replaced the one-year moratorium with a system of graduated exit tax that decreases the longer FIIs stay, in order to penalize short-term capital inflows.

In addition, interest rates were drastically cut to 8 per cent. In a nationwide TV address, Prime Minister Mahathir Mohamad justified the government's decision by making a severe attack on speculators and international fund managers. "There are a lot of things we can now do because we don't have to face their (speculators) actions to stop us. The free market has failed and failed disastrously because of abuses, not because the system is bad," he said. [25]

The fact that as a fallout of the recent currency crisis in the region, the Malaysian economy has gone into deep recession with negative growth in GDP cannot be ignored. In fact, Malaysia's GDP growth at negative 6.6 per cent during 1998 was worse than the prognostications made by many economists. Rising interest rates have had adverse consequences, such as increasing non-performing loans and reducing economic activities. The net non-performing loan ratio of the Malaysian banking system rose to 8.9 per cent at the end of June 1998 compared to 7 per cent three months earlier. A number of companies in Malaysia were facing bankruptcy. Malaysian stocks had lost almost 80 per cent of their value compared to early 1997, when the Kuala Lumpur Stock Exchange composite index stood at more than 1200 points.

Contrary to the apprehensions in the media that the expiry of one-year moratorium on the repatriation of portfolio funds in September 1999 would lead to massive outflows, only a nominal 10 per cent of funds moved out thereby signaling confidence in the Malaysian economy. The buoyant mood of the economy can be gauged from Mahathir's statement, "The (capital flow) controls have not done us any harm. They have not done anybody else any harm, except possibly the currency speculators. So we don't see any reason why we should drop the controls merely because we are doing well."[26] There is no doubt that by insulating its economy from the rapid developments in the international financial markets, Malaysia has, to some extent, restored its relative autonomy in the management of the national economy.

On the positive side, capital controls have given corporate Malaysia some relief as the country is struggling to move out of the deepest recession in its post-colonial history. Lower interest rates have helped throw a lifeline to companies struggling under heavy foreign currency debt. As a result, there is wide support for capital controls from domestic corporate houses. Further, these measures have increased liquidity in the banking system, making it possible to maintain a low interest regime. A series of reductions in the statutory reserve requirement of banking institutions (from 13.5 per cent to 10 per cent on February 16, 1998, to 8 per cent on July 1, 1998 and to 4 per cent effective September 16, 1998) have also provided a boost to liquidity. The foreign reserves of the central bank have also increased following the exchange control measures. Besides, earlier apprehensions that capital controls will result in flight of FDI, proliferation of illegal currency markets and corruption have proved to be without substance.

Some observers, however, are critical of the government program to bailout the politically connected private businesses in the guise of these measures.[27] They have questioned the bailouts of enterprises such as Sime Bank, Renong and Konsortium Perkapalan Berhad that are owned and controlled by people close to Mahathir's family and political party. They have claimed that many small businesses that had been seeking government assistance have not received adequate support. This is an important issue that cannot be ignored by the Malaysian authorities.

The 'breathing space' provided by exchange controls should be used by the Malaysian political leadership to restructure and democratize its economy. This cannot be achieved by bailing out selective enterprises close to the political establishment. It is of utmost importance to ensure the active participation of its citizens in economic decision making processes. Citizens should not be looked upon only as beneficiaries of these controls but also as central actors in the decision making processes. Attempts to protect the business interests of politically well-connected people may prove counter productive and expensive (both economically and politically) and could defeat the very purpose behind the imposition of capital controls. It is high time that the Malaysian authorities also address the issues related to its offshore financial center in Labuan, where capital controls do not apply at all.

China

Thanks to capital controls and non-convertibility of its currency, China not only managed to protect its economy from the contagion effects of the

Southeast Asian crisis but also managed to actually reduce interest rates during the crisis period. Despite the fact that exchange controls have often been abused and corruption has become more pronounced, capital controls still provide the country with policy instruments to deal with capital flows and its impact on the domestic economy. With the help of fixed exchange rate and independent monetary policy, the Chinese authorities have maintained financial stability. This is no less an achievement in the present context when the process of financial globalization has constricted independent policy making at the national level.

Although the Chinese government accepted the obligations of IMF's Article VIII in December 1996 and thereby made the yuan convertible on the current account, it has adopted a very cautious approach towards liberalization of capital account transactions. With emphasis on attracting long-term investment flows, the Chinese authorities have taken special measures to restrict and curb portfolio and other short-term speculative inflows. Capital controls in China are largely in the form of quantitative restrictions. According to Yu Yongding, the key elements of capital controls are universal requirement for registration, strict criteria of approval, tight control over the use of foreign exchange, and severity of the penalty for breaching regulations.[28] Based on his paper, some of these controls are summarized below.

- All inward FDI must seek approval from relevant departments. Chinese enterprises must seek approval from the Ministry of Foreign Economics and Trade and other departments before making investments abroad. Further, all inward and outward FDI must be registered. After mandatory registration and approval, investors can then open special accounts — foreign exchange capital accounts — at designated banks that are authorized to engage in foreign exchange activities. All investment incomes from outward FDI must be repatriated back to China within 6 months of the end of the fiscal year of the host country. Foreign exchange needed for business operations can be kept in the host country after obtaining prior approval of foreign exchange authorities.

- In relation to equities, foreign investors are not allowed to use RMB

(Renminbi) for investing in the stock exchanges inside China. They are only allowed to use foreign exchange to invest in mainland China in certain authorized shares that are called B shares. There are strict guidelines for Chinese companies in terms of listing their shares in international financial markets.

■ Issuers of bonds abroad are limited to 10 authorized window institutions for international commercial loans, Ministry of Finance, and state policy banks. The State Bureau of Foreign Exchanges has to approve the issuance of foreign currency denominated bonds. Chinese residents are not allowed to buy foreign securities. Barring special cases, money raised by issuing bonds abroad have to be repatriated back to China.

■ Chinese residents are not allowed to borrow from foreign banks and other financial institutions. They are also not allowed to open personal foreign exchange accounts abroad.

■ Trade credit above three months have to be reported and registered by foreign exchange authorities.

These capital controls have enabled China to build its foreign exchange reserves which touched $150 billion at the end of 1998. China also registered a $40 billion trade surplus and a $40 billion capital account surplus in 1998. With the help of capital controls, China has been able to keep off short-term capital inflows as 80 per cent of its external debt is long-term and 90 per cent of investments are in the form of FDI. Besides, foreign capital in China has, by and large, complemented domestic savings. Despite these positive features, there are serious shortcomings in the Chinese financial system. For instance, capital controls have been unable to stop capital flight that has taken serious proportions in China, particularly in the nineties. Estimates put the figure of capital flight close to $40 billion. This is a serious matter that cannot be overlooked by the Chinese authorities. It requires rethinking in terms of plugging the loopholes in the existing control regime and ensuring that bureaucracy remains efficient and accountable. Any complacency on the part of Chinese authorities can pose a serious threat to its financial system.

The Renewed Interest in Capital Controls

Gone out of intellectual fashion for over two decades, there is unexpect-
edly, a renewed interest on the question of capital controls. In the wake of
the Mexican and the Southeast Asian financial crises of the 1990s, it is
being once again realized that capital controls can serve as an effective
policy tool to deal with volatile capital flows. The arguments in support of
capital controls are gaining in strength.

Even the die-hard champions of free market ideology are endorsing
the use of some sort of capital controls. The new 'converts' include Jagdish
Bhagwati, Paul Krugman and Joseph Stiglitz. Bhagwati argues that governments should restrict the global flow of capital even while vigorously
promoting free trade in goods and services. Krugman advocates capital
controls largely as a stop-gap measure to allow Asian countries to adopt
more expansionary monetary and fiscal policies for promoting faster
recovery. While Stiglitz favors the use of price-based controls, for instance
those adopted in Chile in the 1990s, to discourage short-term borrowings
without affecting long-term foreign investments.

What is perplexing is the abrupt change in the position of the World
Bank on capital controls. It appears that the Bank has done serious
rethinking on this question in the aftermath of the Southeast Asian
financial crisis. No doubt that the Bank never strongly advocated the
removal of capital controls as its twin, the IMF did, but it had been actively
encouraging liberalization of capital markets in the developing countries
through its affiliate, the International Finance Corporation. In its report
titled *Global Economic Prospects*, the Bank advocates "... better and tighter
domestic financial regulation (and where necessary, restrictions on capital flows) to reduce excessive capital inflows, domestic lending booms,
and risks of financial crises."[29] The Report further notes that, "the benefits
of capital account liberalization and increased capital flows have to be
weighed against the likelihood of crises and their costs."[30] In other words,
the Bank has hinted at the dangers involved in maintaining an open
capital account and therefore is recommending the use of capital controls
whenever necessary. The Report also suggests that those countries with

weak institutional capability and financial systems should proceed carefully with capital account liberalization.

Nowadays, it is increasingly being accepted that capital controls are necessary and desirable. Given a strong political will, the governments can reintroduce capital controls and regulate capital flows, as witnessed recently in Malaysia. Although the task may appear difficult in the present global economic and political scenario, it is by no means unachievable.

While favoring the use of capital controls, one is not arguing that we should go back to the Bretton Woods system of fixed exchange rates and capital controls. Instead, we should learn lessons from the Bretton Woods system and try to emulate the positive features of the system while formulating policies and programs to regulate global capital flows. One of the notable positive features of this system was capital controls which facilitated the pursuit of autonomous economic policy, growth and stability. It is important to stress here that capital controls can only be effective if they are an integral part of the government's developmental plans and intervention strategy. Any wisdom which perceives capital controls as short-term, isolationist, and a quick fix solution to deal with the financial crisis is unlikely to succeed. As Jessica Gordon Nembhard aptly points out:

> capital controls tend to be most successful where governments are credible economic players — serious and specific about their economic goals and capable in their implementation — where plans are detailed and well coordinated, where restrictions complement the plans and each other, and the government and private sector cooperate.[31]

Given the fact that there is wider acknowledgement of the need for capital controls, the debate should move beyond the rhetoric that all capital controls are bad or all capital controls are good. Rather, the debate should be concerned with the wider context of economic development and planning, and therefore, should be centered on what kind of strategies, policies and regulatory controls are required to bring discipline in both markets and governments.

Notes and References

1. C Rangarajan and A Prasad, "Capital Account Liberalisation and Controls: Lessons from the East Asian Crisis," *Money and Finance*, April-June 1999, p. 34.

2. Ibid.

3. Jessica Gordon Nembhard, *Capital Control, Financial Regulation, and Industrial Policy in South Korea and Brazil*, Praeger, 1996, p. 10.

4. Ibid.

5. Natalia T Tamirisa, "Exchange and Capital Controls as Barriers to Trade," *IMF Working Paper*, IMF, June 1998, p. 4.

6. Interest Equalization Tax (IET) was introduced in 1963, with the effect of raising the cost to US citizens of investing in issues by foreigners on the domestic US capital market, US market interest ratios being at that time lower than in most foreign markets. The tax, introduced for the purpose of defending the US balance of payments, duly discouraged foreign capital markets. IET is generally regarded as one of the contributory factors leading to the emergence of the Eurodollar market. IET was withdrawn in 1974.

7. Jeffrey R Shafer, "Experience with Controls on International Capital Movements in OECD Countries: Solution or Problem for Monetary Policy," in Sebastian Edwards (ed.), *Capital Controls, Exchange Rates, and Monetary Policy in the World Economy*, Cambridge University Press, 1995, p. 123.

8. 'Bardepot' was a regulation requiring West German borrowers on foreign markets to deposit a part of the proceeds in a non-interest bearing account at the Bundesbank. It was introduced to deter foreign inflows into West Germany and thereby to contain West German balance of payments surplus. It was withdrawn in the 1970s.

9. *Global Economic Prospects 1998/99*, World Bank, 1999, p. 157.

10. Ibid.

11. Ibid.

12. Ibid.

13. Jessica Gordon Nembhard, op. cit.

14. See, for instance, Alexis Rieffel, "Exchange Controls: A Dead-End for Advanced Developing Countries?," in John Calverley and Richard O' Brien (eds.), *Finance and the International Economy*, Oxford University Press, 1987, pp. 1-19; and Susanne Erbe, "The Flight of Capital from Developing Countries," *Intereconomics*, September-October 1985, pp. 1-11.

15. Jessica Gordon Nembhard, op. cit., p. 3.

16. See, for instance, Alberto Alesina, Vittorio Grilli, and Gian Maria Milesi-Ferretti, "The Political Economy of Capital Controls," National Bureau of Economic

Research, Working Paper No. 2610, 1988; Paul Krugman, "Rationale for Exchange Controls," mimeo, 1987; and G S Lall, *Finance for Foreign Trade and Foreign Exchange*, H P J Kapoor, 1968.

17. Jessica Gordon Nembhard, op. cit., p. 13.

18. Paul Collier and Colin Mayer, "The Assessment: Financial Liberalization, Financial Systems, and Economic Growth," *Oxford Review of Economic Policy*, 1989, pp. 1-12.

19. Francesco Giavazzi and Marco Pagano, "Capital Controls and the European Monetary System," in *Occasional Paper: Capital Controls and Foreign Exchange Legislation*, Euromobiliare, 1985, pp. 19-38.

20. Jessica Gordon Nembhard, op. cit., p. 33.

21. Jessica Gordon Nembhard, op. cit., p. 5.

22. *Trade and Development Report 1998*, UNCTAD, 1998, p. xi.

23. Ibid.

24. "Desperate Measure," *Far Eastern Economic Review*, September 10, 1998.

25. Quoted in Peter Symonds, "Malaysia Erects Currency Barriers as Economy Plunges into Recession," International Committee of the Fourth International, September 4, 1998 (via Internet).

26. Quoted in "Malaysia to Retain Capital Flow Controls," *Business Standard*, October 18, 1999.

27. See, for instance, K S Jomo, "Malaysia Props Up Crony Capitalists," *Asian Wall Street Journal*, December 21, 1998; and Helen E S Nesadurai, "Accommodating Global Markets: Malaysia's Response to Economic Crisis," September 8, 1998 (via Internet).

28. Yu Yongding, "China: The Case for Capital Controls," paper presented at the conference, Economic Sovereignty in a Globalizing World, organized by Focus on the Global South, DAWN and SAPRIN in Bangkok, March 23-26, 1999, p. 2.

29. *Global Economic Prospects 1998/99*, op. cit., p. 135.

30. Ibid., p. 136.

31. Jessica Gordon Nembhard, op. cit., p. 58.

7

Managing Capital Flows:
The Case of Chile

CHILE is often cited as a successful example of restricting 'hot money' inflows in the 1990s — a period characterized by worldwide financial instability and crises. Since the Chilean experience has received considerable attention of many observers and policy makers, this chapter describes in detail the history, policy response, effectiveness and shortcomings of capital controls. Taking the experience of Chile as a test case, this chapter underlines the scope and limitations of capital controls. These controls, implemented as isolated policy measures, are unlikely to yield desired benefits in the long term. It is argued in the succeeding pages that financial regulations, and capital controls in particular, tend to be more successful where governments are credible economic players in their own right.

While highlighting the relevance of curbing short-term financial flows, this chapter probes the so called benefits of long-term flows. It delves into the misspecification of the terms of the debate as to short-term versus long-term investment in the interest of stability along with measures that could mitigate the volatility and vulnerability of the domestic economy, and argues that though restricting short-term inflows is no mean achievement, it does not follow that long-term inflows necessarily work in the interest of the host country. In fact, as in the Chilean case, they may turn out to be acquisitional and subjugative in nature, as evidenced by what follows.

History of Capital Controls in Chile

The debate on capital controls that ensued with renewed vigor in the aftermath of the Mexican currency crisis and the Southeast Asian currency crisis in 1994 and 1997 respectively, has led to a common but erroneous perception among many observers that Chile introduced these controls in the nineties. In fact, Chile had a long tradition of capital controls till the mid-seventies. Till then, the controls were largely in the form of quantitative restrictions. However, with the implementation of neo-liberal economic policies in the mid-seventies, the Chilean authorities replaced the earlier regime of quantitative restrictions with price-based restrictions. Price-based restrictions were implemented on two occasions in Chile — during the late seventies and after 1991. On both the occasions, capital restrictions were in many ways similar and took the form of unremunerated reserve requirements on short-term capital entering the country while a relatively open capital account was maintained to encourage capital outflows and long-term capital inflows. In order to understand the reasons behind the imposition and re-imposition of capital controls in Chile, it is necessary to examine certain political and economic developments that took place in the country since the seventies.

In the post-war period, Chile had a relatively closed and state run economy. Capital controls had been increasingly applied since the early thirties. The socialist government of Salvador Allende during 1970-73 strengthened this trend. With an emphasis on economic redistribution, the Allende government launched a massive nationalization program (more than half of the private commercial banks were nationalized) and adopted an import substitution industrialization policy (ISI) with increased restrictions on trade and finance. The government had complete control over foreign exchange transactions in both the current and the capital account and an estimated 85 per cent of the financial system was under state control in 1973.[1]

The overthrow of the Allende government by the military regime headed by General Augusto Pinochet in 1973, however, marked the beginning of a new phase in the Chilean economy. The Pinochet government quickly dismantled central planning and state led development and transformed the economy into a market led open economy. The earlier policy of ISI was abandoned in favor of trade liberalization under the banner of export led growth and the domestic financial system was liberalized with the authorization of new, unregulated financial intermediaries called *financieras*. Capital controls and restrictions on the banking sector were rapidly removed and interest rates deregulated.

With the macro economy firmly controlled by the 'Chicago Boys,'[2] the Pinochet government adopted an orthodox stabilization program with tight fiscal and monetary policies. Government spending was drastically reduced and public firms were hastily privatized. The budget deficit was cut from 24.6 per cent of the GDP in 1973 to 1 per cent in 1975.[3] The implementation of these drastic and unpopular measures by Pinochet's authoritarian regime was sought to be justified ostensibly by the avowed objective of curbing inflation — an aim which these monetarist privatization policies could not accomplish.

In 1974, the Chilean government took two major steps that significantly opened its capital account. First, it introduced a new investment law called the Decree Law 600. This law, based as it was on the non-discrimination between local and foreign investors, helped in liberalization and inflow of foreign investment. The Pinochet government was so determined to allow foreign banks to open subsidiaries and to allow foreign investment in commercial banks that it decided to abandon the Andean Pact that banned these measures. Besides, the government amended the Foreign Exchange Control Law which allowed non-financial firms to borrow abroad while severe restrictions were placed on banks and financial firms. However, the amended law allowed domestic banks to guarantee the foreign borrowings of non-banking firms that led to a massive surge in foreign loans to non-banking firms.

The implementation of these measures posed new challenges to the Chilean authorities who were finding it extremely difficult to manage the negative impact of capital inflows on the real exchange rate that could have derailed their new development strategy of export led growth. In order to deal with the situation, the Chilean authorities adopted a series of policy mechanisms in 1976. These included: mandatory registration of all capital moving into the country with the central bank; additional restrictions in the form of minimum maturities and maximum interest rates for foreign lenders who wanted to have access to foreign exchange; moratorium on loans with maturities below twenty four months; and imposition of unremunerated reserve requirements ranging from 10 to 25 per cent of the value of the loan with maturities from twenty four to sixty six months. The reserve requirements were to be deposited in the central bank for the complete duration of the loan.[4]

Deregulation of the Banking Sector and Financial Crisis

Till 1980, a major part of the capital inflows was associated with non-banking firms. The turning point came in April 1980 when the Pinochet government removed existing controls and restrictions (for example, a limit on the level of banks' foreign liabilities and the maximum amount by which banks could increase their foreign liabilities each month) on the banking sector thereby allowing the increased channelization of foreign funds by the banks. This led to a surge in capital inflows in the Chilean banks and financial firms even while the reserve requirement and quota for short-term loans remained in place.

In 1981, the process of deregulation and liberalization of the domestic banking system was taken a step ahead with the removal of restrictions on international financial intermediation and sanction for banks to open branches abroad. This led to a further weakening of the already fragile Chilean banking system that became apparent as early as 1976 when a medium sized bank, Banco Osorno, collapsed. Instead of drawing lessons from this event and adopting new regulatory and supervisory mechanisms or at least reverting to the previous ones, more deregulation and liberalization measures were prescribed. This could have only exacerbated the problem.

With an emphasis on *laissez faire* approach towards the financial sector, the Pinochet government paid scant attention to serious issues bedeviling the economy like the concentration of ownership of newly privatized banks. Compared with the situation when over 500 firms were under state control during the Allende regime, only 43 firms continued to remain under state control by 1980. Another factor which was generally ignored by the policy makers was the extent of concentration of capital in the hands of a few big industrialists cum bankers, who owned a large number of industries and financial (banking and non-banking) institutions. The system of guarantees resulted in a greater consolidation of the holdings of these large conglomerates, defeating the very purpose of regulation. Largely owned by conglomerates, the Chilean private banks were used by owners to lend to firms within the same group and shore up their balance sheets. It has been estimated that in some banks more than 40 per cent of the loan portfolio was concentrated in conglomerate owned firms.[5] A substantial part of the loans were used by the owners to finance speculative investments in real estate and to purchase state owned companies at a low price. There is little doubt that without the heavy influx of foreign capital, the much vaunted privatization program would have failed.[6]

A majority of foreign loans (over 80 per cent) was obtained by banks without government guarantees as the foreign banks had absolute faith in the policies of the 'Chicago Boys.' This faith was so strong that many foreign banks did not demand government guarantees in Chile, as they insisted in other Latin American countries. The 'Chicago Boys,' in turn, had unshakable faith in the 'invisible hand' of the market and therefore any kind of regulation was considered an anathema. As a result, the authorities refused to check the growing abuses in the financial system and overlooked the mounting foreign debt.

Simultaneously, a series of measures aimed at increased liberalization and deregulation of the financial system were taken. The central bank of Chile further liberalized the capital account, eased foreign exchange controls, abandoned the fixed exchange rate system and reduced the reserve requirements on short-term capital inflows. The cumulative impact of these measures led to a sudden spurt in foreign borrowings intermediated by domestic banks in Chile. Domestic borrowers shifted from peso to dollar loans to reduce financial costs. The progressive overvaluation of the real exchange rate resulted in a steadily rising trade deficit, which reached 6.7 per cent of the GDP in 1980 and 12.9 per cent in 1981, but this was financed without any drain on government reserves by enormous inflows of private capital.[7]

In the beginning of 1981, the overvaluation of the peso created problems on the export front and many firms were finding it difficult to cover losses through further borrowings, despite a sharp rise in interest rates. At the international level, there was a sharp increase in interest rates and the dollar — to which the peso was linked under the prevalent exchange rate system — rose against major international currencies. Anticipating a crisis, the foreign commercial banks cut off credit to Chile in 1982 and capital inflows fell sharply. As a result, the entire banking sector was affected adversely and a number of banks faced bankruptcy. Two banks, Banco Espanol and Banco de Talca, went bankrupt and were subsequently bailed out by the government. In order to reduce the speculative pressure, the Chilean authorities devalued the peso in June 1982, but this led to further deterioration in the financial health of many firms, which had borrowed heavily in foreign currency. By mid-1983, Chile was in the midst of a full-blown financial crisis. Thereafter, the Chilean authorities launched a massive bank bailout program, which cost the country (at present value terms) more than 20 per cent of the GDP.[8]

According to Sebastian Edwards, the Chilean scenario appears quite akin to the recent financial crisis in Southeast Asia, particularly in Indonesia and Korea, which shared identical features like volatile capital flows, reckless lending by conglomerate controlled banks, asset bubble, high current account deficit and poor regulation of the banking sector.[9] As aptly pointed out by him: "One cannot avoid thinking that, had watchers of East Asia studied the Chilean financial crisis of 1982, they would not have been so shocked by the turns of events in the Asian 'tigers.'"[10]

Unlike the previous two years, this time around, the shortcomings within the policy regimen were taken cognizance of, and the mechanistic understanding that viewed privatization and liberalization as a panacea for all ills in the economy was at least partially modified. In the aftermath of the financial crisis, the Chilean authorities realized the importance of prudential regulation and supervision of the banking system.

The Return of Private Capital to Chile in the late 1980s

Towards the end of the 1980s, private capital inflows began returning to Latin America. According to the United Nations' Economic Commission for Latin America and the Caribbean (ECLAC), net private capital inflows to Latin America were almost seven times higher in 1991 than in 1988. Chile was not only one of the first countries to attract these inflows, but it also received the largest capital inflows, in relation to the size of its economy. Among the five larger economies of the region, Chile received the highest private capital inflow as a percentage of the GDP in 1990 (7.2 per cent) and accounted for 15 per cent of the total private capital flows to the region in that year.[11] In 1990, Chile and Mexico accounted for 78 per cent of the total private flows to Latin America.[12] Total net capital inflows registered an increase from an average of $1 billion during 1985-89 to approximately $3 billion in the first half of the 1990s. Record capital flows were experienced in 1994 and 1996, when the inflows reached close to $5 billion.[13]

The return of capital to Chile in the late eighties and the early nineties was the result of a combination of external and internal factors. The main external factors were relatively lower international interest rates, particularly in the US (compared with higher and increasing rates in Chile); poor economic performance and recession in the industrialized nations; and a significant increase in global finance capital searching greedily for investment opportunities that could provide quick and heady returns due to globalization of financial markets and innovations in financial instruments. The domestic factors which encouraged capital inflows were: adoption of free market policies well before other countries in the region; sharp reduction in external debt through dubious means such as debt-equity swaps; elimination of existing capital and exchange controls; and more importantly, the continuation and legitimization of free market policies by the democratically elected government in 1990. Ironically, the new democratic regime was more committed to neo-liberalism than their authoritarian predecessors. Interestingly, liberalization rode on the back of both the authoritarian and the elected state structures in Chile. It seems as if there was an ideological continuity in the realm of economic policy! This is a revealing aspect of the political economy of development in Chile that merits deeper analysis.

In 1986, the Chilean authorities launched a massive banking reform program in which strict guidelines on banks' exposures and activities were laid down along with a series of supervisory measures. To strengthen the prudential framework of the financial system, the Chilean authorities also amended the General Banking Law and the Organic Law of Superintendency of Banks and Financial Institutions. In October 1989, the Chilean Congress enacted a constitutional law enshrining legal autonomy for the central bank of Chile. This law provided the central bank the mandate to ensure the stability of the financial system. Notwithstanding these new regulatory and supervisory measures, the core elements of Chile's macroeconomic policies during the 1990s have been: the increasing role of market; adoption of flexible policy instruments; extremely conservative fiscal policies; selective financial liberalization; emphasis on market self-regulation; and minimization of volatility.

Compared to the capital inflows of the seventies and the early   eighties, the composition of inflows to Chile during the nineties was quite different. Earlier, Chile largely received foreign credit, mostly in the form of syndicated loans from commercial banks. However, these flows dried up due to the onset of the debt crisis in 1982-83. In the late eighties and the early nineties, syndicated loans were replaced by foreign investments. As such, it included FDI, short-term credit, portfolio investment, long-term loans, and repatriation of capital held by Chileans abroad.

Initially, much of the capital inflows were associated with the debt-equity swap program launched by the Chilean authorities in 1985. The bulk of investments made with debt-equity swaps went into the processing of natural resources, especially forestry, pulp and paper, and into services.[14] In 1990, other forms of capital inflows became significant. The long-term capital flows in the form of FDI in Chile were largely concentrated in the export sector with traditional primary goods such as copper (which accounts for about 40 per cent of exports) and non-traditional primary goods such as fish, forest products, fruit and wine. Portfolio flows began in Chile in the early nineties and were largely in the form of bank lending. Initially, portfolio inflows were very significant and fluctuated between 2 and 3.5 per cent of the GDP between 1990 and 1993.[15] However, portfolio inflows fell sharply as a consequence of the control mechanisms adopted in the early nineties.

The Return of Capital Controls in Chile in the 1990s

With the return of private foreign capital in various forms, the Chilean authorities used a variety of restrictions. As mentioned earlier, the emphasis in the nineties was on market-based restrictions rather than quantitative restrictions which existed till 1973. In reintroducing these restrictions the Chilean authorities had three main objectives.

■   To encourage long-term capital inflows in the form of FDI and discourage short-term speculative capital inflows which makes the country more vulnerable to currency crisis through flight of capital.

Table 7.1: Tax Rate on Short-term Capital Inflows in Chile

Number of months	Tax Rate*	Number of months	Tax Rate
1	95	20	13
2	90	21	12
3	74	22	11
4	67	23	10
5	61	24	9
6	55	25	8
7	50	26	7
8	45	27	7
9	41	28	6
10	37	29	5
11	33	30	5
12	30	31	4
13	27	32	4
14	25	33	4
15	22	34	3
16	20	35	3
17	18	36	3
18	16	48	1
19	15	60	0

* According to maturity (in per cent).
Source: Annual Report, Banco de Chile, 1992.

■ To insulate the domestic economy from the impact of capital inflows thereby gaining greater autonomy in monetary policy.

■ To curb appreciation of the real exchange rate in order to maintain an overall strategy of export led development.

In order to move towards capital account liberalization, capital out-flows were completely freed by the Chilean authorities except for one regulation — a minimum waiting period of one year before repatriation of a foreign investment. On the other hand, new restrictions on capital inflows were introduced to favor equity over debt and long-term capital inflows over short-term 'hot money' inflows. Except for these restrictions, the capital account was fully liberalized as foreigners and local residents were given complete freedom to invest, purchase and sell foreign currencies. In June 1991, the central bank of Chile introduced three main restrictions on the capital account.

Reserve Requirement: In order to discourage short-term borrowing without affecting long-term foreign investments, the Chilean central bank imposed a one-year unremunerated reserve requirement (RR) of 20 per cent on new foreign loans. In simple terms, it meant that local firms in Chile which borrow abroad have to keep 20 per cent of that loan as a deposit at the central bank, without interest, for one year. After one year, the central bank would return the funds. Thus, the RR, which is essentially a price-based mechanism, acted as an implicit tax on capital in-flows, with the rate varying inversely with maturity (see Table 7.1).

In subsequent years, the rate of the unremunerated RR was increased and its coverage extended through several steps to cover most forms of foreign financing except FDI. From time to time, the Chilean authorities have adopted a flexible approach towards the imposition of RR and therefore it underwent several modifications since its introduction. Between 1991 and 1997, a number of modifications were carried out (see Box 7.1). Most of these modifications were meant to plug loopholes that had developed over time or were a response to developments in the domestic and international economy. The RR has been lowered or

Box 7.1

Reserve Requirement in Chile: Changes and Motivation

Measure	Motivations
June 17, 1991: A 20 per cent unremunerated reserve requirement (RR) on new foreign borrowing is introduced (to be held for up to 90 days for 90-day credits; to the maturity of the credit for 90 days to one-year credits; for one year for credits of more than one year). RR is in the same currency as the foreign borrowing, is not remunerated, and is applicable to all foreign loans to banks or others. Commercial credit is not covered, but a maximum period of six months is allowed for shipment.	Give greater flexibility to conduct monetary policy; prevent an appreciation of the real exchange rate; allow a higher interest rate differential; discourage short-term inflows and favor equity and long-term financing.
June 27, 1991: Borrowers allowed to meet RR by entering a repurchase agreement in which central bank of Chile sells and the borrower repurchases immediately a note equivalent to 20 per cent of the foreign loan. Central bank charges discount equal to LIBOR.	Repurchase agreement mechanism allows the tax to be paid up-front, which facilitates enforcement and monitoring.
July 1, 1991: RR extended to current borrowing that is renewed.	Close a loophole.
January 23, 1992: RR extended to foreign-currency denominated deposits by residents and non-residents held by commercial banks.	Close a loophole.
May 28, 1992: RR rate raised to 30 per cent, but in the case of direct borrowing abroad by firms RR is maintained at 20 per cent. RR deposit is to be held for one year for all	Raise cost only for banks, and unify duration of the RR due to difficulty of distinguishing loan maturity.

contd. on next page

borrowing regardless of the loan maturity.

August 19, 1992: RR is raised to 30 per cent for direct borrowing by firms (i.e., uniform 30 per cent requirement); deposit to be held for one year regardless of loan maturity. Discount on central bank notes is raised to LIBOR plus 2.5 per cent.

Close a loophole. Discount rate was raised to increase the cost of the implied tax.

October 30, 1992: Discount on central bank notes is raised to LIBOR plus 4 per cent.

Increase the cost of the implied tax.

November 1994: Starting January 1995, RR deposit must be in US dollars only.

To stop building open positions in domestic currency.

July 1995: Secondary market American Depository Receipts (ADRs) become subject to RR similar to those applicable to foreign borrowing.

Close a loophole (secondary transactions do not constitute a FDI).

December 1995: New foreign borrowing to prepay other loans exempted from RR.

Refinancing of current debt is likely to lower the cost and increase maturity.

December 1996: Foreign borrowing of less than $200000 (or a cumulative $500000 in 12 months) is exempt from RR.

Reduce administrative burden of enforcing the measure.

March 1997: Minimum amount for exemption from the RR is lowered to $100000 (or a cumulative $100000 in 12 months).

Close a loophole.

June 1998: RR reduced to 10 per cent to reduce cost of external borrowing (except for short-term credit, credit lines, and foreign currency deposits).

Adjustment to international capital market environment.

September 1998: RR eliminated. Requirement for foreign investors to keep their money in the country for at least a year maintained.

Adjustment to international capital market environment.

Source: Bernard Laurens and Jaime Cardoso, "Managing Capital Flows: Lessons from the Experience of Chile," *IMF Working Paper*, 1998, pp. 43-44.

increased in response to the prevailing market conditions. For instance, the reduction in the RR in June 1998 to 10 per cent was carried out to counteract the negative effects of shifts in the market sentiment on Chile's country risk premium which occurred in the aftermath of the Southeast Asian financial crisis. As the Asian crisis further deepened, the RR was ultimately eliminated to zero in September 1998.

Minimum Term Before Repatriation: To discourage the entry of speculative capital and to restrict the liquidity of foreign institutional investors, foreign direct and portfolio investments (except for primary and secondary American Depository Receipts[16]) were required to stay in Chile for a minimum one-year period. Malaysia adopted a similar mechanism in September 1998.

Minimum Risk Classification: Chilean firms and banks were allowed to issue bonds and ADRs, access global debt markets only if their credit ratings were of a minimum quality. In May 1992, financial and non-financial corporations were required to secure a favorable rating from the National Risk Classification Commission.

In subsequent years, many modifications have been carried out. For instance, in June 1993, the previous requirement was replaced by requirement to obtain from a foreign rating company a credit rating equal to or better than that assigned to Chile. In April 1994, the earlier requirements for non-financial corporations were replaced by the requirement that they be rated BBB, that is, 'Investment Grade.' In September 1994, the previous requirement for financial institutions was upgraded to BBB+. These measures had several effects. First, domestic corporations borrowing on the international capital market were forced to subscribe to the best-accepted international norms and practices regarding disclosure and accounting standards. Second, only sound corporations with a business structure that enabled reliance on external borrowing without taking excessive risks were allowed to tap international capital markets. Third, the requirement that financial institutions secure a rating higher than non-financial corporations prevented the poorly rated non-financial corporations from borrowing heavily from banks which relied excessively on external financing.

In addition, Chile also introduced prudential limits on domestic corporations borrowing abroad, which helped reduce external vulnerability. The authorities also introduced limits on outward direct investment by financial institutions. In particular, commercial banks, pension funds and insurance companies were allowed to invest only in foreign securities issued or guaranteed by foreign governments or central banks and private enterprises rated 'Investment Grade' by a foreign rating company. The measure was aimed at preventing deterioration in the quality of their assets.

In terms of exchange rate, the use of fixed nominal exchange rate was abandoned after the 1982 crisis. Since early 1992, the central bank of Chile had carried out active sterilized intervention[17] in foreign exchange markets to prevent undue appreciation of the peso. However, the sterilization policy was not effective as it helped maintain a differential between domestic and foreign interest rates thereby perpetuating capital inflows.

Another notable feature of capital account liberalization in Chile is the substantial foreign investment undertaken by Chilean companies and individuals, particularly in Latin American countries, in the 1990s. During this period, the total stock of Chilean investment grew from $181 million in 1990 to almost $10 billion by the middle of 1998. According to the figures provided by the central bank of Chile, in 1997 and the first seven months of 1998 alone, Chilean business corporations invested $6.1 billion abroad. This two way process of financial globalization has led to greater integration of Chilean financial markets with neighboring countries and the US.

The Effectiveness of Capital Controls

Though the debate on the effectiveness of restrictions on capital inflows in Chile during the 1990s remains unresolved, nevertheless there is an emerging consensus that these restrictions have helped in lengthening the average maturity of capital inflows. The support for Chilean type

restrictions comes from a diverse range of people and institutions including progressive economists, the World Bank and the IMF. Joseph Stiglitz,
former Senior Vice President and Chief Economist of the World Bank has
been a vocal advocate of these kind of restrictions. The Bank's report,
Global Economic Prospects 1998/99, commended the use of Chilean type
restrictions in preventing financial crises in the developing countries.

The sudden turnaround in the position of the IMF in recent months
when it started praising Chile for adopting such restrictions sounds quite
flabbergasting. The IMF's Managing Director, Michel Camdessus, in a
recent lecture remarked:

> Although Chile had long abandoned direct controls on capital out-
> flows, it has regulated short-term capital inflows flexibly, using mar-
> ket-based criteria. In this respect, it has given us all food for thought
> as we consider measures appropriate for external debt management
> in the current climate of international financial flows.[18]

The effectiveness of these restrictions in Chile is reflected in a number

Table 7.2: Capital Inflows (gross) to Chile *($ million)*

Year	Short-term	Percentage	Long-term	Percentage	Total	Deposits*
1988	916564	96.3	34838	3.7	951402	—
1989	1452595	95.0	77122	5.0	1529717	—
1990	1683149	90.3	181419	9.7	1864568	—
1991	521198	72.7	196115	27.3	717313	587
1992	225197	28.9	554072	71.7	779269	11424
1993	159462	23.6	515147	76.4	674609	41280
1994	161575	16.5	819699	83.5	981274	87039
1995	69675	6.2	1051829	93.8	1121504	38752
1996	67254	3.2	2042456	96.8	2109710	172320

* Deposits in the Banco de Chile due to reserve requirements.
Source: Sebastian Edwards, *Capital Flows, Real Exchange Rates, and Capital Controls: Some
Latin American Experiences,* Working Paper 6800, National Bureau Of Economic Research,
1998.

of developments. First, the restrictions significantly altered the composition of capital inflows in favor of long-term inflows. The data on the composition of capital inflows into Chile between 1988 and 1996 is given in Table 7.2. The Table clearly shows that there was a sharp fall in the short-term capital inflows after the imposition of these restrictions in 1991. Short-term inflows decreased from 72 per cent in 1991 to 3.2 per cent in 1996 while long-term inflows increased from 27 per cent to nearly 97 per cent during the same period. These variations support the view that the controls have indeed affected the composition of inflows. There is, however, no evidence to support the view that these restrictions had a significant effect on the aggregate volume of capital entering the country.

Second, these controls also helped in altering the short-term component of Chile's external debt. When the controls were initially introduced, the short-term component of the external debt dropped by 5 percentage points in 1991 (i.e., from 26.4 per cent to 21.8 per cent) but climbed back to about 27 per cent in 1992. It was only in 1996 that short-

Table 7.3: Evolution of Chile's External Debt

($ million)

Year	Short-term	Total External Debt	Percentage of short-term External Debt	Debt/GDP Ratio
1988	3462	18914	18.3	78
1989	4367	17645	24.7	63
1990	5027	19070	26.4	63
1991	3952	18116	21.8	53
1992	5496	20263	27.1	47
1993	5665	21364	26.5	47
1994	6497	24109	26.9	46
1995	6254	24559	25.5	36
1996	4356	24701	17.6	34
1997	3078	27639	11.1	35

Source: International Monetary Fund, 1997.

term debt fell below 20 per cent of the total external debt and in the subsequent period, it further declined. In 1997, the short-term component declined to 11 per cent (see Table 7.3). Data from the BIS on the maturity structure of Chile's external debt also support the view that capital controls have had some effect on limiting the short-term component of Chilean external debt. At the end of June 1997, loans with less than one-year maturity represented 43 per cent of Chile's total exposure to banks in the BIS jurisdiction — one of the lowest ratios among the major emerging market economies.

Third, these restrictions helped the Chilean authorities pursue a relatively independent monetary policy and they were able to maintain domestic interest rates that were higher than the international rates. The non-interest bearing reserve requirement substantially increased the cost of bringing in short-term capital, which in turn reduced the differential between external and domestic short-term interest rates. As a result, the opportunities for interest rate arbitrage inflows were drastically reduced. Without the reserve requirement, it was almost impossible for Chilean authorities to maintain a higher domestic interest rate without inviting the attendant inflow of avaricious foreign funds. In a recent study, two Chilean researchers have calculated the tax equivalence of Chile's unremunerated reserve requirement on capital inflows. They found that, as a result of these restrictions, for a 180 days loan the annual tax equivalence has fluctuated between 1.29 and 4.53 per cent.[19]

These restrictions also helped in minimizing Chile's external vulnerability in various other ways. For instance, the one-year time requirement for repatriation of funds acted as a disincentive for inflows into equity markets and thereby prevented the formation of a price bubble in the financial markets of Chile. Even the critics of Chilean restrictions would accept that this is no mean achievement, particularly in the context of developing countries where the formation of unstable and volatile price bubbles is almost an inevitable consequence of the rapid surge in capital inflows. Further, by not allowing financially weak corporations to borrow abroad and by placing a minimum risk rating on foreign assets purchased by domestic financial institutions, the authorities were able to reduce the possibility of a larger borrower defaulting and triggering off an external crisis. The risk of short-term illiquidity was further reduced, as it was mandatory for banks and financial institutions to keep a certain percentage of their foreign currency deposits in the central bank.

Lastly, the effectiveness of these restrictions can also be gauged from the fact that the Chilean economy, compared with other countries in the region, remained largely protected from the contagion effects of the Mexican crisis of 1994-95 and the Southeast Asian crisis of 1997. The country's ability to withstand these two major international financial crises of the nineties is no less an achievement in an era when the financial markets have become a major source of destabilization in the developing countries.

The Chilean experience highlights the need to have a flexible mix of policy tools. It is doubtful whether the use of a single instrument (e.g., reserve requirement or minimum risk qualification) would have deterred speculative capital inflows. While evaluating the effectiveness of Chile's capital controls, Manuel Agosin and Ricardo Ffrench-Davis observed, "a policy package, rather than a single policy tool, is desirable."[20]

Critical Issues

Despite the positive elements discussed above, there are, however, many drawbacks in the capital restrictions policy measures in Chile. A common criticism, which was also echoed in *The Financial Times*, that these restrictions were insufficient to totally eliminate the short-term speculative inflows, deserves serious attention. Despite heavy purchases of foreign exchange by the central bank of Chile, the authorities were unable to prevent a significant real appreciation of the peso, particularly during the period 1996-97 when the capital inflows were very large (over 10 per cent of the GDP). Hence, these policy instruments were of little help in achieving the stated goal of curbing the appreciation of the peso.

Critics of Chilean restrictions further argue that certain types of short-term capital inflows that are not associated with speculative invest-ment (e.g., trade credit) have also been penalized by these restrictions. Carlos Massad, Governor of Chile's central bank, has admitted the fact that there were many loopholes in the controls that were successfully exploited by the market players. "The fact that about 60 per cent of the capital inflow is free from the reserve requirement reflects, in part, a deliberate decision to exempt certain kinds of investment (such as for-eign direct non-financial investment) and, in part, the gaps in the regula-tion," confessed Carlos Massad.[21]

The issues pertaining to the 'durability' of these restrictions in Chile have not been given due attention. Are these transitional mechanisms or will they remain a permanent feature of the Chilean economy? For how long will these restrictions continue in Chile? Already, in the wake of the Southeast Asian currency crisis, the demand for foreign exchange in Chile had risen in 1998, and as a result, the currency band had to be lowered on several occasions. The large inflows of finance capital that had taken place in 1996-97 were giving way to outflows, and the nominal exchange rate had started to depreciate. Hence, there is a need to take a fresh look at the system and to assess the available policy options to manage financial flows in the future. Analysts are also pondering over the question of applicability of these restrictions to other countries. This is an area in which further research is required.

The Other Side of the Chilean 'Success Story'

The sustained economic growth and low rates of inflation coupled with capital controls and macroeconomic stability in the 1980s and the 1990s are often cited as indicators of the Chilean 'success story.' In the first half of the 1990s (1990-95), Chile achieved the highest average GDP growth rate in Latin America to the tune of 7.3 per cent per annum.[22] In 1996, the rate of inflation reached its lowest level in 35 years at 6.6 per cent. During 1987-96, gross domestic investment in Chile increased by an average of 13 per cent per annum.[23] The investment ratio reached a level of 27.5 per cent of the GDP in 1995-96, while the gross domestic saving ratio in 1995 was a staggering 27 per cent of the GDP. As a result, Chile has been successful in eliminating the savings gap and is therefore less dependent on foreign savings than other economies in the region.[24] For this reason, many observers regard Chile as a model for the rest of Latin America. Though capital controls and macroeconomic stability were the main factors behind the 'success story,' there were other important economic and political factors which played a role in attracting capital inflows, and therefore, any comprehensive analysis of the 'success story' should move beyond capital controls and macroeconomic stability. For instance, the Chilean Congress in 1996 ratified the association agreement with Mercosur, the South American free trade zone. A free trade agreement was also concluded with Canada which came into operation in 1997 and Chile is one of the more vocal supporters of the Free Trade Area of the Americas (FTAA) proposal.

Macroeconomic stability (e.g., low inflation, balanced budgets, stable exchange rates, etc.), in fact, tells us little or nothing about the actual well-being of the majority of Chileans in the 1990s. As in other parts of Latin America and in fact most of the postcolonial world, deep rooted social and economic inequalities exist in Chile. Inequality in the distribution of income has been accentuated. In 1989, the poorest 20 per cent of the Chilean population accounted for 3.7 per cent of the total income, a figure that fell to 3.5 per cent in 1994. According to the data provided by the Inter-American Development Bank, the average per capita income of the top 20 per cent in 1993 was more than 17 times the average Chilean per capita income. According to William Robinson, the Chilean 'success story' when seen as a variable isolated from a larger totality serves to mystify real relations of domination and inequalities.[25] He points out, "success and failures are not mutually exclusive; some have benefited and many have lost out from Chile's neo-liberal program."[26] There is enough evidence to show that the 'success story' in Chile has been beneficial for the Chilean upper and middle classes as well as foreign capital — a minuscule proportion of the economy — but has been a great burden on the majority of the Chilean population who have sunk deeper into impoverishment. In other words, the interpersonal distribution of the gains of the Chilean 'success story' have matched and perhaps strengthened the preexisting inequalities in the interpersonal distribution of assets and income.

Undoubtedly, capital restrictions coupled with macroeconomic and political stability in the 1990s provided much needed stability for foreign capital to operate freely in Chile. While the upper and middle classes indulged in voracious consumerism as the shopping malls in Santiago were filled with foreign goods thanks to the lifting of trade controls, 45 per cent of Chile's population living in abject poverty in 1990 was further marginalized and left out of the 'success story'. It is in this context that one has to situate the ongoing debate on the choice of long-term inflows over short-term inflows.

Short-term vs. Long-term Inflows: The Debate

In case of Chile (as also in many other recipient countries), there is a consensus among policy makers to encourage long-term capital inflows in the form of FDI and to discourage short-term capital inflows well known for their quick liquidity, volatility and destabilizing effects on the economy. The capital controls introduced in Chile and Colombia were meant to discourage short-term inflows. While supporting the need to curb short-term inflows, many critics of foreign capital — environmentalists, NGOs, peoples' movements — are equally skeptical regarding the presumed benefits of long-term inflows to the economy, local population and natural resources of the host countries. They argue that the cost of FDI is also high because capital can move out through royalty payments, dividends and various legal and illegal methods including transfer pricing. In Chile, profit repatriation alone was $755 million per year from 1990 to 1997.

The existence of abundant mining reserves is one of the prominent factors behind the surge in FDI in Chile. According to the statistics of the Foreign Investment Committee (CIE), mining activities (particularly copper and gold) received nearly half of the total FDI inflows during the period 1974-96. In 1997 alone, nearly 33 per cent of the total FDI inflows went to the mining sector in Chile (see Tables 7.4 and 7.5). Canada and US account for a large proportion of total foreign investment in the mining sector in Chile. In addition, there are significant FDIs in other natural resource processing activities including agriculture, fishing and forestry. In fact, a large number of foreign companies involved in this sector entered Chile in the late 1980s to take advantage of debt conversion programs. From 1985 to 1990, nearly 40 per cent of the total inflows of $3.23 billion, which entered Chile under Chapter XIX, were directed to the industrial sector (largely paper and pulp). In fact, what is most striking about the sectoral distribution of FDI in Chile and changes in it over time is not only the pre-eminence of the mining and primary sectors, but also the decline in the relative share of the mining (47 to 33 per cent between 1989 and 1997) and manufacturing sectors (22 to 10 per cent between 1989 and 1997), with gains in the share of electricity, gas and water (0 to 27 per cent between 1989 and 1997).

As a large part of long-term inflows to Chile went into mining and agro industries, analysts point out that the long-term negative impact of these investments, particularly on the livelihood of the peasantry and environment, have been ignored. They argue that foreign investment in

Table 7.4: Sectoral Distribution of FDI in Chile, 1974-1997
(Percentages)

Sector	1974-1989	1990-1996	1997
Mining and quarrying	47	47	33
Manufacturing	22	16	10
Shipping and storage	5	7	3
Electricity, gas and water	-	3	27
Agriculture	2[a]	2[a]	1[a]
Other services	23	25	26

[a] Includes agriculture, fishing and forestry.
Source: ECLAC database developed by the Unit on Investment and Corporate Strategies, Division of Production, Productivity and Management, on the basis of information from the Foreign Investment Committee of Chile.

the agri-business sector has led to the proletarianization of the Chilean peasantry and increased urban and rural unemployment. The historic dependence on primary commodity exports has dramatically increased in an entirely unsustainable fashion.[27] Overexploitation of maritime resources has led to extinction of many marine species. As timber reserves have been depleted, overexploitation has triggered a dangerous cyclical process that could ultimately culminate in a severe ecological disaster — rapid soil depletion, decrease in precipitation and an incipient process of desertification.[28] On the other hand, much of the wealth produced in the export sector is going abroad through profit remittances because controls on the outflows have been totally eliminated.

It is an established fact that a substantial amount of long-term capital inflows have not gone into greenfield projects but for taking control of Chilean assets through debt conversion programs in the 1980s and privatization of the few remaining state enterprises in the 1990s. According to a recent report by ECLAC, nearly 40 per cent of FDI in 1997 went into mergers and acquisitions in Chile.[29] Through mergers and acquisitions, foreign companies are increasing their presence in the domestic market, particularly in financial services. Recent examples include the purchase

Table 7.5: Foreign Investment in Chile, 1997

($ million)

Sector	Amount
Mining	1627
Electricity, gas and water	1378
Other services[a]	1487
Other sectors[b]	54
Total FDI under Decreee Law 600	5041

[a] Includes merchandising, construction, transport and communications.

[b] Includes agriculture, fishing, forestry, construction, transport and communications.

Source: ECLAC database developed by the Unit on Investment and Corporate Strategies, Division of Production, Productivity and Management, on the basis of information from Foreign Investment Committee of Chile, the Manufacturers' Association and financial publications.

Box 7.2

Colombia: Following the Footsteps of Chile

Colombia, following the experience of Chile, introduced capital controls in 1993. In both countries, the restrictions were market-based rather than quantitative and in both the cases restrictions on capital movements acted as an implicit tax on foreign financing. While maintaining a fairly open capital account and liberal policy towards long-term inflows, the policy makers in both the countries introduced these restrictions to negate the impact of capital inflows on the appreciation of their exchange rate. Thanks to these controls, both countries have been able to alter the maturity composition of capital inflows.

Historically, Colombia has also had a long tradition of capital controls as it maintained a very strict capital control regime between 1967 and 1991. However, with the implementation of structural adjustment program in 1990, Colombia shifted to a neo-liberal economic policy regime with drastic changes in the areas of trade, labor, foreign investment and financial markets. It was during this period that the Colombian authorities started removing restrictions on the capital account.

Private capital inflows rose sharply in Colombia in the early 1990s in response to tax amnesty, financial liberalization and higher interest rates.[31] Initially, the Colombian authorities responded by a policy of sterilized intervention, which had become the most popular policy response to deal with rapid capital inflows to Latin America, in order to avoid a real appreciation of the peso. However, due to the continued increase in capital inflows and resulting appreciation of the peso, the Colombian authorities abandoned the sterilization intervention policy and replaced it with price-based restrictions. In 1991, withholding taxes were introduced on transfers and non-financial private service income in Colombia. The rate, initially 3 per cent in April 1991, was later increased to 10 per cent in July 1992. This instrument acted as a disincentive to capital inflows. The imposition of withholding taxes on current account transactions discouraged agents to use service transactions and transfers for capital movements. However,

contd. on next page

some quantitative restrictions on capital flows remained in place till 1993. For instance, the domestic use of foreign loans and their maturity was regulated until 1993 along the same lines that prevailed since 1967.

In September 1993, the central bank adopted a one-year 47 per cent unremunerated reserve requirement on all foreign loans with maturities of less than 18 months. The mechanism was based on certificates issued by the monetary authority, denominated in foreign exchange and redeemable in domestic currency after a 12-month lock-in period. Despite this, the authorities were unable to curb short-term capital flows, and therefore, they extended the reserve requirement to loans with maturities below 36 months in March 1994. Further, in August 1994, the central bank extended unremunerated deposits to all foreign loans of less than 5 years. This time, a decreasing reserve ratio was adopted with a holding period identical to the maturity of the loan. For instance, it was 140 per cent for loans with maturities less than 1 month; 88 per cent for 24 months; and 43 per cent for loans with maturities of 60 months (see Table on page 176). Studies have shown that the unremunerated deposits have been successful in inducing a re-composition of foreign liabilities in favor of long-term maturities.[32] FDI and other long-term capital rose from $1.6 billion in 1993 to $4.5 billion in 1994 while short-term private capital inflows declined to $0.1 billion from $0.9 billion.

In addition, the maximum period of payment for imports without incurring a deposit requirement was shortened to four months from six months. Rules for foreign borrowing for real estate purposes were tightened in March 1994, when the minimum maturity of such loans was raised from two to three years, whereas in August 1994 all borrowing related to real estate transactions was prohibited.[33] Another notable feature of the Colombian restrictions is its banking regulation that limits foreign exchange exposure by forcing bank borrowings in US dollars to be re-lent in dollars.

Since 1996, these restrictions have been partially relaxed because of the declining pressure from short-term inflows. In February 1996, reserve ratios were reduced while loans with maturities of more than 4 years were exempted from unremunerated deposits. In March 1996, the exemptions

contd. on next page

Tax Rate on Short-term Capital Inflows in Colombia

Number of months	Tax Rate*	Number of months	Tax Rate
1	140	20	96
2	137	21	94
3	135	22	92
4	132	23	90
5	129	24	88
6	127	25	86
7	123	26	85
8	122	27	83
9	119	28	80
10	117	29	78
11	115	30	77
12	112	31	75
13	110	32	74
14	108	33	73
15	106	34	72
16	104	35	71
17	102	36	69
18	100	48	56
19	98	60	43

* According to maturity (in per cent).
Source: Annual Report, Banco de la Republica, Colombia, 1994.

contd. on next page

were extended to maturities of more than 3 years and a flat deposit rate of 50 per cent was adopted for foreign loans under 3 years of maturity.

In January 1997, the Colombian government declared an economic emergency in response to the deterioration in public finances and the astounding influx of foreign funds. The emergency measures were meant to make foreign borrowing more expensive and to boost fiscal revenues. In March 1997, however, the Constitutional Court struck down these emergency measures and the Banco de la Republica immediately proceeded to extend the 50 per cent legal reserve requirement to apply to all foreign credit having a maturity of less than 60 months. Despite these measures, the country continued to accumulate foreign exchange, and therefore, in May 1997 the Banco de la Republica imposed a 30 per cent deposit requirement on all foreign borrowing operations. A large number of exemptions, for instance, on import of capital goods and short-term loans were granted. It seems likely that these exemptions were misused, which in turn, restricted the effectiveness of the measures. Nevertheless, many analysts view these restrictions as successful, particularly in discouraging short-term flows and improving the term structure of total capital flows.[34]

The fact that the contagion effects of the Mexican crisis of 1994-95 and the Southeast Asian crisis of 1997, by and large, have less impacted both Chile and Colombia cannot be ignored by the critics of these restrictions. However, the long-term effectiveness of these measures is questionable. Since the beginning of 1999, the peso has been under sharp speculative attack and this has depleted Colombia's forex reserves. As a result, the Colombian authorities had to devalue the peso on June 28, 1999, to avoid further depletion. The authorities have also widened the band from a maximum of 14 per cent to 20 per cent. The country is facing an unprecedented debt crisis that consumes about 36 per cent of the national budget. The economy is facing the worst recession in the last 70 years with thousands of companies and small businesses going bust. With unemployment soaring over 20 per cent, there is tremendous backlash against neo-liberal policies pursued by the Colombian government, particularly among the working class and the peasantry. It is high time that the authorities reconsider their commitment to the present policies and give due emphasis to the role of government in steering the economy.

of Banco Osorno by Banco Santander resulting in the creation of the largest bank in Chile; acquisitions of Banco de Santiago and Cruz Blanca Seguros de Vida; sale of a 40 per cent share in Seguros La Construccion to a UK-based firm Royal and Sun Alliance for $122 million; and the sale of a 50 per cent share of Inversiones Previsionales to Citicorp for $80 million.

This trend has gained momentum in recent times and 79 per cent of the funds committed to mergers and acquisitions of Chilean companies came from foreign companies in the first six months of 1998. Of the total $4.2 billion FDI inflows in the first eight months of 1998, 66 per cent correspond to the acquisition of local companies by foreign companies, 12 per cent to privatization of state owned enterprises, 11 per cent to expansions and a mere 11 per cent to greenfield investment. Most prominent among the recent acquisitions are the purchase of the Prosan company (toiletries and hygiene products) by a US-based company, Procter and Gamble for $375 million; the takeover of Banco BHIF by BBV of Spain with an investment of $350 million; the acquisition of the food company Dos en Uno by the Argentine firm Arcor for $200 million; the acquisition of Enersis holding company by Endesa-Espana of Spain for $1179 million; purchase of Embotelladora Andina by Coca-Cola Corporation (US) for $98 million; purchase of Cruz Blanca Seguros de Vida S A by Netherlands-based ING Latin American Holdings for $125 million; acquisition of EMEL by US-based Power Market Development Company (PMDC) for $119 million, etc.[30]

The fact that a major share of the long-term inflows has gone into exploitation of Chilean natural resources as well as acquisition of its public and private sector companies underlines the aims of this capital — what is referred in the literature as the process of primitive accumulation and subjugation. Therefore, it is an opportune time to critically analyze the issues raised by the Chilean experience and move beyond the debate on short-term versus long-term capital inflows.

Notes and References

1. Raul Laban and Felipe Larrain B, "The Chilean Experience with Capital Mobility," in Barry P Bosworth, Rudiger Dornbusch, Raul Laban (eds.), *The Chilean Economy: Policy Lessons and Challenges*, The Brookings Institution, 1994. p. 154.

2. The appellation 'Chicago Boys' refers to a group of Chilean economists, drawn from the upper classes and recruited mostly from the conservative Catholic University of Santiago, who were sent to the University of Chicago to study economics under monetarists such as Milton Friedman and Arnold Hargberger. On their return from Chicago where they familiarized themselves with free market ideology, they were appointed to key positions in the government.

3. Barry P Bosworth et al., op. cit., p. 5.

4. Sebastian Edwards, *Capital Flows, Real Exchange Rates, and Capital Controls: Some Latin American Experiences*, Working Paper 6800, National Bureau of Economic Research, 1998, p. 39.

5. Ibid., p. 41.

6. Sue Branford and Bernardo Kucinski, *The Debt Squads, The US, the Banks and Latin America*, Zed Books, 1988, p. 87.

7. Barry P Bosworth et al., op. cit., p. 8.

8. Sebastian Edwards, op. cit., p. 42.

9. Ibid.

10. Ibid.

11. Raul Laban and Felipe Larrain B, *The Return of Private Capital to Chile in the 1990s: Causes, Effects, and Policy Reactions*, Development Discussion Paper No. 627, Harvard Institute for International Development, March 1998, p. 6.

12. Ibid., p. 7.

13. Ibid., p. 8.

14. Manuel R Agosin and Ricardo Ffrench-Davis, "Managing Capital Inflows in Chile," paper presented at DESA meeting of an Expert Group in New York, United Nations, July 22-24, 1998, p. 6.

15. Ibid., p. 3.

16. ADRs are certificates issued by a US bank to a member of the US public who has bought shares in a non-US-based company in a foreign currency. These certificates are denominated in US dollars and can be traded on the US stock markets.

17. Sterilized intervention refers to those interventions in the foreign exchange market by central bank in which the change in the monetary base caused by foreign exchange intervention is offset by open market operations involving domestic assets.

18. Remarks by Michel Camdessus at the Round Table organized by the Government of Chile on "Institutions and the Market in the Era of Globalization," Paris, March 14, 1999.

19. Salvador Valdes-Prieto and Marcelo Soto, "New Selective Capital Controls in Chile: Are they Effective," Working Paper, Catholic University of Chile, 1996.

20. Manuel R Agosin and Ricardo Ffrench-Davis, op. cit., p. 24.

21. Carlos Massad, "The Liberalization of the Capital Account: Chile in the 1990s," in *Should the IMF Pursue Capital-Account Convertibility?*, Essays in International Finance No. 207, Princeton University, 1998, p. 44.

22. Hartmut Sangmeister, "Is Chile a Model for Latin America?: A Comparative Analysis of the Economic Reforms in Argentina, Brazil and Chile," *Economics*, Volume 58, 1998, p. 123.

23. Ibid.

24. Ibid., p. 124.

25. William I Robinson, *Promoting Polyarchy: Globalization, US Intervention, and Hegemony*, Cambridge University Press, 1998, p. 199.

26. Ibid.

27. Ibid., p. 198.

28. Ibid.

29. *Foreign Investment in Latin America and the Caribbean: 1998 Report*, ECLAC, 1998, p. 109.

30. Ibid., p. 119.

31. Peter J Quirk and Owen Evans, *Capital Account Convertibility: Review of Experience and Implications for IMF Policies*, Occasional Paper 131, IMF, 1995, p. 40.

32. Mauricio Cardenas and Felipe Barrera, "On the Effectiveness of Capital Controls: The Experience of Colombia during the 1990s," *Journal of Development Economics*, Volume 54, 1997.

33. Peter J Quirk and Owen Evans, op. cit, p. 41.

34. See Stephany Griffth-Jones, "Stabilising Capital Flows to Developing Countries," *IDS Bulletin*, Vol. 30, No. 1, 1999, p. 39.

8

Whither International Financial Architecture

IT is being widely accepted that the present international financial system (or rather 'non-system') warrants a fresh appraisal primarily to contain the increasing tide of financial instability and volatility at the global scale. The recurring financial crises in both the developed and the developing countries have foregrounded the need for reform of the international financial system, often termed as the 'international financial architecture.' It is high time that the governments and the international institutions put this issue on top of their agenda. It needs to be emphasized here that the demand for the reform of the global financial system antedates to the eighties, when the debt crisis was at its peak. Since then, several progressive economists have been advocating a complete restructuring of the unregulated international financial system. However, their concerns and alternative proposals towards building a more transparent, rule-based and accountable global financial system were dubbed as biased, non-pragmatic and ideologically driven. As the tenets of the Washington Consensus held sway in the late eighties and the early nineties, the G-7 countries, international financial institutions and the neo-liberal think tanks outrightly rejected any system of regulation on financial markets and cross border flow of capital. However, recent events, particularly the Mexican and the Southeast Asian currency crises coupled with the collapse of some of the prominent financial institutions (like the Barings and the ₵TCM) have underlined the acute necessity of reform of the free market global financial system.

In the aftermath of the Southeast Asian financial crisis, a score of blueprints to reform the global financial architecture have been put forward. Some point to the need for repairing the cracks in the present architecture (like greater emphasis on transparency and better macroeconomic policies) while others suggest a complete redesigning including the abolition of the IMF and re-imposition of capital controls. Yet, some others advocate a return to the Bretton Woods system.

A detailed review of the merits and demerits of each and every blueprint is beyond the scope of this book, as it would require a separate volume, a few are certainly worth mention. Proposals to reform global financial architecture have not only originated from the initiatives of individual nation states but have also been complemented by clubs of nations such as the G-7, G-22 and G-20 as well as the international institutions such as the IMF, the BIS and the UN.[1] The list comprising non-official proposals is quite exhaustive as many economists (Barry Eichengreen among others) and institutions (the US-based Council on Foreign Relations, for instance) have put forth alternative plans. One common strand that binds official and non-official proposals relates to the recognition of inherent instability of the present global financial architecture. While there is general consensus on the desirability of reforming the global financial architecture, there seems to be no unanimity on the nature of reforms and their feasibility. In any case, restructuring of global financial system does not seem to be an easy task, since the obstacles hindering the regulation of global financial flows are primarily political in nature, and not technical or administrative.

George Soros in an article published in the *Financial Times* on December 31, 1997, proposed that an International Credit Insurance Corporation be set up to supply loan guarantees. A number of economists including Jane D'Arista and Jeffrey Garten have advocated the need for establishing an international central bank, while John Eatwell and Lance Taylor have favored the creation of a new multilateral international institution — World Finance Authority — having wide-ranging executive functions.[2] The World Finance Authority, according to its proponents, can act as a forum to not only enact rules for facilitating international financial cooperation but to oversee their eventual implementation as well. The proposed Authority, the authors argue, should have the power to monitor and regulate the activities of international banks, currency traders, and fund managers.

A number of proposals have emphasized the need to reform the IMF. Two of the former US Secretaries of Treasury, namely, George Schultz and William Simon, along with Walter Wriston, a former CEO of Citibank, have termed the IMF as an "ineffective, unnecessary and obsolete" institution.[3] George Soros, in this regard, has proposed that the IMF should be converted into an international central bank. Sebastian Edwards, on the other hand, feels that the IMF should be divided into three separate bodies. Tony Blair and Gordon Brown while asking for greater openness and accountability in the functioning of the IMF and the World Bank, have urged for a new Bretton Woods type meeting to consider radical reforms of these institutions.[4]

Official proposals, particularly those put forward by the IMF, G-7, G-10 and G-22, place extra emphasis on macroeconomic stability and transparency. However, macroeconomic stability, by itself, may not be sufficient to protect the domestic economies from speculative attacks, as amply demonstrated by the recent financial crises. As to the question of transparency, there is no denying the fact that a system of disclosure of information in terms of better quality and timeliness is highly desirable. What is not understandable is that while the principle of transparency is being extended to the official sector with great fervor, no attention seems to have been paid to demand greater disclosure and transparency standards on the part of major market players. It would be worthwhile to extend the principle of transparency to all market participants and international financial institutions that matter in the global financial system. It is naive to believe that financial crises can be dealt with transparency alone. Financial crises of various types have occurred in several countries in the 1990s (e.g., the UK, Sweden and Norway) in spite of stringent disclosure standards. As a matter of fact, it must not be forgotten that 'Black Monday' (when the global stock markets crashed on October 19, 1987) took place while there was no dearth of relevant information. Notwithstanding the adoption of greater disclosure standards, information asymmetry continues to rock financial markets as exemplified in the case of Barings and Orange County.

The Guiding Principles

Any attempt to restructure the present international financial architecture presupposes a set of guiding principles under which several specific steps could be initiated to achieve the desired results. It also requires an understanding of what kinds of reforms are desirable and feasible in the present context. Just as a domestic market is governed by certain rules of the game, a similar set of rules is needed to govern global financial markets. In order to promote a better rule-based international financial system, a few important principles are outlined here.

First, it has to be admitted that there is no single solution to resolve the myriad problems faced by the financial world. As no single measure can resolve all the problems, a combination of measures is required at various levels to reform the present financial architecture. The growing complexity in the working of financial markets (for instance, derivatives) has to be properly understood. It requires a new perspective to look at financial markets in which big financial players (other than the banks) play a major role.

Second, the strategic role of nation states and coordination among them to reduce the economic and political influence of the global financial markets through enforcement of rules and discipline cannot be overstated. It is often argued that since there are no effective policy mechanisms to regulate capital flows, market should be allowed to control itself through self-discipline instead of direct regulatory intervention. It is based on the flawed assumption that the market is the best mechanism to determine how money should be invested; if capital is allowed to move freely, market will reward countries that pursue sound economic policies and pressurize the rest to do the same. But recent financial crises in several liberalized countries have demolished this myth. Countries that were following market-friendly policies were, in fact, pushed to the brink by the very same market forces. History also shows that market has miserably failed to control its own functioning, while the cost of market failure has generally been borne by society.

Historically, regulation of financial system has been residing in the domestic domain. The Bretton Woods system, though reflecting the hegemony of US aspirations, was primarily based on national regulation, supported by international coordination among the participant countries. Given the unruly manner in which financial globalization is taking place, it is doubtful whether a particular country or an institution alone can address the problems emerging from financial instability and systemic risk. It is beyond the capacity of a single nation or institution to regulate global foreign exchange trading which is carried out in OTC markets twenty four hours a day.

Though financial regulation remains within the jurisdiction of national authorities, a well-coordinated regional and international plan with specific norms, procedures and institutional responsibilities can be worked out. The necessity for regional mechanisms is explained in the following pages, wherein it is emphasized that these can serve as a vital link between national and international measures. The need for international supervision and regulation of capital flows is quite in tune with the global nature of these flows and the systemic risks posed by them. However, international measures are relatively much more complex and difficult to implement (as compared to national or regional measures) as it requires the cooperation of a large number of countries and international financial institutions. Yet, importance of global measures cannot be undermined, as the challenges posed by finance capital are also global. Further, the incredible growth in mergers and acquisitions in the financial world calls forth international regulation and supervision. Any measure to deal with such issues requires a high degree of international cooperation. Accomplishing such a level of international cooperation on global financial issues may appear difficult on the face of the clout enjoyed by financiers and speculators, yet it does not seem to be an unattainable task. Eric Helleiner has rightly pointed out that if recent international efforts to combat money laundering can lead to its significant curtailment (if not total elimination), similar regulatory efforts can be launched to deal with the global financial flows.[5]

Third, the envisaged financial architecture should be capable enough to provide adequate space and strength to individual countries to decide appropriate domestic economic policies (such as monetary policy) as well as the level of their participation in the global financial system. While arguing that countries should have greater autonomy in deciding monetary policies, it should not be surmised that central banks should be delinked from political control. In fact, what is being demanded is more transparency and accountability in the operations of the central banks which have remained outside the realm of public scrutiny. Although hue and cry is made against any kind of state intervention in the functioning of central banks, no such concern is shown about the central banks' autonomy from the financial markets.

As the current trend is towards depoliticization of monetary policy issues under the pretext of maintaining independence of central banks, it could give rise to serious consequences and therefore requires further elaboration. By leaving monetary policy in the hands of unelected and often unaccountable technocrats, duly elected governments tend to lose control over the economy. Since powerful financial and business elites benefit from a conservative monetary policy at the cost of other sections of society (such as workers and peasants), the central banks cannot continue to operate in secrecy and remain outside the purview of democratic accountability.

Fourth, although the cracks in the Washington Consensus are becoming apparent, still its key elements (particularly financial liberalization) require thorough reexamination in the light of recent financial crises. An alternative approach which puts restraints on the global finance capital through the use of capital controls should be high on the agenda of nation states. A selective delinking from fly-by-night financiers and 'hot money' flows is not only desirable but also feasible. Countries should strongly resist temptations to set up arrangements such as the BIBF and offshore financial centers. In addition, countries will have to take precautionary measures to strengthen their domestic financial system and closely supervise external debt position, especially the short-term debt.

This could be followed up with a fundamental reorientation of the domestic financial system and the real economy with selective linkages with the globalization processes. The financial system should be modified to serve the needs of the real economy and particularly those sections of society who have been marginalized by the market forces. Though the role of foreign investment cannot be negated, growth must emanate primarily from domestic savings and investment. A progressive direct taxation system has the ability to enhance domestic financial resources. Rather than focusing on export led growth, domestic markets should act as the prime engines of growth. Besides, principle of equity must be on top of the agenda of nation states.

Lastly, as global financial issues affect the lives and livelihoods of vast majority of people, these cannot be left in the hands of rich financiers, international financial institutions and central bankers. There is a need to broaden the debates on global financial issues by seeking participation of people and their representative institutions (e.g., trade unions and peoples' movements) to ensure that the global financial architecture serves the needs of the real economy and people at large. The concept of people's participation should not be restricted to only sharing of information but more importantly, it implies involving people in the decision making processes. In this regard, initiatives have to be taken by civil society institutions to acquaint themselves with the ongoing debates on international financial architecture.

Nine Steps Towards a Better International Financial Architecture

In the following pages, specific policy measures to restructure the present international financial architecture have been proposed at various levels. These measures can serve as a starting point for further debate on the issues posed by financial globalization.

Back to Capital Controls

In the light of recent financial crises, it is increasingly being accepted that capital controls is one of the most effective and meaningful tools available at the national level to protect and insulate the domestic economy from volatile capital flows and other negative external developments. Even the die-hard champions of free market ideology are endorsing the use of capital controls (albeit temporarily). Without the imposition of capital controls, the national authorities will be hard put to handle rapid capital flight, depletion of foreign exchange reserves and loss of autonomy in monetary policy in the wake of massive inflows and outflows of capital.

As discussed in detail in chapter 6, both the developed and the developing countries have extensively used capital controls in the past. Even the critics of Bretton Woods system will admit the fact that capital controls were instrumental in facilitating the pursuit of autonomous economic policy, economic growth and financial stability. In the present context, imposition of capital controls becomes imperative since the regulatory mechanisms to deal with capital flows are national whereas the financial markets have already become global. Undoubtedly, the type of capital controls in place will differ from one country to another, depending on the nature and composition of financial flows and the institution through which capital flows take place.

However, it needs to be underscored that capital controls must be an integral part of state intervention strategy in the financial system in particular and overall economic development in general. Any wisdom that considers capital controls as short-term and isolated measure is unlikely to succeed in the long run. A transparent and an accountable system of regulation and supervision is a prerequisite for the success of capital controls.

Enhancing Regulatory and Supervisory Measures

As capital controls may not have the capacity to resolve all problems associated with global financial flows, they need to be supplemented by other regulatory measures at the national level. While a return to the types of regulatory measures that existed in the fifties and the sixties is not being advocated, what is being emphasized here is that new types of regulations must come into place to address the problems posed by the growing sophistication of global financial markets in the recent years. For instance, regulatory measures related to commercial banks are not only inadequate but also inappropriate for non-banking financial institutions and institutional investors who are nowadays major players in the global financial markets. In a similar vein, stock markets require new regulatory measures (e.g., margins, price-bands and circuit breakers) to curb excessive volatility. Further, problems associated with insider trading, short selling and program trading require new regulations and better understanding by the national regulatory authorities.

Recent experience in the recipient countries suggests that policy makers and regulatory bodies often tend to overlook the problems during the boom periods when massive capital flows is the order of the day, whereas serious note is taken only during the bust periods. The policy makers cannot remain oblivious of the fact that those (usually the upper middle classes and the rich) who benefit during the boom periods are not the real losers during the bust periods. On the other hand, vast sections of the populace (consisting of the poor and lower middle classes) do not gain during the boom period, as their purchasing power is limited. Rather, they are the worst sufferers during the bust periods, which are accompanied by job losses, fall in real wages, high inflation, high taxes, and reduced public expenditure.

In addition to regulatory measures at the level of the recipient countries, enforcement of complementary measures in the source countries acquires cardinal importance to deal with hedge funds and other highly leveraged institutions (HLIs) that pose systemic risk. Nearly 5500 hedge funds are operating worldwide, with an estimated $300 billion of funds under management, without being subject to any meaningful regulations and information disclosures. As mentioned in detail in chapter 4, the role of hedge funds is shrouded in controversy for their role in triggering the ERM crisis in 1992, causing irreparable instability in the international bond market in 1994, and for precipitating the Southeast Asian financial crisis in 1997. Due to increased leverage and unhedged exposure, hedge funds play an instrumental role in bringing the financial crisis of a recipient country to the doors of a source country.

The near collapse of LTCM has significantly exposed the fragility and systemic instability of the much-touted soundness of the financial system in the source countries. Direct regulation of hedge funds and other HLIs, by implication, has to be on the agenda of regulatory authorities. For instance, regulatory measures such as licensing requirements, capital requirements, putting limits on hedge funds on the level of leverage and the fees charged by their managers can be introduced by the authorities. Similarly, a mandatory stipulation for hedge funds to regularly disclose their investments, leverage and derivative positions to the regulatory bodies and the public at large can be instituted. Such regulatory measures, however, should not be restricted only to hedge funds but may be extended to all HLIs.

In addition, a significant restructuring of banks' disclosure and credit assessment practices in relation to the HLIs is necessary. The LTCM episode has already exposed these deficiencies. Banks provide huge amounts of funds to the HLIs without knowing what these institutions are doing with their money. Banks should be asked to disclose publicly their exposure to the HLIs, financial derivatives and other off-balance sheet items. Since 1988, the Basle Accord on capital adequacy and risk norms has been part of banking regulations in more than hundred-odd countries. However, recent events have clearly shown that there are several inherent flaws in the Accord, as it was not sound enough to curb excessive short-term bank lending to several Southeast Asian countries. For non-OECD countries, loans of maturity of up to one year, for instance, had a much lower weightage than loans of over one-year period. By making short-term lending more profitable, this rule encouraged banks to lend recklessly in the region.[6]

Although the IMF insists that there should be greater surveillance of recipient countries, it has so far not shown matching concern vis-a-vis the developed countries from where a majority of such funds originate. Issues of transparency, regulation, supervision and prudential controls in source countries are equally important. There is, undoubtedly, an urgent need for regulatory provisions on investors in the source countries, otherwise controls in the recipient countries will remain ineffective.[7]

The policy makers in the source countries will have to adopt a cautious approach towards the growing trend of mega-mergers and acquisitions in the banking and financial sectors. Due to global deregulation, mergers and acquisitions have become the dominant trend in the financial world, particularly since the mid-1990s. With the emergence of new mega-financial institutions, policy makers are finding it difficult to handle the problems associated with moral hazards. Quite often, big institutions deliberately undertake risky investments with the expectation that the governments or international financial institutions will finally rescue them in the event of a crisis. This trend is increasingly gaining ground in the source countries. The recent bailout of LTCM by the US authorities is a classic example of this trend. Same logic seems to have been applied in the case of the ailing Japanese banks that had a large-scale risky investment exposure in the Southeast Asian region.

By enforcing effective controls, the source countries will not merely protect their own domestic investors but will also be able to ensure global financial stability. As the contagion effects of the financial crises can be regional as well as global, they have the potential to seriously damage the economies of the source countries. Hence, it is in the self-interest of source countries that adequate regulatory mechanisms are adopted.

Stable Exchange Rate Systems

As sharp swings in the exchange rates induce financial instability and hamper economic growth, stable exchange rate systems are quite desirable. In the post-Bretton Woods system, several types of exchange rate systems have been tried but results have been, by and large, disappointing. In the present era of rapid capital mobility, it would be unwise to recommend a particular kind of exchange rate system. With nearly $1.5 trillion moving across the world every day, no exchange rate system can remain perfect and sustainable over a long period.

The choice of selecting a particular type of exchange rate system (fixed, floating or others) is further restricted by the rule of 'trilemma' — countries can achieve only two of the three objectives simultaneously: open capital markets, independent monetary policy and fixed or managed exchange rates. In this context, each country has to seriously reexamine the so-called benefits of open capital markets and free capital mobility, particularly short-term capital flows. Just because free flow of short-term capital across borders benefits a handful of speculators and currency traders, important policy matters related to exchange rates and monetary system cannot be left to the whims and fancies of such forces. To a large extent, countries can sustain a stable exchange rate and monetary autonomy with the help of capital controls, as these have the capacity to reduce volatility in exchange rates by substantially curtailing short-term financial flows.

Analysts have put forward an alternative way for reducing exchange rate instability through the establishment of target zones among the major currencies (the dollar, the euro and the yen), while other countries have been offered the option of either joining the target zone system or following their own exchange rate systems.[8] Under the target zone system, exchange rates can fluctuate within the targets or bands (e.g., 10 per cent on either side) with regular minor adjustments in the targets. There are several advantages with such a regime since it leaves enough space for autonomous monetary policy and prevents speculative attacks on the currencies. While supporting the establishment of target zones among the developed countries, Robert Blecker has argued the need for an International Stabilization Fund to intervene instantaneously to defend the target zones.[9]

Box 8.1
Is Dollarization the Answer?

Unable to defend national currency from speculative attacks, a number of countries are seriously considering the proposal to replace their currencies with the US dollar. In simple terms, dollarization means a policy of accepting US dollar as legal tender or issuing a national currency (e.g., balboa of Panama) that is legally equivalent to the US dollar. This trend is becoming apparent in Latin America where several countries are seriously examining the possibilities of dollarization. In January 1999, Argentina's central bank submitted a report detailing steps to complete the dollarization process. Ecuador, the first country to default on the Brady bond debt, announced its plan for dollarization in January 2000. If financial media reports are to be believed, some kind of dollarization will take place in Mexico and Canada in the near future.

There are several problems related to dollarization. It is nothing but a total surrender of monetary independence to the Federal Reserve of the US. If implemented, dollarized countries will not be able to control their economies, as the important policy measures (e.g., interest rates) will be decided by the US. What is good for the US economy may not be good for the dollarized countries. While it will yield foreign policy benefits to the US, there is no guarantee that dollarization would lead to higher economic growth or prevent the occurrence of financial crisis in these countries. Hence, it would be naive to think that by dollarizing their currencies, countries will be able to replicate the US model.

The target zone proposal received considerable media attention when Oscar Lafontaine, the then German Finance Minister, supported the target zone idea between the euro, the dollar and the yen at the G-7 forum in early 1999. In order to adopt a more proactive approach to currency management, France and Japan had also extended support to this proposal within the G-7. Not surprisingly, the US opposed the establishment of target zone regime on ideological grounds as such an agreement has the possibility of subverting its avowed policy of free market financial liberalization and open capital markets.

The Rationale for Regional Cooperation

With the sole exception of the European Union which has a comprehensive regional mechanism in the form of EMU, there are no regional institutional mechanisms in existence to deal with the issues emerging from the financial crises. In the face of increasing instability of global financial markets, the need for regional institutions to dampen financial contagion is being increasingly acknowledged. There are several reasons signifying the necessity of regional mechanisms. First, as individual countries lack resources and capacity to face severe financial crises, regional mechanisms can be useful in complementing national mechanisms. Regional institutional mechanisms can serve as a vital link between national and international mechanisms. Second, greater attention must be paid at the regional level due to the regional concentration of financial and trade flows. Third, the contagion effects of the financial crises are more disastrous

Table 8.1: Regional Contributions in the IMF-led Bailout Programs

	Regional ($ billion)	IMF ($ billion)	Regional/IMF (per cent)
Thailand	11.0	3.9	280
Indonesia	14.0	10.1	140
Korea	11.0	21.0	52

Source: Stephen Grenville, "The Asian Crisis and Regional Co-operation," Talk to International Seminar on East Asian Financial Crisis, Beijing, April 21, 1998, (via Internet).

for countries within the region. This fact has been highlighted by the ERM crisis in 1992, the Mexican peso crisis in 1994 and the Southeast Asian currency crisis in 1997, where the contagion effects were substantially regional. Recent studies have also confirmed the regional dimension of financial crises.[10] Lastly, in comparison to the international mechanisms, regional mechanisms could be more appropriate, efficient and quick in preventing financial crisis in a particular country as well as to limit and control the contagion effects of the crisis. For instance, regional institutions (with fewer members) can quickly provide financial assistance to a country facing a crisis than the IMF that has to take into consideration the interests of all its 182 members. Besides, international rescue plans may lack country-specific knowledge and the severity of financial crisis faced by individual countries.

In the aftermath of the Southeast Asian financial crisis, the debate on regional mechanisms at the Asian level has been revived. While there is a renewed interest in strengthening regional cooperation through the existing forums such as the EMEAP,[11] several new regional initiatives have already taken concrete shape whereas some other proposals are under discussion. The need for a regional response in Asia has been further strengthened by the fact that regional contributions to the IMF led bailout programs for Thailand and Indonesia were much higher than the IMF's own contribution (see Table 8.1). Much before the Southeast Asian financial crisis erupted, B W Fraser, the then Governor of Reserve Bank of Australia, called for an Asian version of the Bank for International Settlements (BIS) in 1995.[12] As the BIS continues to be a Euro-centric institution, with 13 of its 17 board members from Europe, the proposal has several merits.

By and large, there is wide acceptance regarding monitoring and surveillance mechanisms (the Manila Framework Group, the Asian Surveillance Group, etc.) both within Asia and outside. But, when it comes to creating a new regional institution in Asia, there is stiff opposition particularly from the US, Europe and the IMF in spite of considerable support for such a proposal within the Asian region. The idea for an Asian

Box 8.2

Japan, Asian Monetary Fund and Geopolitics

In September 1997, the Japanese government unilaterally proposed the establishment of an Asian Monetary Fund (AMF). The initial proposal was to have a funding of $100 billion, half of it was to be contributed by Japan and the remainder by China, Hong Kong, Singapore and Taiwan. The purpose of the AMF was to provide liquidity to forestall speculative attacks on the region's currencies. Unlike the IMF loans, the financial support from the AMF was to be with low conditionality.

In spite of widespread support within the region, the proposal did not materialize. Within two months after the proposal was made by the then Japan's Vice Minister of Finance for International Affairs, Eisuke Sakakibara (often dubbed 'Mr Yen'), Japan backtracked in a meeting held in Manila in November 1997. Realizing that the AMF has the potential to undermine the authority of the IMF as a global crisis manager as well as the US role in the region, the proposal was defeated in this meeting in favor of a US-backed 'Framework for Enhanced Asian Regional Cooperation to Promote Financial Stability.' Popularly known as the 'Manila Framework,' it is no substitute to the AMF as it deals with only monitoring and surveillance activities. However, during the annual meeting of the IMF and the World Bank in 1998, Japan put forward a conservative bilateral proposal, the Miyazawa Plan. Under this Plan, a $30 billion package for the region was worked out to facilitate short-term trade financing and economic recovery through medium- and long-term projects. Initially meant for crisis-hit economies of Indonesia, Korea, Thailand, Malaysia and the Philippines, the Plan has been extended to Vietnam. As the Miyazawa Plan is quite akin to the basic tenets of 'Washington Consensus,' it received the support of the US and other G-7 countries.

Notwithstanding several positive elements, one cannot overlook the fact that the proposal for the creation of an AMF and the Miyazawa Plan are instruments in the hands of Japanese authorities to subserve the interests of their corporations and financial institutions in the Asian region — just as the US uses the IMF to extend the interests of its corporations and financial institutions. Challenged by the growing influence of the US and China, Japan wants to reassert its power and domination in the Asian region through such regional mechanisms. Therefore, these efforts should be seen in the context of regional geopolitical and economic exigencies.

Monetary Fund (AMF), as proposed by Japan in 1997, was turned down at the behest of the US and the European nations primarily because it challenged the monopoly of the IMF over crisis management, and besides, it did not envisage a role for the US (see Box 8.2). Given the IMF's flawed handling of the Asian crisis and substantial financial resources residing within the Asian region, the proposal for the creation of an AMF is well worth consideration.

In fact, several Asian countries are thinking in terms of evolving regional monetary and exchange rate cooperation. For instance, Thailand, Malaysia and India are considering a proposal to trade in a local currency in order to avoid dependence on the US dollar as the preferred currency for conducting trade.[13] If such proposals are implemented, the monopoly of the US dollar in trade in the region will be weakened substantially and regional cooperation may well be further strengthened.

While supporting the need for new regional institutional mechanisms, several important questions — who calls the shots, what is the *modus operandi* of decision making and who ultimately benefits from such decisions — have to be reckoned with.

It's Time for Tobin Tax

Professor James Tobin in his Janeway Lectures at Princeton first proposed a tax on global foreign exchange transactions in 1972, it came to be popularly known as Tobin tax. In the subsequent years, James Tobin has modified and further elaborated his earlier proposal. Realizing the need for "throw(ing) some sand in the wheels" of global financial markets, Tobin advocated the tax as a mechanism for discouraging speculation in short-term foreign exchange dealings. He proposed a 0.25 per cent tax on currency transactions in order to control volatility in the international currency markets and to preserve some autonomy in national monetary policies. Essentially a Keynesian proposition, the underlying logic of Tobin tax is to slow down speculative, short-term capital flows, as they will be taxed each time they cross the border. The cost of Tobin tax for commodity trade and long-term capital investments will be negligible.

According to Tobin, a tax of 0.2 per cent on a round trip to another currency costs 48 per cent a year if transacted every business day, 10 per cent if every week, 2.4 per cent if every month. In other words, there would be a high surcharge on short-term flows as it has been calculated that over 80 per cent of spot foreign exchange transactions have a maturity of less than seven days.

In the seventies and the eighties, neither the mainstream economists nor the political establishments evinced any interest on the proposal. "It did not make much of a ripple. In fact, one may say that it sunk like a rock. The community of professional economists simply ignored it," lamented Tobin.[14] However, the case for Tobin tax has gained urgency in the nineties as the recent financial crises highlight the growing instability and fragility in the global financial markets. Its revenue potential has further enhanced the attractiveness of Tobin tax. A number of NGOs and peoples' movements have also launched campaigns urging for a Tobin tax (see next chapter).

There are several justifications for the adoption of Tobin tax. As the global foreign exchange transactions have surpassed many times over the global trade in goods and services and even the GDP of all the nations put together, the need for such a tax has become paramount. Given the fact that majority of flows is short-term, speculative and extremely volatile, this tax can curb interest rate arbitrage and other speculative activities that contribute towards the destabilization of the financial system. Besides, Tobin tax is expected to preserve the autonomy of national authorities in formulating monetary policy and also ensure insulation from the deleterious effects of volatile international financial markets. Such autonomy is particularly valuable for the developing countries, as they are more vulnerable to external capital flows.

The revenue potential of a Tobin tax provides another justification for its adoption. A number of estimates of the amount of revenue that can be generated from a Tobin tax have been calculated. The revenue potential of a 0.25 per cent tax in the 1970s was relatively modest; with the 1998 global forex volume, the annual tax revenue that could be generated is over $350 billion. This amount is quite tempting, given the fact that international official aid has declined over the years, and the national governments are constrained with less financial resources for social sector spending. These financial resources can also be used when capital flight occurs. A part of these resources may be used to support international bodies (e.g., the UN) which are facing serious resource crunch.

An additional advantage of the tax is that it could facilitate the monitoring of international financial flows by providing a centralized database on such flows, which is the need of the hour. This could be particularly valuable to the developing countries where large information gaps exist.

Much of the criticism relating to Tobin tax have centered on the question of its practicability and technical feasibility. Quite often it is argued that the regulation of currency trade through measures such as Tobin tax is a difficult proposition since the volumes traded are too high. However, analysts have stressed that the obstacles to put restrictions on currency trading are not technical, but political.[15] If the modern electronic system can enable massive cross border flow of foreign exchange in trillions, why can't the same technology be used to collect taxes?

Critics of Tobin tax further argue that it is almost impossible to get all the countries to agree on a common tax. Nevertheless, a beginning can be made with a few countries coming together on this issue even if a generalized consensus across territories is not possible. For instance, a nominal Tobin tax can be instituted through an agreement among seven major centers of currency trading, namely, the US, the UK, Japan, Singapore, Switzerland, Hong Kong and Germany, which account for 80 per cent of all currency transactions. An agreement among these seven countries to levy and supervise the collection of tax is a feasible idea. This would also contain the threat of relocation of funds, as the various offshore financial centers are mere booking addresses that function because the mainland authorities have, so far, tolerated such evasive tactics. Another common criticism of Tobin tax is related to evasion. All taxes (e.g., income tax and property tax), for that matter, are open to evasion but this is not sound enough reason for not having them.[16] Concerted efforts should be made to check loopholes, as no policy measure can be foolproof.

It is often ignored that not long ago, taxes on financial transactions (though not necessarily on foreign exchange transactions) have been imposed in several countries including the US, Germany and the UK. During 1963-74, the US imposed the Interest Equalization Tax to discourage residents from investing in foreign bonds. Germany followed the 'Bardepot' regulation till the 1970s. Many of these taxes had enabled authorities to strictly regulate financial markets. The proposal for levying Tobin tax, in comparison, seems to be a market-friendly instrument. Stephany Griffith-Jones has provided another example of the securities transaction tax, known as 'stamp duty' in the UK.[17] According to her, the stamp duty collected a very high yield — $1300 million in the fiscal 1993. Interestingly, there was no major flight from spot transactions into futures and options and London continues to remain one of the major financial centers.

The issues raised by Tobin tax are more political than technical or administrative. Its adoption requires political will, particularly among the G-7 countries, as well as better coordination at the international level. The recent experience (for instance, money laundering related to drug trafficking, etc.) shows that international cooperation among countries is possible if there is a political will. A similar approach (with a higher degree of concern) is required to deal with the issues related to Tobin tax. As the proposal for a Tobin tax is progressive and willy-nilly goes against the avowed neo-liberal ideology, it has not received support from the G-7 countries, international banks, the World Bank and the IMF. In the US, surprisingly, the idea for Tobin tax faced 'political censorship' when senators led by Bob Dole introduced a bill in the Senate to prohibit UN agencies and its officials from developing or promoting Tobin's proposal, or any other international taxation scheme.[18] The bill expressly prohibited "foreign transaction fees."[19]

There is no denying the fact that the idea of a Tobin tax needs to be suitably updated and modified to be relevant in the present context. In this regard, several suggestions have been made recently. For instance, in

1996, Tobin proposed to bring derivatives under the tax net. Similarly, Paul Spahn has suggested a two-tier structure for a Tobin tax.[20] Under this proposal, in addition to a low tax on all foreign exchange transactions, there would be a penal tax on transactions outside a specified band. Analysts have also suggested new institutions to administer Tobin tax. Tobin tax is one of the instruments on which a lot of work has already progressed.[21] In the coming days, it could become an important symbol for campaigns to restructure international financial architecture. Various citizens' groups and NGOs have already announced their plans to launch a global campaign by linking up with other like-minded groups.

While supporting the case for a Tobin tax, it is not being argued that all problems related to global finance capital would be resolved by it. In the present context, no one single instrument by itself can perform miracles. Nevertheless, Tobin tax can certainly serve as a first step towards developing a more stable global financial system. If it is used in conjunction with other policy instruments (for instance, capital controls), Tobin tax does offer an attractive mechanism to deal with the multiple issues related to volatility and instability of global financial flows.

A Reformed IMF

Although the IMF had lost its *raison d' etre* with the collapse of Bretton Woods system in the early 1970s, not only has it managed to reinvent itself, but more importantly, it has also assumed the role of an international lender of the last resort, particularly in the aftermath of the Mexican financial crisis. Over the years, the IMF has moved away from its original mandate of providing short-term stabilization loans to countries facing balance of payments problems. Particularly, since the 1980s, the IMF has moved into medium-term adjustment programs advocating structural reforms such as privatization, financial liberalization and relaxation of labor laws. Recent attempts such as increase in quotas under the Eleventh General Review of Quotas, the New Arrangements to Borrow and the adoption of Contingent Credit Lines are moves aimed at transforming the IMF as an international lender of the last resort.

In the wake of the Southeast Asian crisis, the IMF has come under severe criticism for its flawed approach. Critics belonging to the right and the left have called for the total abolition of the IMF. Even its twin sister, the World Bank has also questioned the IMF's role in dealing with the Asian crisis in its publication, *Global Economic Prospects and the Developing Countries*. In the present global economic and political context, the proposal to reform the IMF has a far higher degree of international support than any other proposal. Several steps could be undertaken to reform the IMF. For instance, the IMF should be made to stick to its original mandate and competence. As countries often need liquidity to tide over external imbalances, the IMF can continue to provide short-term stabilization lending. It must stop prescribing medium- and long-term structural adjustment reforms. Further, the IMF should not pursue the role of an international lender of the last resort and should also refrain from the proposed amendment in its Article of Agreement to include capital account liberalization.

Although the IMF prescribes greater disclosure of information and transparency standards to governments and central banks, it is perhaps the only multilateral institution (with 182 members) which still maintains secrecy about its operations. Outside the IMF, no one has any clue how the institution works out the size of its loan package as its internal records related to loan evaluation and policy recommendations are kept secret. Deliberations and operations of the IMF, therefore, need to be more transparent and accountable to the public.

This could be followed up by a radical democratization of the IMF. Unlike the UN, the membership of the IMF is not based on one nation-one vote criterion. Instead, voting power is based in proportion to the quotas of subscription that member-countries make to the IMF. Consequently, the US and other developed countries have been able to control the IMF. By adopting the principle of one nation-one vote, the overarching influence of the US and other developed countries could be minimized and some form of democratic accountability ushered into the functioning of the IMF.

Regulate Financial Derivatives

The recent growth of financial derivatives (particularly OTC derivatives that are informal agreements between two parties and therefore carry heavy risk) and their extensive use for speculative purposes pose a serious systemic risk. Although financial derivatives are supposed to help reduce risk, in reality, they have become one of the biggest sources of volatility and instability in the global financial markets. Largely because financial derivatives are off-balance sheet items, the task of market participants to assess risks faced by the counterparties becomes more difficult and therefore requires additional regulations to bring discipline in the derivative markets.

Financial derivatives are quite sophisticated, risky and highly leveraged instruments and a slight mishandling of trading can lead to huge losses. Besides, much of trading is carried out by a handful of banks and financial institutions. It has been estimated that 10 largest banks are counterparties in nearly half of all derivative contracts. A failure or default by one bank could lead to a series of defaults leading to a systemic failure. Since much of derivatives involve cross border trading, systemic failure in one country can have a spread effect on a global scale. We have already witnessed how the financial crisis of Russia was brought to the doors of Wall Street *a la* LTCM.

In recent years, several proposals have been made to address the problems associated with financial derivatives. The proposals range from more information disclosure and transparency in OTC derivatives by creating clearing associations (as in the case of exchange traded derivatives) to greater regulation of the banks and financial institutions who are the main players in the realm of financial derivatives. In this regard, the suggestion made by David Felix, noted economist, to impose appropriate capital requirements on the derivative-issuing banks for equalizing the prices of OTC derivatives with those of the organized markets is worth consideration.[22]

Curb Dubious Activities of Offshore Financial Centers

It is high time that international community pays serious attention to the world of offshore financial centers (OFCs) as they provide legitimate space for unregulated financial players such as trust companies, shell companies, hedge funds and brokerage houses. Because of lax regulations, OFCs are used not only to launder the proceeds of drug trafficking and other crimes but also aid and abet certain kinds of financial crime. The BCCI and the EUB scandals are glaring examples reflecting this trend. Further, the role of OFCs in catalyzing the financial crises in Latin America and Southeast Asia in the 1990s is well documented, and therefore, does not need any reiteration.

In the past, the onshore regulatory authorities have tolerated the evasive tactics of their banks and financial institutions and allowed them to establish offshore branches and subsidiaries with little or no regulation. Onshore authorities, to begin with, can initiate tough measures against such banks and financial institutions. As the dubious operations of OFCs hinder the working of direct controls on financial institutions, an international policy initiative for curbing regulatory and tax evasions could be chalked out in consultation with the OFCs.

Bailing in Private Sector

Since the 1980s, the entire burden of private debt, from private lenders to private borrowers, has been transferred to the public domain with the financial support from the IMF and other official lenders. This has created a moral hazard problem that encourages private sector lenders to carry out reckless lending because they know that they will remain unscathed, if things go sour. This trend became more evident in the recent financial crises. Under the bailout programs orchestrated by the IMF and the US government in the aftermath of the Mexican and the Southeast Asian financial crises, all private sector lenders were repaid in full and without any 'haircut' or delay. Such bailout programs are unethical because for every imprudent borrower, there is an imprudent lender as well. There is no reason why taxpayers' money should be squandered to bailout imprudent private lenders.

In the event of a financial crisis, there has to be a mechanism for better crisis resolution through orderly debt workouts and bailing in, rather than bailing out, private sector creditors. By enforcing a compulsory 'haircut,' the authorities can address not only the immediate problems of debt repayment, but more importantly, also those related to moral hazard.

Notes and References

1. Besides putting forward a number of proposals, the G-7 has also created a Financial Stability Forum. G-20 is a new group of member states that has been formed in the annual meeting of the IMF in September 1999, after several developing countries highlighted the need for their participation in the discussions on the global financial system. G-20 includes the G-7 countries plus a number of important developing countries from Latin America, Asia and Eastern Europe including Argentina, Brazil, China, Korea, India, Australia, Venezuela, Mexico and Turkey. The European Union will also be represented at the G-20 meetings through its President. G-20 replaces the G-22 which was created after the Mexican Peso crisis in the 1980s as a forum for crisis management and the restructuring of the financial system.

2. See John Eatwell and Lance Taylor, *International Capital Markets and the Future of Economic Policy*, Working Paper No. 9, Center for Economic Policy Analysis, September 1998; and John Eatwell, "From Cooperation to Coordination to Control?," *New Political Economy*, Vol. 4, No. 3, 1999, pp. 410-415.

3. George Schultz, William Simon and Walter Wriston, "Who Needs the IMF?," *Wall Street Journal*, February 3, 1998.

4. Speech made by Prime Minister Tony Blair to the New York Stock Exchange, September 29, 1998 (via Internet); and Speech by the Chancellor of the Exchequer, Gordon Brown to the Commonwealth Finance Ministers Meeting in Ottawa on September 30, 1998 (via Internet).

5. Eric Helleiner, "The Myth of All-powerful Financial Markets," in Isabelle Grunberg (ed.), *Perspectives on International Financial Liberalization*, Discussion Paper Series No. 15, Office of Development Studies, United Nations Development Programme, 1998, pp. 33-37.

6. For a detailed discussion, see Stephany Griffith-Jones,"A New Financial Architecture for Reducing Risks and Severity of Crises," *International Politics and Society*, 3/1999, pp. 263-278.

7. For a detailed discussion on the need for regulations in the source country, see Stephany Griffith-Jones, "Regulatory Challenges for Source Countries of Surges in Capital Flows," in Jan Joost Teunissen (ed.), *The Policy Challenges of Global Financial Integration,* FONDAD, 1998.

8. See, for instance, John Grieve Smith, "Exchange Rate Instability and the Tobin Tax," *Cambridge Journal of Economics,* Vol. 21, No. 6, 1997, pp. 745-752; and Robert A Blecker, *Taming Global Finance: A Better Architecture for Growth and Equity,* Economic Policy Institute, 1999.

9. Robert A Blecker, op. cit., p. 136.

10. See, for instance, J Frankel and S Schmukler, "Crisis, Contagion, and Country Funds: Effects of East Asia and Latin America," *Working Paper No. 96-04,* Center for Pacific Basin Monetary and Economics Studies, Federal Reserve of San Francisco; and Reuven Glick and Andrew K Rose, "Contagion and Trade: Why are Currency Crises Regional?," *Working Paper No. 98-03,* Center for Pacific Basin Monetary and Economics Studies, Federal Reserve of San Francisco.

11. The Executives' Meeting of East Asia and Pacific Central Banks (EMEAP) is a cooperative organization of central banks and monetary authorities in the East Asia and Pacific region. Established in 1991, the EMEAP was set up in response to under-representation of Asian countries in the international financial fora (such as the G-10). It comprises the central banks of Australia, People's Republic of China, Hong Kong, Indonesia, Japan, Republic of Korea, Malaysia, New Zealand, the Philippines, Singapore and Thailand. Apart from organizing Governors' Meetings and Deputies' Meetings, EMEAP has set up three working groups on Payment and Settlement Systems, Financial Markets and Banking Supervision.

12. B W Fraser, "Central Bank Co-operation in the Asian Region," *Reserve Bank of Australia Bulletin,* October 1995.

13. See, for instance, recent news reports, Dexter Cruez, "Hegde dubs dollar dependence suicidal," *Business Standard,* September 10, 1998; and T S Vishwanath, "India, Malaysia keen to trade in local currencies," *The Economic Times,* September 7, 1998.

14. James Tobin, "Prologue," in Mahbub ul Haq, Inge Kaul and Isabelle Grunberg (eds.), *The Tobin Tax: Coping With Financial Volatility,* Oxford University Press, 1996, p. x.

15. Kavaljit Singh, "Tobin Tax: An Idea Whose Time Has Come," *Economic and Political Weekly,* May 1, 1999, p. 1019.

16. Inge Kaul, Isabelle Grunberg and Mahbub ul Haq, "Overview," in Mahbub ul Haq and others, op. cit., p. 7.

17. Stephany Griffith-Jones, "Institutional Arrangements for a Tax on International Currency Transactions," in Mahbub ul Haq and others, op. cit., p. 146.

18. Kunibert Raffer, "The Tobin Tax: Reviving a Discussion," *World Development*, Vol. 26, No. 3, 1998, p. 529.

19. Ibid., p.532.

20. Paul Bernd Spahn, "The Tobin Tax and Exchange Rate Stability," *Finance and Development*, June 1996, pp. 24-27.

21. In addition to above references, see, for instance, Alex C Michalos, *Good Taxes: The Case for Taxing Foreign Currency Exchange and Other Financial Transactions*, Dundurn Press, 1997; Heikki Patomaki, *The Tobin Tax: How to Make it Real*, The Network Institute for Global Democratisation, 1999; and Rodney Schmidt, *A Feasible Foreign Exchange Transaction Tax*, The North-South Institute, 1999.

22. David Felix,"Repairing the Global Financial Architecture: Painting over Cracks vs. Strengthening the Foundations," *Foreign Policy in Focus*, Interhemispheric Resource Center and Institute for Policy Studies, September 1999, p. 10.

9

Financial Globalization: New Challenges for Peoples' Movements

FINANCIAL crises, specifically in the recent years, have been an inevitable outcome of the unfettered and mindless liberalization of finance, and truly there is an urgent need to restructure the present international financial architecture. It is increasingly being admitted that if the international financial system is not regulated, there is little possibility of any country remaining immune from the catastrophic impact of the recurring financial crisis. Despite the fact that the restructuring of the global financial architecture is the key motif of the ongoing international debates, peoples' movements, NGOs, and labor organizations in the developing and the developed countries are yet to respond — effectively and critically — to the issues emerging from globalization of finance.

There are innumerable activists, social movements, NGOs, women's and labor groups representing different sections and interests of society throughout the length and breadth of the globe. Since the 1980s, these groups have emerged as a significant force in the national and global arenas. In the recent past, several NGO campaigns have been responsible for forcing international financial institutions to incorporate transparency and public participation in their functioning. For instance, the Inspection Panel at the World Bank was created largely under the pressure of NGOs and peoples' movements.

By and large, the areas where peoples' movements have made vivid progress are limited to social and environmental issues. Despite the fact that financial globalization has a considerable impact on poor people, labor and issues of human rights and environment, very little attention seems to have been paid to this issue by the activist groups. Table 9.1, generally speaking, charts out some of the positive and negative contours of financial globalization.

It is only in the 1990s that a significant number of groups and movements have started campaigns on international trade issues (e.g., GATT, WTO and NAFTA). As regards global financial issues, these groups have largely concentrated on either official capital flows (e.g., the World Bank, ADB and bilateral aid) or FDI. Not much attention seems to have been paid to issues related to global finance capital. There could be two important reasons underlying such a state of affairs. Firstly, global finance capital and financial markets comprise a new field for peoples' movements. Secondly, and perhaps more importantly, there has been lack of information and comprehension on issues related to global finance. No doubt, financial matters are very complex and a thorough understanding of them requires a considerable amount of expertise and experience, which unfortunately, many groups do not possess. Therefore, a well-thought out and coordinated action program by the social movements at various levels is yet to emerge.

However, it is encouraging to note the recent attempts by some groups to closely work on financial issues, particularly in the context of how international economic relations and institutions profoundly affect the national economic policies and projects. In the wake of the Southeast

Table 9.1: Financial Globalization: A Balance Sheet[1]

Positive for	Negative for
Short-term investments	Long-term investments
Casino economy	Real economy
Creditors	Debtors
Institutional investors, speculators, currency traders and fund managers	Small investors
Professional and managerial people	Workers and non-skilled labor
People with financial assets	People without financial assets
Global financial supermarket	National sovereignty
Offshore financial centers and funds	National tax revenues
Self-regulated markets	Regulatory bodies
'Efficient' markets	Welfare state
Risk takers	Stable financial system
Promoting neo-liberal economic policies	Promoting state intervention and public interest
Promoting authoritarian regimes[2]	Promoting genuine democratization[3]
	Environment

1. These are rough approximations.

2. Rapid capital inflows can legitimize the authoritarian regimes and thereby delay the transition to a democratic regime (e.g., Indonesia till recently).

3. Rapid capital outflows, which are followed by a severe balance of payments crisis, can discredit even democratic regimes. Further, it forestalls the possibility of the transition towards a more democratic regime by curtailing the rights of pro democracy groups such as organized trade unions (e.g., South Korea).

Asian financial crisis, a number of social movements and NGOs have started paying attention to issues pertaining to global finance capital. This is evident from the increasing number of national, regional and international workshops and training programs held in Asia and elsewhere on financial issues since 1997.[1]

In the post-1997 period, environmental groups have also launched issue-based campaigns highlighting the environmental hazards associated with projects financed by global capital.[2] Thanks to the recent campaigns by NGOs and peoples' movements in the developed countries that exposed the dangers of the MAI, this agreement has been shelved for the time being.

People's Response: A Case Study of India

At the political level, except for a handful of issues such as the question of allowing free entry of private insurers into the insurance sector, there seems to be a growing consensus among mainstream political parties to throw open India's financial markets. This is reflected in the advocacy and continuation of financial 'reforms' by the three successive governments of the center-left, center and right in the 1990s. The absence of an alternative political process at the national level has reduced the potential for expression and advocacy of alternative policies and strategies. This gives unsound policy decisions the appearance of a *fait accompli.*

On the other hand, social movements, NGOs and labor groups, operating in the non-party political space have yet to critically respond to issues related to finance capital and its presence in India. Since the territory of finance capital is new to Indian groups, they are increasingly realizing the importance of comprehending such issues.[3] As global financial issues are quite complex, Indian groups need requisite expertise to tackle them.

Although a number of research institutes work on financial matters, most of them serve the corporate sector. Since the reports and journals published by these institutes are quite expensive, the grassroot movements are unable to access them, and therefore, the task of providing timely and relevant information to movements has been left to a handful of independent research groups and socially committed intellectuals. With their limited resources and reach, they are hardly able to provide information and campaign tools to activist groups crisscrossing the country. In the recent past, there have been some well-intentioned efforts to demystify the complex issues related to globalization of finance.[4] Such efforts need to be supplemented through preparation and publication of educational material for the common people, especially in the vernacular languages.

It is not surprising that there is little, if any, input from Indian groups at the international level on these issues as compared to the earlier animated debates on environment, gender, poverty and sustainable development. Social movements and groups in India are yet to familiarize themselves with the ongoing debates on financial globalization.

There is no denying the fact that in recent years Indian groups have demonstrated that mass campaigns can be successfully launched against the might of World Bank funded projects (e.g., Narmada dam and Singrauli power projects). Several struggles and campaigns focusing against the ill effects of FDI have also been carried out in India (examples include campaigns against Union Carbide, Cargill, Enron, Nestle and deep-sea fishing). However, the same campaign strategies cannot be employed in the case of finance capital, which is by and large, footloose in nature. Regarding finance capital, popular movements will have to take into cognizance the nature and working of regulatory agencies such as the Securities and Exchange Board of India and the Reserve Bank of India.

At the international and regional levels, a series of discussions on the need to regulate financial flows and restructuring of international financial architecture are taking place at both the official (e.g., G-7, G-15, Group of 22 and the Commonwealth) and non-official circles (e.g., World Economic Summit). But a handful of economists, experts, concerned officials and market players from India who can be counted on the finger tips are able to take part in these deliberations.

What should be the Agenda of Peoples' Movements?

Given the present geopolitical conjuncture, one cannot expect major structural changes in the global financial system to take place without mass mobilization and empowerment of people in both the developed and the developing countries. Perhaps more so in the developed countries where most of these financial flows originate in the first place.

As mentioned before, previous successful strategies of campaigning and lobbying against official capital flows (World Bank and ADB) are unlikely to pay dividends in the case of finance capital. While the World Bank and other institutions (multilateral and bilateral) have a mandate for poverty alleviation and sustainable development (although their intent, commitment and approach to such issues are open to question), private finance capital is only interested in reaping profits, has no people oriented developmental agenda, and is accountable only to its own shareholders. Moreover, there is little or no transparency worth comment in their operations given their fear of disclosing information that could be exploited by their competitors.[5] Hence, activists and groups should seriously heed the advice of Brent Blackwelder of the Friends of the Earth, "NGOs need a 'quantum leap' from Washington to Wall Street."[6]

It is easier to target campaigns and monitor the funding activity of the World Bank, the IMF and the ADB since they are centralized institutions. However, the same strategy can not be deployed in case of global financial capital as it is liquid, decentralized and footloose in nature, moving from one country to another in no time. This makes monitoring an extremely difficult task. Earlier strategies of campaigning (e.g., labor, legal or environmental and community action) against private capital flows are unlikely to work in the case of footloose finance capital.[7]

An action program calling for total delinking of domestic economy from global financial flows, in the given economic and political context, is unlikely to succeed. Action programs based on curbing unbridled international financial liberalization and selective delinking from short-term and speculative funds may have better chances of success. The terms and conditions of linkages with global financial flows should be decided by the nation states rather than by global financial markets and financial institutions. If peoples' movements are strong, alert and influential, there is every possibility of devising an investment strategy that allows only such financial flows that are beneficial to the domestic economy. This does not mean that one should blindly attract long-term FDI and other types of financial flows. Experience shows that the cost of FDI can be debilitating as capital can move out through royalty payments, dividends, imports as well as other legal and illegal means.

Strategies will vary from country to country depending on the specific context, yet a number of common action programs could be planned in both the recipient and the source countries. Some common action programs that can be employed are outlined in the succeeding pages. These may not be definitive but can serve as a starting point for further debate and refinement.

Action Programs in the Recipient Countries

We often hear the refrain that "global financial markets are too powerful and nation states are helpless." While the power of the nation state has undoubtedly been weakened in the era of financial globalization, it must be remembered that governments in most parts of the world are active participants in the global financial system. Financial globalization is not merely technologically driven. Power and politics, within the nation state, define the context of international capital mobility.[8] If countries are losing autonomy in economic decision making, much of this loss is, in fact, self-inflicted. By stating "globalization is beyond our reach and we cannot do anything about it," the political elite is surrendering national sovereignty to foreign capital. Despite globalization, there is every possibility that nation states can restore relative autonomy in the management of their economies, as witnessed recently in Malaysia. Since the existence of nation state cannot be wished away, activists and groups should make renewed efforts to make it accountable and democratic.

Policy makers and regulatory bodies in the recipient countries have generally ignored the problems faced by vast sections of society while inviting massive capital inflows. During the boom phase of inflows, majority of the populace (consisting of the poor and the lower middle classes) does not seem to gain, as they have limited purchasing power. Whereas they bear the brunt during the bust phase which is accompanied by fall in real wages, high inflation, higher taxes, job losses and reduced social sector spending by the government. Ironically, upper sections of the society while reaping a bonanza during the boom period do not seem to lose much during the bust phase.

At the national level, the activist groups must advocate greater regulations. Concentrated efforts must be made to enforce capital controls on the flows of speculative funds in order to prevent the occurrence of financial crisis. In this context, it will be worthwhile to emulate policy measures adopted by Malaysia in 1998. Nation states have much to learn from the use of capital controls in China and India, which have safeguarded these economies from the vagaries of finance capital. Tax-based policy mechanisms (e.g., Tobin tax, capital gains tax, etc.) could also be tried to curb the onrush of such speculative flows.

Action Programs in the Source Countries

Sooner or later, NGOs and peoples' movements in the source countries will have to take serious note of global finance capital. Serious efforts have to be made to exert public pressure on regulatory bodies for the implementation of stringent regulatory mechanisms and disclosure standards. Certain types of financial instruments (e.g., hedge funds) are highly unregulated in their source countries. There are over 5500 unregulated hedge funds operating in the international financial markets. Recent collapse of the US-based international hedge fund, LTCM, illustrates this point.

In the source countries, any campaign against global finance capital is unlikely to succeed without the support of middle class investors who invest their savings in the mutual funds, pension funds, bonds and other financial instruments. Since this community running into millions is very large, the capital contributed by it is in trillions of dollars. In the US alone, the proportion of investment of households/individuals in mutual funds accounts for over 35 per cent. The American mutual fund industry, with assets touching $4 trillion, accounts for over half of the world's mutual fund assets. Admittedly, a substantial amount of capital — which the international fund managers move across the border with impunity — belongs to this community.

In recent years, attempts have been made by NGOs in some western countries and the US to sensitize the investor community to the wider implications of their investment. A number of funds (popularly known as socially responsible funds) which invest only in socially and environmentally sound projects have also burgeoned. However, experience shows that some socially responsible funds do not behave differently from other profit seeking funds. These funds also have a tendency to overreact on 'herd instinct.' To illustrate this point from the perspective of a recipient country, the Thai example is quite relevant. When the speculative attack on the Thai baht was launched in early July 1997, all kinds of funds including socially responsible funds, quickly moved out of the region, thereby catalyzing the crisis. Thus, from the perspective of a recipient country, these socially responsible funds are no different. NGOs and citizens' groups, particularly in the source countries have to keep this in mind while extending support to such funds.

Need for International Action

While working at the national level (both in the recipient and the source countries), peoples' movements have to address the issues at the regional and international level. The need for activism at the international level is necessitated by the fact that financial globalization is bound to cause serious damage to world financial markets and the real economy. The growing trend towards megamergers and acquisitions in the banking and financial sectors calls for international regulation and supervision.

As the financial crises are increasingly taking global dimensions, social movements likewise have to take a global stance. Although the arena of mass movements may remain national, cross border alliances and linkages with international groups need to be developed and strengthened. The battle against global financial system cannot be fought in exclusivity, rather it has to be an integral part of wider cross sectional movements against neo-liberalism and global capitalism.

In the short run, ongoing campaigns against the OECD proposal for a MAI and new issues at WTO including financial liberalization needs to be strengthened. Similarly, campaigns against the rewriting of IMF articles favoring full capital account liberalization as well as the liberalization of trade in financial services under the WTO agreement must be launched without delay by NGOs and peoples' movements.

In the long run, some of the proposals to cope with the financial issues at the international level are worth consideration by the peoples' movements. The idea of Tobin tax, for instance, has already generated avid interest among many economists, NGOs, trade unions and political groups in recent years. It was evident during the World Social Summit in 1995, when various activist groups and movements demanded the imposition of Tobin tax to raise additional resources to finance developmental projects. The NGOs also endorsed a Tobin tax at Rio + 5, a 1997 review of the Rio Summit. In the near future, Tobin tax could become a key motif for launching an international offensive against global finance. In the last couple of years, a host of campaigns advocating the imposition of Tobin tax have been launched by peoples' movements and NGOs in many parts of the world, particularly in the developed countries such as Canada, France, UK, Finland and US (see Box 9.1). There is an urgent need for similar campaigns in the developing countries as well.

Simultaneously, the activists and peoples' movements are required to closely follow the developments related to the creation of new institutions like World Financial Authority to deal with global finance issues. At this juncture, there is little hope that such an institution will come into being, given the hostility of global financial institutions, particularly the IMF and international fund managers, towards a supranational body overseeing

Box 9.1

International Campaigns on Tobin Tax

Canada: A sustained public education campaign on Tobin tax was launched by Halifax Initiative, a coalition of Canadian organizations, with the support of a number of citizens' groups, NGOs and trade unions in 1998. In the campaign, millions of Canadian citizens, with the help of labor, church, academic, environment and development organizations, sent a message in favor of the Tobin tax to their Members of Parliament directly through an open letter or by signing a citizen's declaration. In December 1998, a petition asking their elected representatives to reflect on this matter was signed by over 50000 citizens. Due largely to this campaign, on March 23, 1999, the House of Commons in Canada adopted a motion calling for an international tax on financial transactions.

The Canadian Parliament is the first parliament in the world to pass such a motion. The motion (M-239) for a new tax on all transactions in the international financial markets was put forward by Lorne Nystrom of National Democratic Party in the House of Commons. Except for the Liberal and Conservative parties, the motion received the support and backing of all other parties, and was adopted by a vote of 164 to 83. Even the Finance Minister, Paul Martin, who had earlier expressed reservations about the effectiveness of such a tax, finally supported the motion.[10]

By passing a motion on Tobin tax, Canada has shown that efforts can be made to deal with volatile financial flows. This move has democratized the contemporary debate on the restructuring of international financial architecture and widened the scope for public participation in major economic decision making.

Using democratic methods, the Canadian people have displayed the supremacy and legitimacy of politics (the politics of public interest and public good) over the financial markets. The Canadian groups have already announced their plans to extend their campaign at the global level by linking up with like-minded groups besides pushing their agenda in international fora.

contd. on next page

France: A group of citizens, associations, trade unions and newspapers founded the Association for the Taxation of Financial Transactions for the Benefit of Citizens (ATTAC) in June 1998. As many as 27 local municipalities have also joined ATTAC. The organization not only calls for an updated version of Tobin tax but also advocates regulation of capital flows and democratic control over finance capital. In order to build a platform for diverse movements against neo-liberalism, the ATTAC took the initiative and launched an International ATTAC Movement in December 1998. ATTAC chapters now exist in Argentina, Austria, Belgium, Brazil, Greece, Ireland, Italy, Quebec, Senegal, Spain and Switzerland. The ATTAC brings out a weekly newsletter titled *Sand in the Wheels*.

UK: War on Want, a UK-based group launched a new campaign called 'It's Time for Tobin' in April 1999 for a global speculation tax. Aimed at the City of London, one of the main financial centers of the world, the campaign is directed towards taming speculative financial flows. The campaign identifies mobilization of citizens as the top priority and seeks to coordinate activities with other groups at the global level. Recently, the group published a report titled *The Global Gamblers*, identifying major banks in the UK which are big players in currency speculation. Meanwhile, another NGO, Oxfam, has published a study called *Time for a Tobin Tax?*

Finland: A coalition of over 200 organizations launched a campaign on Tobin tax in 1999. As part of the campaign, a book *The Tobin Tax: How to Make it Real* was published. The campaign has received support from various political parties and their representatives in the Finnish Parliament. Besides, the Finnish government decided to make assessments of financial transaction arrangements, including Tobin tax.

US: The Tobin Tax Initiative is a project of the International Innovative Revenue Project, US. Formed in 1998, its mission is to generate awareness of Tobin tax among grassroot activists and groups. The group publishes a monthly newsletter titled *Tobin Tax Update*. In the recent past, the City Council of Arcata has adopted a proclamation urging the national governments world over to cooperate for instituting Tobin style taxes on foreign currency transactions to curb speculation.

their operations at the global level. Nevertheless, NGOs and movements will have to ensure that in case a new institution comes into existence, it should function under the overall United Nations system, have a developmental agenda and be guided by open democratic processes. Likewise, NGOs and peoples' movements should also closely follow developments related to the forthcoming international conference on Financing for Development being organized by the UN.

In the future, NGOs and peoples' movements have to grapple with two major international institutions that deal with finance capital. These institutions are BIS and IOSCO (The International Organisation of Securities Commissions). Located in Basle, BIS is the oldest international financial institution. Its mandate is to monitor and regulate private bank lending. IOSCO, based in Montreal, works on securities issues. Unfortunately, both these institutions have not come under close public scrutiny, unlike the World Bank and the IMF.[9]

Towards A New Strategy

It is clear that global finance capital is all set to institutionalize an international regime driven by the market forces. Controlled by a grow-ing alliance of transnational capital, bureaucratic surrogates and political elites, this regime is neither accountable to elected governments nor to the people. The power of central banks to operate independently of elected bodies puts the issues of control over money, credit and interest rates outside the realm of democratic accountability. The real challenge before peoples' movements resides in enforcing the adoption of a genuinely participatory agenda in the operations of international finance capital and its allied institutions. Citizens and their representative bodies will have to take such initiatives so as to bring discipline and accountability in the operations of both the market and the state. It could perhaps be achieved by increasing the participation level of citizens in decision making processes and creating effective control mechanisms that were earlier not accessible to ordinary citizens. Assertion of the primacy of social control over global financial flows by citizens and their representative bodies can only act as a bulwark against the present trajectory of financial globalization.

In the coming days, one is sure to witness a growing interest among diverse sections of society on global financial issues. Peoples' movements, therefore, have to be galvanized for devising new tools of analysis and action to ensure that global finance capital serves the interests of citizens and democratic states and not the avarice of owners and managers of capital. In order to forge such a counter hegemonic project, activist groups and peoples' movements have to come to terms with the terminology, procedures and operations of global finance capital.

Notes and References

1. For instance, meeting organized by eight regional Hong Kong-based NGOs on the theme, "Financial Crisis: Our Response," during June 15-18, 1998 in Hong Kong; International Training Program on International Private Finance, organized by Friends of the Earth and National Wildlife Federation in Washington during July 15-19, 1998; "Creating Common Wealth: Dealing with World Debt and Financial Crises," public forum organized by Halifax Initiative, Jubilee and In Common in Ottawa on September 28, 1998; "Towards a Progressive International Economy: A Working Conference," organized by Friends of the Earth, International Forum on Globalization and Third World Network in Washington during December 9-11, 1998; "Reform of the Bretton Woods Institutions: A Transatlantic Progressive Dialogue," organized by Heinrich Boll Foundation and Friends of the Earth in Washington during December 14-15, 1998; and "Economic Sovereignty in a Globalized World," conference organized by Focus on the Global South, DAWN and SAPRIN in Bangkok during March 23-26, 1999.

2. For instance, Quantum Leap Project, a joint project of National Wildlife Federation, US and Friends of the Earth, US. The project monitors the international private finance capital in the context of environmental impact. The project also brings out a regular newsletter titled, *The Bull and Bear Newsletter.*

3. Shripad Dharmadhikary, "Campaign Against Narmada Bonds," in Kavaljit Singh, *The Globalization of Finance: A Citizen's Guide,* Madhyam Books and Zed Books, 1999 (a), p. 163.

4. See, for instance, Kavaljit Singh, op. cit., 1999 (a); Kavaljit Singh, *The Southeast*

Asian Currency Crisis and India: Impact and Implications, PIRG Occasional paper No. 5, 1999 (b); and Arun Ghosh, *Asian Currency Turmoils and WTO Issues: Lessons for India,* CSGTSD, 1998.

5. Welcome speech by Brent Blackwelder at International Training Program on International Private Finance organized by Friends of the Earth and National Wildlife Federation in Washington on July 15, 1998.

6. Ibid.

7. Kavaljit Singh, *Capital Controls, State Intervention and Public Action in the Era of Financial Globalization,* PIRG Occasional Paper No. 4, 1998, p. 24.

8. Gerald Epstein, "International Capital Mobility and the Scope for National Economic Management," in Robert Boyer and Daniel Drache (eds.), *State Against Markets: The Limits of Globalization,* Routledge, 1996, p. 221.

9. See, for instance, Kavaljit Singh, op. cit, 1999 (a), pp. 159-160; and speech by Kavaljit Singh at International Training Program on International Private Finance, organized by Friends of the Earth and National Wildlife Federation, Washington on July 19, 1998.

10. For a detailed discussion on the developments in Canada, see Kavaljit Singh, "Tobin Tax: An Idea Whose Time has Come," *Economic and Political Weekly,* May 1, 1999, pp. 1019-1020.

Bibliography

Ajit Singh, "The Stock Market and Economic Development: Should Developing Countries Encourage Stock-Markets," *UNCTAD Review*, No. 4, 1993.

———, *Corporate Financial Patterns in Industrializing Economies: A Comparative International Study*, Technical Paper No. 2, International Finance Corporation, World Bank, 1995.

———, *Pension Reform, the Stock Market, Capital Formation and Economic Growth: A Critical Commentary on the World Bank's Proposals*, Working Paper No. 2, Centre for Economic Policy Analysis, New School of Social Research, 1996.

Ajit Singh and J Hamid, *Corporate Financial Structures in Developing Countries*, Technical Paper No. 1, International Finance Corporation, World Bank, 1992.

Alberto Giovannini, "Saving and the Real Interest Rate in LDCs," *Journal of Development Economics*, Vol. 18, No. 2-3, 1985.

Alberto Giovannini and M de Melo, "Government Revenue from Financial Repression," *American Economic Review*, No. 83, 1993.

Alex C Michalos, *Good Taxes: The Case for Taxing Foreign Currency Exchange and Other Financial Transactions*, Dundurn Press, 1997.

Andrew Large, *The Future of Global Financial Regulation*, Group of Thirty, 1998.

Andrew Sheng, *Bank Restructuring: Lessons from the 1980s*, World Bank, 1996.

Arun Ghosh, *Asian Currency Turmoils and WTO Issues: Lessons for India*, Centre for Study of Global Trade System and Development, 1998.

A V Rajwade, *Foreign Exchange, International Finance and Risk Management*, Academy of Business Studies, 1996.

Bank for International Settlements, *Annual Report*.

———, *Survey of Foreign Exchange Market Activity*, 1998.

Barry Eichengreen, *Globalizing Capital: A History of the International Monetary System*, Princeton University Press, 1996.

———, *Towards a New International Financial Architecture: A Practical Post-Asia Agenda*, Institute for International Economics, 1999.

Barry Eichengreen and Charles Wyplosz, *The Unstable EMS*, CEPR Discussion

Paper No. 817, Centre for Economic Policy Research, 1993.

Barry Eichengreen and Donald Mathieson, with Bankim Chadha, Anne Jansen, Laura Kodres and Sunil Sharma, *Hedge Funds and Financial Market Dynamics*, Occasional Paper No. 155, IMF, 1998.

Barry Eichengreen, James Tobin and Charles Wyplosz, "Two Cases for Sand in the Wheels of International Finance," *Economic Journal*, 1995.

Barry Herman (ed.), *Global Financial Turmoil and Reform: A United Nations Perspective*, United Nations University Press, 1999.

Barry Herman and Krishna Sharma (eds.), *International Finance and Developing Countries in a Year of Crisis*, United Nations University Press, 1998.

Barry P Bosworth, Rudiger Dornbusch and Raul Laban (eds.), *The Chilean Economy: Policy Lessons and Challenges*, The Brookings Institution, 1994.

Benjamin J Cohen, *The Geography of Money*, University of California Press, 1998.

Bernhard Fischer and Helmut Reisen, *Towards Capital Account Convertibility*, OECD Development Centre Policy Brief No. 4, 1992.

Beverly Chandler, *Investing with the Hedge Fund Giants: Profit Whether Markets Rise or Fall*, Financial Times Management, 1998.

Carlos Diaz-Alejandro, "Good-bye Financial Repression: Hello Financial Crash," *Journal of Development Economics*, 1985, pp. 1-24.

Charles Goodhart, Philipp Hartmann, David Llewellyn, Liliana Rojas-Suarez and Steven Weisbrod, *Financial Regulation: Why, How and Where Now?*, Routledge, 1998.

Charles Kindleberger, *International Capital Movements*, Cambridge University Press, 1987.

——, *Manias, Panics and Crashes: A History of Financial Crises*, Macmillan, 1990.

Charles R Morris, *Money, Greed and Risk: Why Financial Crises and Crashes Happen*, Times Business, 1999.

C Rangarajan and A Prasad, "Capital Account Liberalisation and Controls: Lessons from the East Asian Crisis," *Money and Finance*, April-June 1999.

Charles Wyplosz, "Capital Controls and Balance of Payments Crises," *Journal of International Money and Finance*, 1986, pp. 167-197.

Dani Rodrik, *The New Global Economy and Developing Countries: Making Openness Work*, Policy Essay No. 24, Overseas Development Council, 1999.

David Felix, "Developing Countries and Joint Action to Curb International Financial Volatility," *UNCTAD Bulletin*, 1993, pp. 7-9.

———, *Financial Globalization vs. Free Trade: The Case for the Tobin Tax,* UNCTAD Discussion Paper No. 108, UNCTAD, 1995.

———, "Repairing the Global Financial Architecture," *Foreign Policy in Focus,* Special Report No. 5, 1999.

Department of Finance, Canada, "Finance Minister Announces Six-Point Canadian Plan to Deal with Global Financial Turmoil," Press Release, September 29, 1998.

Dominic Casserley and Greg Gibb, *Banking in Asia: The End of Entitlement,* John Wiley & Sons (Asia) Pvt. Ltd., 1999.

Doug Henwood, *Wall Street,* Verso, 1997.

ECLAC, *Foreign Investment in Latin America and the Caribbean: 1998 Report,* 1998.

Edward S Shaw, *Financial Deepening in Economic Development,* Oxford University Press, 1973.

Eric Helleiner, *States and the Re-emergence of Global Finance: From Bretton Woods to the 1990s,* Cornell University Press, 1994.

———, "Explaining the Globalization of Financial Markets: Bringing States Back in," *Review of International Political Economy,* 1995.

Franklin R Edwards, "Hedge Funds and the Collapse of Long-Term Capital Management," *Journal of Economic Perspective,* Vol. 13, No. 2, Spring 1999.

F M Mwega, "Saving in Sub-Saharan Africa: A Comparative Analysis," *Journal of African Economies,* Vol. 6, No. 3, October 1997.

Graciela L Kaminsky and Carmen M Reinhart, "The Twin Crises: The Causes of Banking and Balance of Payments Problems, *The American Economic Review,* Vol. 89, No. 3, June 1999.

Geoffrey R D Underhill (ed.), *The New World Order in International Finance,* Macmillan Press Ltd., 1997.

George Soros, *The Alchemy of Finance: Reading the Mind of the Market,* John Wiley, 1987.

———, "Avoiding a Breakdown: Asia's Crisis Demands a Rethink of International Regulation," *Financial Times,* December 31, 1997.

———, *The Crisis of Global Capitalism,* Public Affairs Press, 1998.

Gerald Epstein, "International Financial Integration and Full Employment Monetary Policy," *Review of Political Economy,* 1995, pp. 164-185.

Group of Thirty, *International Insolvencies in the Financial Sector,* 1998.

Gulnur Muradoglu and Fatma Taskin, "Differences in Household Savings Behavior: Evidence from Industrial and Developing Countries," *The*

Developing Economies, Vol. 34, No. 2, June 1996.

Ha-Joon Chang, "Korea: The Misunderstood Crisis," *World Development,* Vol. 26, No. 8, 1998.

Ha-Joon Chang and Chul-Gyue Yoo, "The Triumph of the Rentiers?," *Challenge,* Vol. 43, No. 1, January/February 2000, pp. 105-124.

Heather D Gibson and Euclid Tsakalotos, "The Scope and Limits of Financial Liberalisation in Developing Countries: A Critical Survey," *The Journal of Development Studies,* Vol. 30, No. 3, April 1994, pp. 578-628.

Helmut Reisen, *After the Great Asian Slump: Towards a Coherent Approach to Global Capital Flows,* Policy Brief No. 16, OECD, 1999.

IMF, *Annual Report on Exchange Agreements and Exchange Restrictions,* 1998.

——, *International Capital Markets: Developments, Prospects, and Key Policy Issues,* annual.

——, *World Economic Outlook,* biannual.

Isabelle Grunberg, "Double Jeopardy: Globalization, Liberalization and the Fiscal Squeeze," *World Development,* No. 4, 1998.

—— (ed.), *Perspectives on International Financial Liberalization,* Discussion Paper Series, No. 15, Office of Development Studies, UNDP, 1998.

Jagdish Bhagwati, "The Capital Myth: The Difference between Trade in Widgets and Dollars," *Foreign Affairs,* May/June, 1998, pp. 7-12.

James Crotty and Gerald Epstein, "In Defense of Capital Controls," *Socialist Register,* 1996, pp. 118-149.

James Tobin, "A Proposal for International Monetary Reform," *Eastern Economic Journal,* 1978, pp. 153-159.

Jan Joost Teunissen (ed.), *The Pursuit of Reform: Global Finance and the Developing Countries,* FONDAD, 1993.

—— (ed.), *Regulatory and Supervisory Challenges in a New Era of Global Finance,* FONDAD, 1998.

—— (ed.), *The Policy Challenges of Global Financial Integration,* FONDAD, 1998.

Jessica Gordon Nembhard, *Capital Control, Financial Regulation, and Industrial Policy in South Korea and Brazil,* Praeger, 1996.

J Frieden, "Invested Interests: the Politics of National Economic Policies in a World of Global Finance," *International Organization,* 1991, pp. 425-451.

John C Edmunds, "Securities: The New World Wealth Machine," *Foreign Policy,* Fall 1996.

John Dillon, *Turning the Tide: Confronting the Money Traders,* Canadian

Centre for Policy Alternatives, 1997.

John Eatwell, *International Financial Liberalization: the Impact on World Development*, United Nations Development Program Discussion Paper Series No. 12, United Nations, 1997.

John Gray, *False Dawn: The Delusions of Global Capitalism*, Granta Books, 1999.

John M Keynes, *The General Theory of Employment, Interest and Money*, Harcourt Brace Jovanovich, 1936/1964.

John Williamson and Molly Mahar, *A Survey of Financial Liberalization*, Essays in International Finance, No. 211, International Finance Section, Department of Economics, Princeton University, 1998.

Jose M Fanelli and Rohinton Medhora (eds.), *Financial Reform in Developing Countries*, Macmillan Press Ltd., 1998.

J Stopford and S Strange, *Rival States, Rival Firms*, Cambridge University Press, 1991.

Kavaljit Singh, *Capital Controls, State Intervention and Public Action in the Era of Financial Globalization*, PIRG Occasional Paper No. 4, 1998.

——, *Globalization of Finance: A Citizen's Guide*, Madhyam Books and Zed Books, 1999.

——, *The Southeast Asian Currency Crisis and India: Impact and Implications*, PIRG Occasional Paper No. 5, 1999.

——, "Tobin Tax: An Idea Whose Time Has Come," *Economic and Political Weekly*, May 1, 1999, pp. 1019-1020.

Kenneth M Morris, Alan M Siegel and Beverly Larson, *Guide to Understanding Money and Investing*, Dow Jones Publishing Company (Asia) Inc., 1997.

Leslie Elliott Armijo (ed.), *Financial Globalization and Democracy in Emerging Markets*, Macmillan Press Ltd., 1999.

Linda Weiss, "Globalization and the Myth of the Powerless State," *New Left Review*, September/October 1997, pp. 3-27.

L Pauly, *Who Elected the Bankers? Surveillance and Control in the World Economy*, Cornell University Press, 1997.

Luca Errico and Alberto Musalem, "Offshore Banking: An Analysis of Micro-and-Macro Prudential Issues," *IMF Working Paper*, No. 99/5, IMF, 1999.

Mahathir Bin Mohammad, *Currency Turmoil*, Limkokwing Integrated, 1998.

Mahbub ul Haq, Inge Kaul and Isabelle Grunberg (eds.), *The Tobin Tax: Coping With Financial Volatility*, Oxford University Press, 1996.

Manuel F Montes and Vladimir V Popov, *The Asian Crisis Turns Global*,

Institute of Southeast Asian Studies, 1999.

Manuel R Agosin, "Capital-Account Convertibility and Multilateral Investment Agreements: What is in the Interest of Developing Countries," *International Monetary and Financial Issues for the 1990s*, Research Papers for the Group of Twenty-Four, Volume X, UNCTAD, 1999.

Marcel Cassard, "The Role of Offshore Centers in International Financial Intermediation," *IMF Working Paper No. 94/107*, IMF, 1994

Mauricio Cardenas and Felipe Barrera, "On the Effectiveness of Capital Controls: The Experience of Colombia in the 1990s," *Journal of Development Economics*, No. 54, 1997, pp. 27-58.

M Bowe, and J L Dean, *Has the Market Solved the Sovereign Debt Crisis?*, Princeton Studies in International Finance No. 83, 1997.

M Deane and R Pringle, *The Central Banks*, Hamish Hamilton, 1994.

Michel Camdessus, Report of the Managing Director to the Interim Committee on the International Monetary System, IMF, 1998.

——, "Capital Account Liberalization and the Role of the Fund," Remarks to the IMF Seminar on Capital Account Liberalization, March 9, 1998.

——, "Toward an Agenda for International Monetary and Financial Reform," Address to the World Affairs Council, November 6, 1998.

Miles Kahler (ed.), *Capital Flows and Financial Crises*, Cornell University Press, 1998.

Patricia Cayo Sexton, "Con Games and Gamblers on Wall Street," *Dissent*, winter 1999.

Paul Hirst and Grahame Thompson, *Globalization in Question: the International Economy and the Possibilities of Governance*, Polity Press, 1996.

Paul Krugman, *Exchange-Rate Instability*, The MIT Press, 1989.

——, *The Return of Depression Economics*, The Penguin Press, 1999.

Stanley Fischer et al., *Should the IMF Pursue Capital Account Convertibility?* Essays in International Finance No. 207, International Finance Section, Department of Economics, Princeton University, 1998.

Peter J Quirk and Owen Evans, *Capital Account Convertibility: Review of Experience and Implications for IMF Policies*, Occasional Paper No. 131, IMF, October 1995.

Peter Warburton, *Debt and Delusion*, Allen Lane The Penguin Press, 1999.

P G Cerny (ed.), *Finance and World Politics: Markets, Regimes and States in the Post-Hegemonic Era*, Edward Elgar, 1993.

Reuven Glick (ed.), *Managing Capital Flows and Exchange Rates: Perspectives from the Pacific Basin,* Cambridge University Press, 1998.

R Ffrench-Davis and S Griffith-Jones (eds.), *Coping with Capital Surges: The Return of Finance to Latin America,* Lynne Rienner, 1995.

R Germain, *The International Organization of Credit: States and Global Finance in the World Economy,* Cambridge University Press, 1997.

Richard O'Brien, *Global Financial Integration: The End of Geography,* Pinter, 1992.

Richard Roberts, *Inside International Finance,* Orion Business Books, 1998.

Robert A Blecker, *Taming Global Finance: A Better Architecture for Growth and Equity,* Economic Policy Institute, 1999.

Robert Boyer and Daniel Drache (eds.), *State Against Markets: The Limits of Globalization,* Routledge, 1996.

Robert Wade, " The Asian Debt and Development Crisis of 1997-?: Causes and Consequences," *World Development,* Vol. 26, No. 8.

Robert Wade and Frank Veneroso, "The Asian Crisis: The High Debt Model Versus the Wall Street-Treasury-IMF Complex," *New Left Review,* No. 228, March/April 1998, pp. 3-23.

——, "The Gathering World Slump and the Battle over Capital Controls," *New Left Review,* No. 231, September/October 1998, pp. 13-42.

Ronald I Mckinnon, *Money and Capital in Economic Development,* Brookings Institution, 1973.

Ronen Palan, Jason Abbott and Phil Deans, *State Strategies in the Global Political Economy,* Pinter, 1996.

R T Naylor, *Hot Money and the Politics of Debt,* Unwin Hyman, 1987.

Salvador Valdes-Prieto, "Capital Controls in Chile Were a Failure," *Wall Street Journal,* December 11, 1998.

Sebastian Edwards (ed.), *Capital Controls, Exchange Rates, and Monetary Policy in the World Economy,* Cambridge University Press, 1995.

——, *"Capital Flows, Real Exchange Rates, and Capital Controls: Some Latin American Experiences,"* Working Paper 6800, National Bureau of Economic Research, 1998.

——, "Capital Controls Are Not the Reason for Chile's Success," *Wall Street Journal,* April 3, 1998.

——, "A Capital Idea?: Reconsidering a Financial Quick Fix," *Foreign Affairs,* May/June 1999, pp. 18-22.

S L Key, *Financial Services in the Uruguay Round and the WTO,* Group of Thirty Working Paper No. 54, 1998.

S Sassen, *Losing Control? Sovereignty in an Age of Globalization,* Columbia University Press, 1996.

Stephany Griffith-Jones, *Global Capital Flows: Should They Be Regulated,* Macmillan Press Ltd., 1998.

——, "A New Financial Architecture for Reducing Risks and Severity of Crises," *International Politics and Society,* 3/1999.

Sue Branford and Bernardo Kucinski, *The Debt Squads, The US, the Banks and Latin America,* Zed Books, 1988.

Susan George, *A Fate Worse than Debt,* Penguin, 1988.

Susan Strange, *Casino Capitalism,* Blackwell, 1986.

——, *The Retreat of the State: the Diffusion of Power in the World Economy,* Cambridge University Press, 1996.

——, *Mad Money,* Manchester University Press, 1998.

Tariq Banuri and Juliet Schor, *Financial Openness and National Autonomy: Opportunities and Constraints,* Oxford University Press, 1992.

Torben M Anderson and Karl O Moene (eds.), *Financial Liberalization and Macroeconomic Stability,* Blackwell Publishers, 1996.

Tremont Partners, Inc. and TASS Investment Research Ltd., *The Case for Hedge Funds,* 1999.

UNCTAD, *Trade and Development Report,* annual.

——, *World Investment Report,* annual.

UNDCP, *Financial Havens, Banking Secrecy and Money-Laundering,* United Nations, 1998.

——, *World Drug Report,* Oxford University Press, 1997.

UNDP, *Human Development Report,* annual.

Wendy Dobson and Pierre Jacquet, *Financial Services Liberalization in the WTO,* Institute for International Economics, 1998.

William Greider, *Secrets of the Temple: How the Federal Reserve Runs the Country,* Simon and Schuster, 1987.

——, *One World, Ready or Not: the Manic Logic of Global Capitalism,* Simon and Schuster, 1997.

William I Robinson, *Promoting Polyarchy: Globalisation, US Intervention and Hegemony,* Cambridge University Press, 1998.

World Bank, *World Development Report,* annual.

——, *Global Development Finance,* annual.

——, *Managing Capital Flows in East Asia,* 1996.

——, *Private Capital Flows to Developing Countries: The Road to Financial Integration*, Oxford University Press, 1997.

——, *Global Economic Prospects 1998-1999 and the Developing Countries*, World Bank, 1999.

——, *Proceedings of the World Bank Annual Conference on Development Economics*, 1993.

Yilmaz Akyuz, *Issues in Financial Policy Reform: Myth and Reality*, UNCTAD, 1994.

List of Newspapers and Journals

Business Standard, daily, New Delhi.
Business Week, weekly, Hong Kong.
Cambridge Journal of Economics, monthly, Oxford.
Capital and Class, three times a year, London.
Economic and Political Weekly, weekly, Mumbai.
Economic Journal, monthly, London.
Euromoney, monthly, London.
Far Eastern Economic Review, weekly, Hong Kong.
Finance and Development, quarterly, Washington.
Fortune, biweekly, New York.
Global Finance, monthly, New York.
International Economic Review, quarterly, Philadelphia.
International Finance, three times a year, Oxford.
Journal of Development Economics, monthly, Amsterdam.
Journal of Economic Issues, monthly, Pennsylvania.
Journal of International Money and Finance, bimonthly, North Holland.
Journal of Money, Credit and Banking, monthly, Ohio.
Money and Finance, quarterly, New Delhi.
Monthly Review, monthly, New York.
New Left Review, bimonthly, London.
The Asian Wall Street Journal, daily, Hong Kong.
The Banker, monthly, London.
The Developing Economies, monthly, Tokyo.
The Economic Times, daily, New Delhi.
The Economist, weekly, London.
The Financial Times, daily, London.
The Hindu Business Line, daily, New Delhi.
The World Economy, monthly, Oxford.
World Development, monthly, Oxford.

Index